'The whakataukī/proverb "Ka titiro ki muri, ka haere ki mua – I walk backwards into the future with my eyes fixed on my past" instills in us the importance of remembering who we are. Carl Rogers' original ideas have always been foundational to Keith's discussion of person-centred psychology (PCP) throughout his career, and he has led the invitation to reimagine PCP with the hope of creating new pathways for practitioners. This book provides another disruption to our familiar and comfortable notions of PCP, and extends our considerations to include cosmological landscapes.'
        Shirley Rivers (Ngāi Takoto, Ngāpuhi, Waikato), *Head of Mission, Methodist Mission Northern, Auckland, Aotearoa New Zealand*

'What a treat to have this book as a legacy to Bernie Neville's lived presence in this world: a fitting tribute to his life as an embodied being, sharing his unique contribution to our "we-ness" and experiences of understanding and healing our relationships ecotherapeutically.

Neville's co-author Keith Tudor has done a fabulous job of honouring their interweaving theories and ideas and bringing this book to fruition: a generous gift to our world. They provide a depth of understanding, an academic rigour and the radical hopefulness we need to understand our pain and anxiety and to find healing, active and growthful ways forward. Accompanied by the soundtrack of Archie Roach, poems, images and voices of colleagues and Neville's daughter, Alisoun, this book sets us free to imagine and re-vision what is possible.

The book reflects my meetings with Bernie over the years at international gatherings: the embodied excitement of sharing life-changing ideas; the incredible depth of processing and reflection; the challenges of facing and accepting hopelessness and despair and the down to earth, every day practicalities of living as humans; and delighting in each other's company and the fact of being alive. This book has a lot to say about daring to live a meaningful life.'
        Suzanne Keys, *Person-centred practitioner and environmentalist, UK*

'This is a deeply moving book on multiple levels. Firstly, there is a profound sense of care and deep respect from Keith and associated secondary authors as they strive to articulate the final published words of Bernie. It is deeply moving in the way this is managed, knowing from the start that this book represents the culmination of Bernie's lifetime of academic work, yet he was unable to see the project through to its end. Secondly, the book "moves deeply" through its subject matter. We are entering an age of growing awareness of the enormity of the challenge to our very existence from our "planetary emergency". This book offers not just a theoretical framework to grapple with our place in this, but also fosters a deep "hope", informed and grounded in Rogers' person-centred approach. As such, this book will be of profound relevance to contemporary person-centred academics, students and practitioners, and indeed all of humanity, as like it or not we are all in this together.'
        Dr Brian Rodgers, *Senior Lecturer, Te Kura Tauwhiro Tangata, School of Counselling, Human Services & Social Work, Waipapa Taumata Rau, The University of Auckland, Aotearoa New Zealand*

'This is an amazing book. It encompasses and connects us with somatic, psychological, anthropological, and interpersonal phenomena in the whole of nature. Specifically addressing the field of psychotherapy and therapists, the authors gently and firmly invite us to think about who and what we are, essentially. The book offers us a guide to discovering and confirming the universal relating principle(s) in universe, including ourselves, who are never the centre of this planet.'
Izumi Kadomoto, *Professor, Department of Clinical Psychology, Taisho University, Japan*

'In this time of ecological crises, too much in our psychotherapeutic traditions appears feeble, unsuited to the problems of our age, or, worse, complicit in those very problems. In *Eco-centred Therapy: Revisioning Person-Centred Psychology for a Living World*, Bernie Neville and Keith Tudor dive deep into Carl Rogers' thought and emerge with something novel and urgently needed: a vision of a psychotherapy for both person and planet. This book looks to the past, yet it is about our future.'
Dr Rhys Price-Robertson, *Gestalt therapist, researcher, and educator, Australia*

Eco-Centred Therapy

Offering a much-needed update of Rogerian theory and practice, and based on insights from cultural studies and ecopsychology, this book breaks new ground by questioning the relevance of certain ways of thinking about counselling and psychotherapy not least in the current planetary emergency.

In response to the growing need for therapists to address increasing anxieties about the climate crisis, Bernie Neville and Keith Tudor address the issue in terms that help therapists reflect on their practice. Based on the authors' previous publications and incorporating new material, this book presents and explores ideas that have been largely neglected in person-centred literature. It re-visions person-centred psychology (PCP) from what has become predominantly its application to individuals to a broader perspective on and about life and the living world. Further, it takes a philosophical and cultural perspective to re-present and re-vision PCP as a 'we' psychology, an eco-psychology, and an eco-therapy.

This book will be of interest to those working in the fields of person-centred therapy, ecopsychology, and ecotherapy as well as those involved in the education, training, and supervision of counsellors and psychotherapists.

Bernie Neville (1938–2021) was a De La Salle Brother before marrying and having a family, an academic, counsellor, and author with a deep interest and presence in person-centred psychology, Jungian psychology, and process philosophy. He was a Professor in the Faculty of Higher Education, Swinburne University of Technology, and at the Phoenix Institute, both in Melbourne, Australia.

Keith Tudor is Professor of Psychotherapy at Auckland University of Technology, Auckland, Aotearoa New Zealand, where he is also co-lead of a Group for Research in the Psychological Therapies. He is an internationally-recognised author; his latest books include (with David Key) *Ecotherapy: A Field Guide* (Karnac, 2023).

Eco-Centred Therapy
Revisioning Person-Centred Psychology for a Living World

Bernie Neville and Keith Tudor

LONDON AND NEW YORK

Designed cover image: Mt Toolebewong at dusk (Photo: Alisoun Neville)

First published 2024
by Routledge
4 Park Square, Milton Park, Abingdon, Oxon OX14 4RN

and by Routledge
605 Third Avenue, New York, NY 10158

Routledge is an imprint of the Taylor & Francis Group, an informa business

© 2024 Bernie Neville and Keith Tudor

The right of Bernie Neville and Keith Tudor to be identified as authors of this work has been asserted in accordance with sections 77 and 78 of the Copyright, Designs and Patents Act 1988.

All rights reserved. No part of this book may be reprinted or reproduced or utilised in any form or by any electronic, mechanical, or other means, now known or hereafter invented, including photocopying and recording, or in any information storage or retrieval system, without permission in writing from the publishers.

Trademark notice: Product or corporate names may be trademarks or registered trademarks, and are used only for identification and explanation without intent to infringe.

British Library Cataloguing-in-Publication Data
A catalogue record for this book is available from the British Library

ISBN: 978-1-032-49621-4 (hbk)
ISBN: 978-1-032-50282-3 (pbk)
ISBN: 978-1-003-39773-1 (ebk)

DOI: 10.4324/9781003397731

Typeset in Galliard
by Taylor & Francis Books

Contents

List of illustrations ix
Additional author biographies x
Foreword xi

Introduction 1

PART 1
Ground 9

1 Taking Rogers seriously 13
2 The mind of things 30
3 We is: The ground of being 48
4 Person-centred psychology and therapy, ecopsychology and ecotherapy 65

PART 2
Conditions 81

5 We cannot imagine without the other: Contact and difference in therapeutic relating 83
6 Crying for the loss of nature: Incongruence and alienation 96
   LEN GILLMAN
7 Being anxiously congruent, and congruently anxious 105
8 Accepting hopelessness as a hopeful process 117
9 Five kinds and four modes of empathy 130

10	Experiencing and perceiving	146
	KEITH TUDOR AND ALISOUN NEVILLE	

PART 3
Freedom—with responsibility 163

11	Setting therapy free	165
12	Setting therapists free	
		180

Epilogue 180

13	Setting Bernie free: A eulogy	193
	KEITH TUDOR	

	References	201
	Index	224

Illustrations

Figures

0.1	The book on the wall	xii
8.1	Hope, Charity, and Faith—Stained glass windows by Sir Edward Burne-Jones (1887), in the Lady Chapel, All Saints' Church, Leek, UK	119
8.2	Still from *The Third Man*	127
10.1	Mt Toolebewong at dusk	149
10.2	Mt Toolebewong—The Shed	149
10.3	Toolebewong Trees	155
10.4	The Lake District, Cumbria, England	156
10.5	Striding Edge towards High Spying How	158
10.6	Helvellyn—Striding Edge, Red Tarn, Red Tarn Beck, Swirral Edge, and Castye Cam	160
10.7	Helvellyn—The Eastern side, looking down onto Red Tarn from Striding Edge	161
13.1	Bernie Neville—on Mt Toolebewong	196

Tables

2.1	Gebser's model of layered consciousness	45
8.1	The whence, thence, and hence of hope, and the challenges of hope	121

Additional author biographies

Len Gillman is a retired Professor of Conservation Biogeography and Evolutionary Ecology. He lives in Laingholm on the fringe of the Waitakere Ranges in Aotearoa, where he is active in local conservation restoration projects. In the 1980s, he was involved with the Native Forest Action Council, and in the 1990s with the Environmental Defence Society, and is currently co-chair of the Waitakere Ranges Pest Free Alliance, a member of the Regeneration Independent Advisory Group to NZ Carbon Farming, and a founding member of Restoration Ruatuna. He has published in the fields of global ecology, biogeography, species diversity theory, genetic evolution, Antarctic ecology and conservation, indigenous names within scientific nomenclature, the use of drones for conservation and behavioural biology, climate change mitigation, and global biotic homogenisation; his current research projects include the effects of glacial retreat on Antarctic vegetation; and he has developed a free-to-use App for identifying all 230 mainland New Zealand native trees species.

Alisoun Neville is a practicing Arts Therapist living on Boon Wurrung Country, Milowl/Phillip Island. Her vision for her work is to support and strengthen mental health and disability practices that can respond more effectively to the impacts of society and its systems. Prior to therapeutic practice, Alisoun worked extensively in health and community services including most recently through Aboriginal community-controlled organisations. In 2006, she was awarded her PhD, combining Law, English, and Cultural Studies/Critical Theory, with a thesis focussing on the stolen generations and the law. In 2016, she returned to study for her Masters in Therapeutic Arts Practice. She loves working with creative arts and experiential practitioners and hopes to represent the profession with the values she strives for in practice: accountability, equity, inclusivity, reciprocity, collaboration, and joy.

Foreword

Alisoun Neville

Bernie, my Dad, loved to spar. Widely known as generous, kind, funny, and wise, he was brutal at times in the game of ideas. "What's wrong with being small-l liberal?" he once laughed, and I scrambled through my lessons and fury to find an adequate retort.

I don't know if he did this with everybody, but he certainly did it with me. When he died, a friend said she had never seen two people be more honest with each other, speaking in the moment without the usual filters.

> "Have you read my book yet?"
> "Have you read my thesis yet?"
> "I've read your thesis!"
> "Only in draft."
> "*You* haven't read *my* thesis."

He is with me as I read this book. But it is often hard for me to read his writing. The ideas are those he shared with me over dinner tables, café tables, park benches, parking brakes, fallen logs, fast and slow stories, repetition, and laughter. They are too familiar in the reading—and I have taken them for granted.

This was not always the case. When he crucified me in the early '90s, not only for studying psychology but for doing it at the (upper-crust) University of Melbourne, I listened with starry eyes to his critiques and mysterious ways. He was, without doubt, a magician of the mind. I even read the books he gave me. But then, as children do, I travelled my own path. I have landed relatively recently as an arts therapist and practitioner, and am learning new things about the revolutions he offered.

The chapter titles of this book are on the living room wall, at Dad's place on Mt Toolebewong, as evidence of a long week of ideas, friendship, sparring (there must have been), humour, and collaboration. Dad continued the writing when I stayed with him through COVID-19, picking up books and philosophies I still hope to comprehend.

On behalf of our family, heartfelt thanks go to Keith for his dedication in bringing this book together. There is nothing easy about finishing it alone. I know from my own contributions how keenly Dad's absence is known throughout the

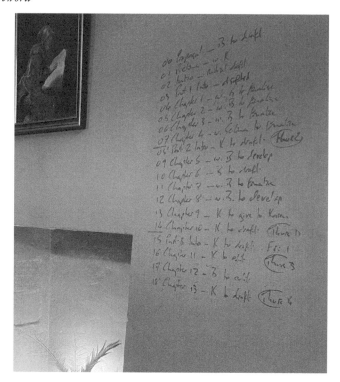

Figure 0.1 The book on the wall

process, and how heavy the pressure to do honour to who he was. We are grateful that Keith spoke with Dad before he died, and know that he was very happy for Keith to finish what they started.

We are also grateful that Dad had Keith and so many others around him who engaged with him to the end, with whom his alive and generative nature was both expressed and deeply valued.

Dad did not have a final say on the content of this text, a chance to spar with Keith's ideas right down to the last word, but he didn't choose to spar when it most mattered, when the heart of the piece called for love, generosity, and the space to simply be.

I hope you enjoy his visits through the reading.

Introduction

This book is about the organic paradigm that underlies person-centred psychology (PCP) and its approach to therapy and, more broadly, to life itself. It is about not necessarily accepting the premise of questions, statements, or arguments made about human nature, nature (or 'Nature'), and therapy.

> ANNABETH: [The] Press is here for the Q&A. Now remember, you control the conversation. You don't like what they ask, don't accept the premise of the question.
> LEO: That's my line, you know. You're quoting me.
> ANNABETH: I thought it was Toby.
> LEO: Where do you think he got it? I've been rejecting the premises of questions since the Hoover Administration.
>
> (Wells et al., 2005)

Thus, we bring together ideas from phenomenology, process philosophy, cultural philosophy, psychology and, specifically, PCP, and ecology.

Some people who identify with PCP, its theory and practice, may find the ideas in this book surprising. However, while a number of the ideas we explore are largely neglected in person-centred literature, we think that they are essential to a comprehensive understanding of Carl Rogers' contribution to psychology, specifically because his worldview takes him beyond individual person-to-person therapy to an interest in people-in-context and, thus, to cosmology.

For a long time, the two of us have been writing about the person-centred approach (PCA) and person-centred therapy (PCT) and, along with other colleagues, especially Maureen O'Hara, Carol Wolter-Gustafson, Ivan Ellingham, and Mike Worrall, would be seen as organismic theorists within the approach (see Tudor, 2021, 2022). Bernie and I had known of each other's work for some time but only met in person in 2006 at the conference of the World Association of Person-Centered & Experiential Psychotherapy & Counseling, held in Potsdam, Germany. That meeting led to a friendship that has grown over the years and has been facilitated by the fact that, in 2009, Keith emigrated to Aotearoa New Zealand—so, as we now live only 2,561 kilometres apart, separated by the Tasman Sea (or 'the Ditch' as it is more commonly and affectionately known in this part of

DOI: 10.4324/9781003397731-1

the world), we are near neighbours! We—that is, each and both of us—have various motivations for writing this book.

For me (Keith), I wanted to develop ideas that Mike Worrall and I had articulated in *Person-Centred Therapy: A Clinical Philosophy* (Tudor & Worrall, 2006), which, amongst other things, had reclaimed Rogers as an organismic theorist and the root metaphor of person-centred theory as the organism. Subsequently, I wrote about PCP as an eco-psychology and PCT as an eco-therapy (Tudor, 2013b; Chapter 4 in this book), and about 'we psychology' (Tudor, 2016). I knew that I wanted to explore more about the nature of human nature and of nature itself. I also knew that I wanted to collaborate with Bernie on a writing project and, as I had been involved with two books about colleagues and elders who had died—Evan Sherrard in 2015 (Sherrard, 2020) and Claude Steiner in (Tudor, 2020a)—I wanted to do this with Bernie while he was still alive! Sadly, this wish was not fulfilled or, at least, was significantly curtailed (of which more anon). Reflecting on this journey over the past five years, and having come across Bill Plotkin's (2008) wheel of life while staying with Bernie, I would say that I have been the stage of early elderhood, walking in the grove of elders. In the same taxonomy I would say that Bernie is in the stage of late elderhood, characterised by being a sage in the mountain cave—though, as late as December 2020 he was still out and working on (his) land in country (see Chapter 10).

For me (Bernie [writing in May 2019]), it's good to be reminded by Keith that I am still alive, and still able to write. Writing has become an occasional obsession for me in the past few decades—occasional, because the energy for writing comes to me intermittently, but when it comes it takes over my life. I'm grateful to Keith, a much more consistent writer than me, for stimulating the current takeover. I'm also grateful, in a different way, to the conservative politicians who, in 2019, won an Australian federal election after a dishonest campaign based on fear of change, fear of refugees, fear of the implications of compassion, and fear of the truth, particularly the truth about global warming. I am grateful to them, and the brain-dead voters of Northern Queensland, for stimulating my anxiety and my sense of urgency. I am grateful to them for challenging my complacency and poking at the presumption of hope which resides deep in my soul. Existentialist philosophers since Kierkegaard have argued that it is anxiety, particularly anxiety about our approaching death, which is the stimulus for taking action in the world (see Chapter 7). That is certainly close to the truth for me as I write this. There are things I need to say, and I find that they match the things that Keith has been saying in his recent writing.

The thinking we try to articulate in this book revolves largely around the view that Carl Rogers expressed time and again: that we need to take seriously the evidence that human beings are organisms, not machines. Further, our individual organisms are not independent of each other and the so-called environment; rather, are manifestations of something larger, a greater organism which has both life and directionality.

We have each worked for years—in counselling, social services, psychotherapy, organisations, and education—and thought about our work in terms of the person-centred framework, initially developed by Rogers and then others. We both take Rogers seriously, not only in his psychology but also in his cosmology.

However, it seems that not all person-centred theorists and practitioners are open to the full implications of Rogers' ideas. This book aims to acknowledge and engage with these ideas.

When I (Bernie) try to put this writing into the context of my professional career, I find a starting point in a specific memory. I was a young teacher in a small Catholic school in Adelaide in 1965. Carl Rogers, the celebrated psychologist, had recently visited Australia, and his visit had stimulated a lot of talk in Catholic Education circles about what was being called 'developmental counselling'. One day the principal called me into his office and told me that he had decided that it would be a good idea to have a school counsellor, and would I like to take on the task (a rhetorical question). I accepted the challenge and, without training or other preparation, added the occasional counselling of adolescent boys to my teaching duties. I immediately got hold of *On Becoming a Person* (Rogers, 1961, 1967c) and looked around for opportunities for training in the PCA. I found that Rogers' way of placing relationship at the centre was a guide to effective counselling and provided a robust justification for the approach to teaching which I had been developing. This led eventually to my completing a PhD on Rogers (Neville, 1976) and gaining an academic position in which I was involved in the training of both teachers and counsellors. Conversations with colleagues led to my discovering the process philosophy of Alfred North Whitehead, the cultural philosophy of Jean Gebser, the ecophilosophy of Arne Naess, and the consequent readjustment of my approach to counselling.[1] I could no longer avoid perceiving the practice of counselling within the context of a planet in grave trouble. In 2012, I managed to get my ideas together in a book, *The Life of Things: Therapy and the Soul of the World* (Neville, 2012). In collaboration with Keith, I am taking these ideas a little further here.

Although I (Keith) had been introduced to Rogers' work as a therapist during my social work training in the late 1970s, it wasn't until the early 1990s, when I was offered the opportunity to do training on what was claimed to be a person-centred counselling course, that I studied PCP more fully. I say 'claimed', as I soon realised that this was much more of an eclectic course, designed by people unfamiliar with the detail and depth of the PCA. The result was, in effect, 'person-centred lite'. For the days (modules) for which I was responsible, I took it upon myself to study the approach and, with the support of engagement with the person-centred community in the UK, further training and supervision, made the modules and, indeed, that course person-centred. I became personally and professionally more identified with PCP, which included publishing—Embleton Tudor and Tudor (1996, 2002); Tudor (1997a, 1997b, 2000); Sanders & Tudor (2001); Tudor & Merry (2002); and Tudor (2002, 2007, 2008a, 2008b). A major part of this was with my partner, Louise Embleton Tudor, founding Temenos in Sheffield, UK (www.temenos.ac.uk), an education/training organisation committed to the PCA (Tudor & Embleton Tudor, 1999) which, amongst other things, developed the first postgraduate training programme in person-centred psychotherapy and counselling in the UK that was validated at Master's level (by Middlesex University), thereby breaking what had been a glass ceiling regarding the PCA and psychotherapy. It was as result of my collaboration with Mike Worrall and others associated with Temenos—

4 *Introduction*

Embleton Tudor et al. (2004), Tudor and Lewin (2006), Tudor & Worrall (2004a, 2004b, 2006, 2007), and N. Rogers et al. (2012)—and my reading of Bernie's work, that I became particularly interested in the organismic base of PCP, and hence my interest in taking this further.[2]

The book itself

The book is the result of our collaboration over some years, much discussion, some re-reading of each other's earlier work, and a lot of new reading. In 2019, we chose a number of our previously published articles and chapters, met up in Melbourne, Australia and retreated to Bernie's place (which he referred to ironically as his 'dacha') on Mt Toolbewong on/in Yarra country, and started to edit them. This process inevitably led to further discussion which, originally, we wanted to reflect in interleaving each chapter with a commentary from the other. In the end, and mainly due to our interest to represent an approach that genuinely reflects a 'we' psychology, we (both) decided to re-edit our individual papers (which form Chapters 2, 4, 5, 7, 9, 11, and 12) or presentations (Chapters 1, 3 and 8) in one voice, and thus co-author all of them as part of a genuinely co-influenced and co-produced piece of work (which has included editing to avoid repetition, and bringing together all the references from individual chapters in one list of References). Nevertheless, we acknowledge the individual origins and publication details of the original contributions to and basis of each of these chapters as follows:

- Chapter 2—An edited version of most of Chapter 5 from Neville, B. (2012). *The Life of Things: Therapy and the Soul of the World*, published by PCCS Books, reproduced with permission.
- Chapter 4—Based on Tudor, K. (2013c). Person-centered psychology and therapy, ecopsychology and ecotherapy. *Person-Centered & Experiential Psychotherapies*, 12(4), 315–329, reproduced with permission.
- Chapter 5—Based on Tudor, K. (2008d). We cannot imagine without the other: Contact and difference in psychotherapeutic relating. *Forum* [The Journal of the New Zealand Association of Psychotherapists], 14, 46–61, reproduced with permission.
- Chapter 7—Based on Neville, B. (2013a). Anxiously congruent: Congruently anxious. *Person-Centered & Experiential Psychotherapies*, 12(3), 223–236, reproduced with permission.
- Chapter 9—Based on Neville, B. (1996). Five kinds of empathy, a chapter originally published in *Client-Centered and Experiential Psychotherapy: A Paradigm in Motion*, published by Peter Lang, reproduced with permission.
- Chapter 11—Based on Neville, B. (2013b). Setting therapy free. *Person-Centered & Experiential Psychotherapies*, 12(4), 382–395, reproduced with permission.
- Chapter 12—From Tudor, K. (2014). Back to the future: Carl Rogers' 'new challenges' reviewed and renewed. *Self & Society*, 41(2), 17–24, reproduced with permission.

By re-editing, re-working, updating, and ultimately co-authoring each of these contributions, we think that our dialogue and thesis is more embedded in the book as a whole—a process which both parallels and embodies the thesis of the book itself. To that end, the book is structured as follows:

- Part I—Four chapters in which we lay the theoretical ground of our argument, based primarily in Rogers' thinking and work but also drawing on cultural psychology, new science, and ecopsychology, and which, respectively, represent the methodology, epistemology, ontology, and initial method of the argument we advance in the book.
- Part II—Six chapters, each of which reflects Rogers' (1957, 1959) necessary and sufficient conditions for therapy, and represents our reworking of these conditions with regard to thinking about different theory and practice that accounts for our relationship with the ecological, and the environment, including the climate emergency.
- Part III—Two chapters which represent our thinking about how both therapy and therapists could and need to be freed from the shackles of old, paradigmatic thinking about individual helping relationships in favour of those that heal the people and the land.
- An Epilogue—In which a final chapter concludes the book.

In writing this book, we have been inspired by the four tasks that Andy Fisher (2013) identified as constituting and furthering the project of ecopsychology: the psychological task—'to acknowledge and better understand the human–nature relationship as a relationship' (p. 7); the philosophical task—'to place psyche… back into the natural world' (p. 9); the practical task—'to develop therapeutic and recollective practices toward an ecological society' (p. 12); and the critical task—'to engage in ecologically based criticism' (p. 16). In bringing our work and ideas together, we had a number of conversations about the book title. Bernie favoured 'Belonging, Becoming, and Being', which reverses the more usual order in PCP of referencing 'being and becoming' and adds 'belonging', placing it first in order to emphasise our thesis of decentring human beings in favour of their/our belonging to something greater (i.e., the planet). Pursuing this theme, Keith liked 'The Organism Bites Back' or even 'Gaia Bites Back'. In the end, and with advice from the publisher, we settled on the current one.

To complete the thesis and structure of the book, we intended to write new chapters. Unfortunately, a planned second writing week at Keith's home then in Titirangi, West Auckland was delayed by restrictions placed on travel by both the Australian and New Zealand governments in response to the global coronavirus pandemic, and so we talked about finishing with each of us working online at a distance. However, given our interest(s) in the ground and field of theory and practice, we decided that it was important for Bernie to come and be welcomed to Aotearoa New Zealand, and so had planned our second and final writing time together in June 2020, after the World Conference of the World Association of Person-Centered & Experiential Psychotherapy & Counseling, held in Auckland.

Unfortunately, this was postponed by a year, during which Bernie's health deteriorated; in January 2021 he was diagnosed with bone cancer and, on 18th February 2021, he passed away, as he wished, at home, and surrounded by the love of his family.

I was able to speak with Bernie before he died and he knew that I intended to complete this project, which I have done, with the support of Len Gillman (Chapter 6); Alisoun Neville (Chapter 10); and Jeff Cornelius-White, Ross Crisp, Louise Embleton Tudor, Patricia McCann, Maureen O'Hara, Brian Rodgers, and Alberto Segrera (Chapter 13), to whom both Bernie and I owe our profound thanks—tēnā koutou katoa | thanks to you all. The last time I spoke to Bernie (12th February 2020), when he was settled at home, he said: "When I'm through all this, I might write a paper about it", adding wryly "It'll be very virtual!"

Completing the book has been a strange experience and a poignant process, and, for me, somewhat virtual as I have felt Bernie's presence. Ever since I knew that we would not be meeting in person, I knew that I wanted to complete as much of the book as possible while Bernie was alive. Bernie was aware of the final structure of the book and heard some of what is written in Chapter 13. I worked through the points I had made to discuss with Bernie, most of which I had to let go or, at least, to decide for myself, and all the editorial queries, most of which paled into insignificance in the context of his ill-health and death. I listened to the music of Archie Roach, an Aboriginal Australian musician, whom Bernie, Louise, my wife, and I all like and admire, and who epitomises what Rogers (1977/1995a) refers to as being in tune with 'the pulse beat of the world' (p. 313).[3] As I edited what Bernie had written, and wrote more passages which link and update what we had previously written, I felt his presence: an uncanny, poignant, and, ultimately, rather beautiful experience of 'we'ness. In the end, only Chapter 6 was completely written after his death by my colleague and friend Len Gillman—tēnā koe | thank you, Len. Finally, I asked Bernie's daughter, Alisoun, to join me in completing Chapter 10—tēnā koe, Alisoun. My determination to complete as much as possible led me to edit much of the book in the four weeks mid-January to mid-February 2021 with, as it were, Bernie beside me. In the week immediately after Bernie's death, I felt both the loss of him and his presence in equal measure—or, rather (as he would have appreciated), in an unquantifiable mix of particles! Ultimately, I ended up completing the book December 2021/January 2022 (around the first anniversary of Bernie's death); and, in May–June 2022, during a period of research and study leave when I was finally able to focus entirely on the book—and to let it go!

Apart from writing as a 'we' and, despite our different styles, finding a genuinely joint voice (in all but the two chapters noted above), we have also adopted a number of conventions. The first is to use the present tense when citing people and their ideas (e.g., 'Rogers argues') in order to emphasise the present sense of argument, debate, and continuing dialogue. The second is to use the plural person pronouns 'they' to stand for 'she' and 'he' and 'their' for 'her' and 'his', both to challenge binary thinking and referencing, and encourage pluralistic thinking that includes the environment. The third is to use the generic term 'therapy' to refer to a range of psychological therapies, including counselling, clinical, counselling, and rehabilitation psychology, and psychotherapy in order to be inclusive and challenge the narcissism of small and mostly Western differences between these practices and their professions and disciplines. The fourth is to use lower case for 'self', 'nature', and 'god' (or gods) in order not to reify them any further than they have been. Finally, during the production of this book, I (Keith) was told that there was a restriction on the use of epigrams, which is why the quotations which summarise and synthesise the subject of some chapters appear as hypograms, the distinction between which would have amused Bernie, and a new convention he would have appreciated.

Acknowledgements

In addition to the acknowledgements we have already made, we would like to acknowledge the wider 'we' that makes writing and publishing a book like this possible: our respective families, friends, and colleagues; for me (Keith) my university, and especially Dr Shoba Nayar for her initial copy-editing, Angie Strachan for her further and thorough copy-editing, and Rebecca Wise for her final work on preparing the manuscript for production; Vilija Stephens, Georgia Oman, and the team at Routledge for their faith in and flexibility with regard to this project; and Suzanne Keys, Izumi Kadamoto, Rhys Price-Robertson, Brian Rodgers, and Shirley Rivers (Ngāi Takoto, Ngāpuhi, Waikato) for their support and beautiful endorsements of the book.

Finally, we each and both wish to acknowledge the land on which we wrote this book—in two countries and over some years. Bernie's acknowledgement of country is represented in Alisoun Neville's contribution. In Aotearoa New Zealand, I (Keith) say 'Kei te whenua o Te Kawerau ā Maki māua kainga ināianei | Our house sits on the land of the iwi (tribe) Te Kawerau ā Maki'. All royalties from this book will go to projects led by Aboriginal people and Māori, designed to repair the rupture caused by the alienation of these lands and their peoples, including that of aspects of Western—and Northern—psychology.

Mt Toolebewong, Yarra, Australia
May 2019
Titirangi, Waitakere, Aotearoa New Zealand
February 2021
Ruatuna/Laingholm, Waitakere, Aotearoa New Zealand
May 2022

Notes

1 See Neville (1997, 1999, 2000, 2005, 2007); Hall & Neville (2011); Neville & McCann (2013); Neville & Varney (2014).
2 Since emigrating to Aotearoa New Zealand, my (Keith's) thinking about and application of PCP has continued to develop (Tudor, 2010, 2011a, 2011b, 2011c, 2013b, 2017/

8 *Introduction*

  2020b, 2021, 2022), and has involved further collaborations, especially in relation to PCP and culture—Komiya and Tudor (2016); Ioane and Tudor (2017, 2022); Haenga-Collins et al. (2019); Rodgers and Tudor (2020); Tudor and Rodgers (2020); Rodgers et al. (2021); Rivers et al. (2022); Tudor et al. (2022).
3 Originally, I included relevant lyrics from Archie Roach's songs as epigrams for each chapter, which thus formed the sound track of the book. Unfortunately, we were not able to use them in the final publication but, for those readers who are interested, they were, from 'Too many bridges' (Roach, 2007) (Chapter 1), from Mother's heartbeat' (Roach, 1997) (Chapter 2), from 'Into the bloodstream' (Roach, 2012a) (Chapter 3), 'Heal the people, heal the land' (Roach, 2018b) (Chapter 4), from 'We won't cry' (Roach, 2012c) (Chapter 5), from 'Native born' (Roach 1990b) (Chapter 6), from 'I've lied' (Roach, 1990a). (Chapter 7), from 'Let love rule' (Roach, 2016b) (Chapter 8), from 'All men choose the path they walk' (Roach, 2022) (Chapter 9), from 'Place of fire' (Roach 2019) (Chapter 11), from 'Dancing' (Roach, 2018a) (Chapter 12), and from 'Wash my soul' (Roach 2012b) (Chapter 13).

Part 1
Ground

The four chapters in this first part of the book represent the ground of the theory we are advancing in the book.

Who are 'we'?

If we (Bernie and Keith) refer to 'we' in the context of this writing, we are referring to: ourselves and you, the reader. Looking more broadly, and given our background (s) and purpose in this book, our we might include anyone who is interested in the PCA to therapy, organismic, humanistic, and eco psychology, and environmentalists. At a stretch, it might include all therapists, even those who reject this approach, because the 'we'ness comprises shared interests, shared professional responsibilities, and a certain shared self-image.

However, the boundaries of the we are flexible. Our we may extend to all humanity or be narrowed to include only those with whom we share gender, ethnicity, nationality, or tribal affiliations. Whether a particular group of people are we or 'they' depends on context. We may say and use 'we' because we also perceive a 'they' who don't share these identities, responsibilities, and interests. If Argentinians are talking about an international football match, Brazilians will be 'they'. If they are talking about the activities of the CIA in Latin America, Brazilians become 'we' and otherness is attached to the perceived enemy. Despite such relatively local rivalries, it is not difficult to argue that all human beings are essentially 'we'—but, then again, it is not quite so simple. Do we include terrorists, torturers, and tyrants in our we? Almost universally, no. Then, further, do we go beyond our species and include the cat and/or dog who is/are part of our family? Generally, yes, because we see them as a part of the family and not another species—though I (Keith) don't! Do we include the apes and gorillas with whom we largely share our genes? After all, we have 98% of our deoxyribonucleic acid (DNA) in common with chimpanzees. Generally, no, though people such as the scientist and naturalist, Dian Fossey (of *Gorillas in the Mist* [1983]) would probably say yes. Other mammals, crocodiles, snakes, beetles, moebae?, Bacteria, viruses? Surely the boundary we put on our 'we' is arbitrary? Why not include trees, flowers (we have 35% of our DNA in common with daffodils), grass, and algae? Why not go further and include minerals?

DOI: 10.4324/9781003397731-2

Once we start thinking of the universe as an organism and alive, this changes everything and we have to deal with questions of consciousness, subjectivity, and interiority, and the nature of the individual—what used to be referred to as the mind–body problem—as well as the role of the therapist. The four chapters in this first part of the book do that.

We psychology

This sense and use of 'we' draws on we psychology—a psychology that focuses on and, indeed, derives from a perspective that considers 'we' before 'I' or, as G.S. Klein (1976) puts it, 'we-go' before ego. In Western psychology, this perspective has its origins in the social psychology of Mead (1934) and Vygotsky (1962), the organismic psychology of Goldstein (1934/1995) and Angyal (1941), and has become the focus of research among developmental psychologists such as Stern (1998). As a term, we psychology is attributed to Fritz Künkel, who drew on the work of Freud, Adler, and Jung in synthesising an explicitly religious psychology (see Künkel, 1984).

The ontological assumption of we psychology is characterised by Winnicott's (1947/1957) famous phrase 'there is no such thing as a baby' (p. 137). The most extreme example of which we are aware is reported by Alford (1994), who writes about the Wolini, a now extinct tribe who lived in the Amazon rain forest on the border between Venezuela and Brazil. They were distinguished in the anthropological literature by the absence in their language of the first-person singular pronoun 'I'; instead, the Wolini were known to each other by a combination of birth order and family name. Taking this further, and paraphrasing Winnicott, we might say that there is no such thing as a relationship, only relationships-in-context. Thus, we psychology acknowledges context and, therefore, social and political worlds as well as personal and interpersonal worlds.

The methodology of we psychology—that, is the philosophical underpinnings of the method—are reflected in theories of relationship. Various philosophers, such as Martin Buber, John Macmurray, and, arguably, Carl Rogers, have contributed to our thinking about the centrality of relationship. In his work, Macmurray (1957/1991a, 1961/1991b) challenges the assumptions of a theoretical and ego-centric view of the (reified) self:

> Against the assumption that the self is an isolated individual, I have set the view that the Self is a person, and that personal existence is constituted by the relation of persons… The idea of an isolated agent is self-contradictory. Any agent is necessarily in relation to the Other. Apart from this essential relation he does not exist. But, further, the Other in this constitutive relation must itself be personal. Persons, therefore, are constituted by their mutual relation to one another. 'I' exist only as one element in the complex 'You and I.'
> (p. 12)

As early as 1942, Rogers referred to his then newer psychotherapy as relationship therapy, a term he credited to Taft (1933/1973) and that prefigured the more recent relational turn in psychotherapy (see Ellingham, 2011; Tudor, 2022). Noel and DeChenne (1974) write about a we dimension in therapy that 'involves discussion of processes occurring between the client and the therapist, processes which are co-owned and must be dealt with collaboratively' (p. 253). Saner (1989) names the 'we'ness of the therapeutic relationship itself as the medium for human development and change, while Summers and Tudor (2000) discuss 'we'ness as one of the principles that underpins co-creative transactional analysis and the practice of exploring and expanding new relational possibilities.

The method or practice of we psychology that follows from this relational methodology focuses on working with and within relationships. As Schmid (2006) puts it,

> Dialogue is an irreversible principle and condition of being human. Humans do not only substantially rely on dialogue, they are dialogue. [Moreover,] dialogue is the authentic realization and acknowledgement of the underlying We... The restoration of the underlying We is the therapy in psychotherapy.
> (p. 251)

The chapters

In the spirit of taking Rogers seriously, the first eponymous chapter focuses on the formative tendency, and sets the ontological and epistemological basis for the book. It is based on an unpublished keynote speech that Bernie delivered in July 2017 at the conference of the World Conference Association of Person-Centered & Experiential Counseling in Vienna, and which I (Keith) had the privilege of introducing. It is especially synchronous that this forms the first chapter of the book as it was the last keynote speech that Bernie delivered.

As we are concerned with establishing the philosophical basis of the thesis of this book and especially the ontological basis of things, in Chapter 2 we set out the nature of the embodied mind and its cultural/historical development. This is particularly important as we are challenging the tendency to identify our individual self with our individual mind.

We build on this in the third chapter by addressing the more collective view of and from 'we', and critique notions of individual identity and self as subject. This suggests and marks a movement from self to organism, from process that focusses on 'the self' to organic process, and from I to we and us, and the living universe.

Having established our ground in the first three chapters—or, rather, having posited a few ideas which are unconventional and, in any case, shifting—in the fourth and final chapter in the first part of the book, we turn to PCP as the basis for an ecopsychology. This chapter, based on an article originally written by Keith, offers theoretical and conceptual links between PCP and ecopsychology, and PCT and ecotherapy. It argues that Rogers' core concepts of the organism and the formative tendency are useful and congruent ones for thinking about human beings, other beings, and the earth; and that Rogers' therapeutic conditions for change and the concept of encounter are useful in developing a person-centred ecotherapy and contributing to an eco-centred therapy.

1 Taking Rogers seriously

Philosophy

Carl Rogers (1957) insists that our approach to therapy is based on our personal philosophy:

> One cannot engage in psychotherapy without giving operational evidence of an underlying value orientation and view of human nature. It is definitely preferable, in my estimation, that such underlying views be open and explicit, rather than covert and implicit.
>
> (p. 199)

Rogers made no claim to be a philosopher; and it is not conventional, even in person-centred circles, to refer to him as such. It probably didn't occur to him. Gaining and maintaining credibility in the American psychological establishment during the 1940s–1970s was a sufficient challenge, without also asking to be accepted as a philosopher. Nonetheless, here we argue that taking Rogers seriously means taking him seriously as a philosopher or, at least, a clinical philosopher, in the sense that his reflections on the nature of the universe, of science, and of the good life, what it means to be human, the ethics of helping, the essence of human relationships: all are the stuff of philosophy—and, therefore, that Rogers should get credit for his contribution to the way we think about such 'stuff', matter, and the things of life.

In a report about his work and study (written between July 1951 and March 1952), Rogers commented: 'I made it my purpose during the Winter Quarter to get some perspective on my work and to extend my thinking into the theoretical and philosophical implications of what we are doing' (quoted in Kirschenbaum, 2007, p. 224). Rogers notes his reading of significant books in psychology, and modern physics, yet states:

> the most rewarding reading was in the field of philosophy. Kierkegaard was a most exciting discovery to me, and Buber very stimulating. Sartre and Whitehead each contributed something. Now that I have returned I am beginning to realize the impact that this reading, and the opportunity for

DOI: 10.4324/9781003397731-3

leisurely thinking has had on me. I know that it will sharply influence my work and my writing.

(p. 224)

Some commentators have taken Rogers seriously in this respect, notably Van Belle (1990, 2005) who traces the philosophical roots of PCT back to Ancient Greek philosophy; and Tudor and Worrall (2006), who discuss Rogers' philosophical influences as comprising humanism, existentialism, empiricism, and Christianity.

Rogers' philosophy points towards a positive future and, even if we find it difficult to go all the way with him in this, we still need to take him seriously. It is not enough to accept those of his ideas which can be fitted comfortably into the mechanistic paradigm which has dominated scientific thinking for the past 400 years, and ignore the ideas that challenge it. The current planetary emergency is forcing us to abandon the ways of imagining the world that have led us to that emergency. We need a new way of thinking about life, the world, and everything—Rogers' contribution to this revisioning is an important one.

Early in his work as a therapist, Rogers encountered Rank's ideas and method of 'relationship therapy', through Jessie Taft (1933/1973). Although his direct contact with Rank's ideas was brief (in one workshop), Rogers' engagement with these ideas put listening at the centre of his theory and practice (for discussion of Rank's influence on Rogers, see Ellingham, 2011; Kramer, 1995; Tudor, 2022b). With regard to Whitehead, Rogers (1963/1995e) makes only one secondary reference to him, citing Whitehead's influence on Ilya Prigogine; nevertheless, we detect Whitehead's influence in Rogers' focus on organism and process. Whitehead's organic philosophy, later renamed process or process-relational philosophy, was finding a solid base in the University of Chicago at the same time Rogers worked there (1945–1957), and we may assume that his ideas found their way into Rogers' conversations with his colleagues in philosophy and divinity. Tudor and Worrall (2006) note:

> We see [Whitehead's] *Process and Reality* as the *philosophical* ground for organismic psychology and for the theory and practice of person-centred therapy. Although complex and dense, it gives philosophical weight to the importance in person-centred therapy of experience, process and perception.
>
> (p. 49)

Whitehead (1925/1997) points to three fallacies which, he claims, undermined the credibility of science: the fallacy of misplaced concreteness; the fallacy of simple location; the fallacy of dogmatic finality. We find in Rogers' writing plenty of evidence that he was keen to avoid all three fallacies. For instance, by acknowledging ourselves—and clients—as process(es) rather than substance(s), we avoid the fallacy of misplaced concreteness. Similarly, in abandoning the notion of a particular boundary between *the personhood of* the therapist and client, Rogers is avoiding the fallacy of simple location. I (Keith) have been particularly mindful of this in re-editing this chapter for production without Bernie, as I have also experienced him being with me. I can see him smiling and laughing, and experience being in dialogue with him, even though, right now (1:41pm on 6th February, 2021), he is still alive but not very conscious and a few thousand kilometres away. Finally, when Rogers (1978/1995b; and others) question reality, truth, and certainty (Tudor, 2018c), we avoid the fallacy of dogmatic finality.

Since Whitehead's and Rogers' ideas run counter to the assumptions on which mainstream thinking in both psychology and philosophy has been based for most of the past 150 years, it is not surprising that they have not been taken seriously within 'scientific' psychology. It is more surprising, however, that they have not been taken seriously, or have been distorted by many who claim to have been influenced by Rogers' work or who identify as 'Rogerian' or 'person-centred'. There are many within the PCT community who are more comfortable with a conventional humanistic understanding of Rogers' position, as articulated in his earliest formulations; and those who think that Rogers 'lost it' in his later years and exchanged his solid, scientific, evidence-based approach for an interest in transcendence and mysticism. Many carry on their work as person-centred therapists while happily ignoring the concept of the formative tendency, which Rogers (1963/1995e) insists 'definitely forms a basis for the person-centred approach' (p. 133).

Many therapy trainers and educators go no further than the instrumental approach to the 'core conditions' promoted by Truax and Carkhuff (1967), Gerald Egan (1980), and others, an approach from which Rogers distanced himself (see Kirschenbaum, 2007). There are many who find it hard to take Rogers seriously simply because he wrote with great clarity and simplicity. Others refuse to take him seriously because he offers us a utopian vision which conflicts with our need to feel depressed, and they find his invitation to look to the future with hope somewhat naïve (Masson, 1989; Quinn, 1993).

We have plenty of reasons to conclude that human society and, indeed, the planet, is on the edge of destruction. We might blame all this on a minority of evil people who have too much power, or we can acknowledge that we are all involved. We can hope that things will get better, that good will prevail, that our children and grandchildren will avoid the calamity, that someone or something will save us, etc. However, the problem with hope is that when we hope we are generally waiting for something to happen, for someone to do something, for things to change. In the context of an emerging catastrophe, hope seems both futile and dangerous. The current planetary emergency demands that we overcome our paralysis and act, yet simply thrashing around desperately hardly qualifies as action. Thus, we need to be inspired by hope: we need to appreciate who we are, and have a vision for the future (see Chapter 8). We may need to stand beside Rogers in his appraisal of our situation in the final pages of *A Way of Being*. Writing about the new and desirable world he saw emerging, a world whose outlines are 'dimly visible', he suggests that 'unless we blow ourselves up, that world is inevitably coming' (Rogers, 1980/1995j, p. 355). The 'unless' and the 'inevitably' cancel each other somewhat: we may well blow ourselves up, or starve, poison, roast, or drown ourselves to death. Nevertheless, it is central to Rogers' vision, and worth taking seriously, that, notwithstanding and even despite our (human) worst endeavours, there is a dynamism impelling the world towards positive change, to which we can make a contribution (see Chapter 4).

Carl Rogers has often been accused of being a romantic or, more accurately, a Romantic, as if this were a moral failing or, at best, a personality disorder. We argue that we need to take Rogers' version of Romanticism seriously and acknowledge the intellectual tradition to which it belongs. Rogers' writings have their roots in a radical intellectual tradition which goes back to philosophers of the Renaissance and beyond, and within this company he is a creative and significant thinker.

The other Enlightenment: An alternative intellectual tradition

When we speak of 'The Enlightenment' we are usually referring to and thinking of the intellectual and cultural movement which emerged in Europe in the 17th century Common Era (CE)[1] and flourished in the 18th century. The Enlightenment philosophers celebrated reason and argued that truth was not to be sought in divine revelation but in objective observation and logic. We associate this movement with names such as Isaac Newton, John Locke, and François-Marie Arouet (better known as Voltaire), and trace its trajectory as it became the dominant paradigm for exploring reality. We may be inclined to think of the Enlightenment as a unitary phenomenon, but it took more than one form. Since the 1980s, a distinction has been made between the moderate Enlightenment—the intellectual tradition which dominated scientific thinking in the 18th century and most of the 20th century—and what has been called the radical Enlightenment (see Gare, 2007/2008, 2014, 2017; Israel, 2002; Jacob, 1981/2006), a tradition that had its origin in Renaissance Italy in the 15th century, in the work of humanist philosophers such as Marsilio Ficino and Giordano Bruno. They believed in the human capacity to find truth through reason and observation rather than religious dogma, but their beliefs led them to quite different conclusions from those of René Descartes, Isaac Newton, and John Locke a century or so later. The philosophers of the radical Enlightenment were by no means opposed to rationality, but their thinking was based on holistic assumptions which were challenged by the Enlightenment philosophers who emerged in the 17th century and who claimed the high ground as far as rationality was concerned. The philosophers of the radical Enlightenment tended to be sympathetic to the naturalistic, vitalistic pantheism which the Catholic Church associated with Paganism and was determined to suppress. The radical Enlightenment did not separate creator from creation: nature simply *is* and everything that exists is part of this greater all. By contrast, the moderate Enlightenment was grounded in belief in a mechanistic 'clockwork' universe supervised by a transcendent deity. For the radical philosophers, the universe was alive and perpetually becoming, in contrast to what became the conventional Enlightenment view that it was a machine set in motion by a creator—and gradually slowing down.

The radical Enlightenment found a voice in the Romantic movement of the 19th century, but this voice was quietened as scientific materialism took hold and psychology descended into the absurdities of behaviourism, including its latest manifestation, cognitive behavioural therapy (for a searing critique of which, see Dalal, 2018). Nevertheless, we hear it in the 20th century thinkers cited by Rogers in his chapter on 'The foundations of a person-centered approach' (1963/1995e), including: Lancelot Whyte (an historian); Jan Smuts (a soldier, scholar, and politician); Alfred Adler (a psychoanalyst); Fritjof Capra (a theoretical physicist); Magoha Murayama (a philosopher of science); Ilya Prigogine (a chemist and philosopher); Alfred North Whitehead, Kurt Goldstein, Abraham Maslow, Andreas Angyal, and Albert Szent-Gyoergi (organismic theorists); Stanislav Grof, Christina Grof, and John Lilly (researchers into altered states of consciousness). We hear it in the 'alternative intellectual history' documented by Hans Hakl (2014); and we hear it again in the writings and words of the process philosophers (George Herbert Mead, John Dewey, Charles Peirce, William James, Alfred North Whitehead, and Charles Hartshorne); creation theologians (Martin Buber and Pierre Teilhard de Chardin); the 'new scientists' (Kurt Goldstein, Ilya Prigogine, and Fritjof Capra); some humanistic and transpersonal psychologists; and ecophilosophers (notably Félix Guattari and Arne Naess).

It is significant, and not surprising, that the vast majority of these influences are male. Male contributors to our understanding of the sciences and humanistic psychology have had a much higher profile than their female counterparts. Rogers did refer to Jessie Taft when discussing early influences on his theory and practice, though he didn't refer to Charlotte Bühler, who contributed theoretically to the development of humanistic psychology from her research in the 1930s, and wrote the first book on humanistic psychology (Bühler, 1972), and whom Rogers met at the conference at Old Saybrook, Connecticut, in November 1964. Isabelle Stengers who unfortunately did not share Ilya Prigogine's Nobel Prize should also be noted. Finally, we acknowledge inspiring women in the next generation of process philosophy, namely Catherine Keller, Sally McFague, and Danah Zohar.

The voice of the radical Enlightenment may be found beyond Rogers' later writings such as *A Way of Being* (Rogers, 1980/1995i). His organic philosophy and, ultimately, his cosmology; his radical empiricism; his conviction that inner experience must be included in the domain of science; and his acknowledgement of alternative realities: all place him firmly in the company of the philosophers and scientists of an alternative intellectual tradition that has challenged, and challenges, the clockwork paradigm.

The cultural philosopher Jean Gebser (1949/1986) suggested that the rational consciousness which emerged in Europe in the 17th century reached a dead end in the middle of the 20th century, as it was no longer able to deal with the kind of universe we inhabit. He argued that the collapse of rational consciousness opened the way for the re-emergence in Europe of the magical/mythical consciousness which had dominated European culture before the Enlightenment, a consciousness which supported Nazism, Fascism, and the tribal conflicts which were plaguing Europe. However, he also documented the emergence of a different kind of consciousness which he calls integral, a consciousness which embraces myth and soul without abandoning rationality; a consciousness which has a new understanding of time, self, and space, and moves beyond rational thinking to acknowledge the paradoxical nature of reality. He observed in both arts and sciences evidence of a new human experience of reality. Poets, philosophers, biologists, physicists, artists, musicians were addressing a reality which was space-free, time-free, ego-free, arational, and multi-perspectival. He argued that the kind of consciousness which had led us to an imminent catastrophe was incapable of finding a remedy for the state of the world, and that only a new kind of consciousness could save us. We suggest that this provides another context for viewing Rogers' writings as philosophical.

Rogers is occasionally accused of inconsistency and self-contradiction in his theorising. We suggest that what appears as inconsistency in Rogers' theorising represents his struggle to honour his intuitive understanding of human existence and experience without abandoning the assumptions and methods of modern science (see Rogers, 1959). In Rogers' later writings, we no longer see this struggle. He embraces the alternative intellectual tradition which applies a critical mind to a different image of the universe: an organic, living, non-dualistic, directional universe of which humans are creative participants, rather than detached observers. He does not abandon reason and he does not abandon objective observation; he simply applies them to a different vision of the universe, a vision which he shares with some of the best minds of the past 3,000 years. Rogers saw himself as an empirical scientist; however, could best be categorised as a 'radical empiricist', a term which both William James and Alfred North Whitehead applied to themselves. While, like mainstream scientists, they believed that knowledge must be based on evidence, and that theory must be grounded in observation and experience, they did not limit their definition of evidence to what our five—or more—senses can observe and measure. Reality, they believed, has an interior as well as an exterior, an invisible dimension as well as a visible one.

Rogers was serious about science. His contributions to empirical research into the conditions for successful therapy (Rogers, 1957, 1959) are well known, and both pre-date and prefigure more recent research in therapy in 'common factors' (Asay & Lambert, 1999). However, he rejected the logical positivism which framed the research of most of his contemporaries and welcomed the discussion of 'new paradigm research' which emerged in the 1970s (see Reason & Rowan, 1981). The critical point distinguishing Rogers' understanding of research from that of his more conventional colleagues was his conviction that subjectivity is at the centre of all observation, and hence of all scientific knowledge, and, therefore, that subjectivity has to be taken seriously. Here his ideas were in tune with the 'hard sciences' of the 20th century in a way that mainstream academic psychologists, who were desperate for psychology to have credibility as a science, were not.

By way of setting the scene for the rest of the book, we turn to discussing some implications and applications of Rogers' radical, Enlightenment thinking with regard to the universe, the formative tendency, the human organism, the therapeutic relationship, intuition, and 'the good life'.

The universe as alive: Being and becoming

One strand of thinking in the alternative intellectual tradition is grounded in the view that the universe is alive and becoming. This may be found in Spinoza and his followers in the 17th century. Currently we find it in post-positivist science, in biology, process philosophy, complexity theory, and evolutionary psychology. In this way of thinking, the universe is an organism, is alive, and has within itself a tendency to move towards greater complexity and harmony. Rogers clearly embraces this way of thinking, and it was central to the thinking of Otto Rank and Alfred North Whitehead—two of the major influences on Rogers' world view.

For most of human history it was taken for granted that the universe is alive. It was only in 17th-century Europe that this idea was seriously disputed and the notion that the universe consisting of dead matter entered scientific discourse as a fact. Even with the flourishing of mechanistic science in the 19th century, the idea of the universe as organic and living retained some currency, finding particular expression in the Romantic movement. Nevertheless, 20th-century mainstream science opted for the clockwork metaphor and paradigm. American and British psychological science became seriously addicted to it, to the extent of dehumanising human beings. This was the context in which Rogers found himself developing his radical approach to therapy.

In the clockwork paradigm, the universe consists essentially of dead matter. In the process of evolution, some of this matter has accidentally gained an additional quality we call life. Later, a smaller portion of this (life) gained an additional quality we call experience; and later still, an even smaller portion of this (experience) gained an additional quality we call awareness. Finally, an even smaller portion of awareness became capable of rational thought. Miraculously, we human beings are alive, experiencing, aware, and thinking (if not thoughtful); and a rock is not. However, in the organic paradigm, life is not an add-on; it has not arrived through random mutations; it is not simply a quality of matter—or a matter of additional qualities. Life is at the very centre: the material world we experience—the rocks, trees, and animals—are the ways in which life manifests itself; and hence *The Life of Things* (Neville, 2012).

In the preface to *Client-Centered Therapy*, Rogers (1951) states that:

> [This book] is about both the client and me as we regard with wonder the potent and orderly forces which are evident in this whole experience, forces which seem deeply rooted in the universe as a whole… The book is, I believe, about life, as life vividly reveals itself in the therapeutic process—with its blind power and its tremendous capacity for destruction, but with its overbalancing thrust towards growth, if the opportunity for growth is provided.
>
> (p. xi)

This kind of thinking, combined with the personal tone and the use of the first person personal pronoun, did not have a place in professional writing in the field of psychology in 1951. Rogers (1961/1967i) comments that the publishers of *Client-Centered Therapy* thought that his preface was 'most unsuitable' (p. 26). The fact that Rogers got this preface published is another reason we should take him seriously: it makes all the difference to the way we read him.

The recognition that the universe is alive has profound social and political consequences. It has most obvious consequences in our treatment of the planet. The shift from an environmental awareness which sees the earth as an object which we can either preserve or destroy to an awareness that there is no gap between us and what we call 'the environment' is a critical one. Life flows on and we are caught up in it, along with the rest of the cosmic organism—the rocks and the trees and the planets and the stars. Every action of ours which disrespects the greater organism works to destroy us.

A larger, creative formative tendency

A second, key area in which Rogers is not taken seriously enough, either in person-centred theory or person-centred practice, is his concept of the formative tendency. Yet he insists that there are two foundations of the PCA. In both theory and practice, we find a tendency to focus on the first: the actualising tendency. Regarding this, Rogers (1963/1995e) asserts: 'For me it is meaningful to say that the substratum of all motivation is the organismic tendency towards fulfilment… towards actualization, involving not only the maintenance but also the enhancement of the organism' (p. 123). The other foundation is the formative tendency. As Rogers puts it: 'I hypothesise that there is a formative, directional tendency in the universe… This is an evolutionary tendency towards greater order, greater complexity, greater interrelatedness' (p. 133). In their discussion of this tendency, Tudor and Worrall (2006) clarify the use of language: 'As with the organism's tendency to actualise, the language we use is significant. The universe does not *have* an actualising tendency. It *is* a tendency to form, or it tends to form' (p. 98).

Rogers (1963/1995e) writes of this second foundation of the PCA as 'an evolutionary tendency' (p. 133), scanning the evolution of humanity from its single cell origin to complex organic functioning, culminating in 'a transcendent awareness of the harmony and unity of the cosmic system, including humankind' (p. 133). Immersing oneself in the flow of life presumably carries one in this direction. We should note that an organic philosophy like that of Spinoza, Whitehead, or Rogers does not construct a dualistic separation of matter and spirit. There are plenty of complexity theorists and others who see the evolution of consciousness in a similar light, but Rogers' thought is distinctive in relating this evolution to the phenomenon of the human relationship. This cosmic tendency is actualised in each individual's tendency to seek fulfilment which, in turn, is concretised in the deep relationship that characterises the genuine therapeutic encounter.

Strangely enough, this concept, which 'definitely forms a basis for the person-centred approach' (Rogers, 1963/1995e, p. 133), seems to be ignored by many PCT practitioners who are comfortable with the conventional understanding of therapy as an interaction bounded by the personalities and behaviour of two individuals in the complementary roles of therapist and client. If they were genuinely to perceive it as an interaction embedded in the creative advance of the universe, they could not escape the demand to carry this awareness into and through their work. For further discussion of this, see Tudor and Worrall (2006), Cornelius-White (2007), Neville (2007), and Bazzano (2012).

An organic philosophy

From quite early on in his work, Rogers refers to and talks about the human organism (although, interestingly, it is rarely indexed in his work). As early as 1951 (in *Client-Centered Therapy*), he refers to 'organic experience', and, in his theory of personality and behaviour (written as a series of propositions) he elaborates:

> II) *The organism reacts to the field as it is experienced and perceived....* III) *The organism reacts as an organized whole to this phenomenal field....* IV) *The organism has one basic tendency and striving—to actualize, maintain, and enhance the experiencing organism....* V) *Behaviour is basically the goal-directed attempt of the organism to satisfy its needs as experienced, in the field as perceived.* VI) *... the intensity of the emotion [is] related to the perceived significance of the behavior for the maintenance and enhancement of the organism.* X) *The values attached to experience, and the values which are part of the self structure, in some instances are values experienced directly by the organism....* XII) *Most of the ways of behaving which are adopted by the organism are those which are consistent with the concept of self....* XIII) *Behavior may, in some instance, be brought about by organic experiences and needs which have not been symbolized....* XIV) *Psychological maladjustment exists when the organism denies to awareness significant sensory and visceral experiences....* XV) *Psychological adjustment exists when the concept of the self is such that all the sensory and visceral experiences of the organism are, or may be, assimilated....* XIX) *As the individual perceives and accepts into his self-structure more of his organic experiences, he finds that he is replacing his present value system—based extensively on introjections which have been distortedly symbolized—with a continuing organismic valuing process.*
> (Rogers, 1951, pp. 484, 486–487, 491, 493, 498, 507, 509–510, 513, 522, original emphasis)

It is difficult for us now to appreciate just how naïve and unscientific this language would have appeared to enthusiastic behaviourists in the 1940s and 1950s. Rogers even controversially suggested that human behaviour involved something other than reaction to external stimuli, and that the cause/effect model did not offer an adequate explanation for human experience. It was only within the developing framework of humanistic psychology that it became credible to think in terms of 'growth', a concept which is meaningless if we cling to the notion that we are machines. The language of actualisation—and actualising—depends on an image of growth. Machines cannot actualise; they can only wear out.

As person-centred therapists, teachers/educators, or consultants, we don't set out to change people or organisations the way we might improve or repair a machine. We accept Rogers' proposition that change is not imposed or manipulated. As Godfrey Barrett-Lennard (2013) puts it, 'significant change is an organic process that has its own energy and basic direction, a process that [we] may at best help to release or enable' (p. 103). Rogers understood that our role is not a passive one, and that the key to a liberating process outcome is the establishment of a truly organic relationship between the therapist/facilitator and the client(s).

We are relational beings; so, too, are our clients and students. Rogers (1955/1967d) writes of the immediacy of a relationship 'in which it is my total organism which is sensitive to the relationship, not simply my consciousness', a relationship that is based 'on my total organismic sensitivity to this other person' (p. 202). We are not individual selves who connect with other individual selves to form relationships. Relationship is prior to individual identity—which is why we argue that the experience (and concept) of belonging is prior to becoming and being. We emerge moment-by-moment from the web of relationships in which we are entangled. This understanding is shared by contemporary philosophers in the same intellectual tradition, such as Christian de Quincey (2005), who argues that: 'all individuated subjects co-emerge, or co-arise, as a result of a holistic field of relationships. The being of any one subject is thoroughly dependent on the being of all other subjects with which it is in a relationship' (p. 281).

For Rogers, it is the relationship between therapist and client which enables the actualising tendency—the directional tendency evident in all organic and human life—which enables healing and creativity. Tudor and Worrall (2006) observe that PCP and practice have tended to ignore the centrality of the organism in Rogers' thinking, focussing instead on his concept of the self, and argue that his contribution to organismic theory and psychology is more significant than his contribution to self-psychology. They point out that when Hall and Lindzey included a chapter on Rogers in their *Theories of Personality* (1957), they identified him as an organismic theorist, yet in the later editions of their book (1970, 1978) they refer to him as a self-theorist, even though, by 1961, in *On Becoming a Person*, Rogers was arguing that there is no such thing as a substantial self.

If we take Rogers seriously when he uses the language of organism, we are inevitably led to consider the human individual as a whole, to avoid mind-body dualism, to reflect on the interdependence of organism and environment, and to challenge conventional notions of the self, one of the implications of which is to view belonging and connection as healthy and maintaining separateness from others as pathological. However, while we (Bernie and I) might think this is beyond argument, I (Keith) think that psychological health is still predominantly understood in terms of a 'strong ego', 'psychological adjustment', an 'internal locus of control', 'autonomy', etc.

In *Client-Centered Therapy*, Rogers (1951) defined the self in terms of our subjective perception of who we are, and proposed that we should stop thinking of 'self' as stopping at our skin and realise that any boundary we put on or to our 'self' is an arbitrary one. Ten years later, in *On Becoming a Person*, he collapsed this subject/object dichotomy, suggesting that there is no such substantial 'thing' as the self at all, for, as he put it, at a certain stage of process in psychotherapy (the sixth stage), '*Self as an object tends to disappear*':

The self, at this moment, *is* this feeling. This is a being in the moment, with little self-conscious awareness, but with primarily a reflexive awareness, as Sartre terms it. The self *is*, subjectively, in the existential moment. It is not something one perceives.

(Rogers, 1958/1967e, p. 147)

In this book, Rogers writes of 'being one's organism', 'being one's experience', 'not being a fixed quantity of traits', 'being a flowing river of change', 'being a participant in a fluid, ongoing process', and so on. Such an understanding of the self is in tune with Whitehead's process philosophy. In this understanding, the universe does not consist of 'things' at all, but of events. We are a succession of 'drops of experience', whilst the 'self' with which we are inclined to identify, is simply our recollection of our past moments of experience, a recollection which, of course, is part of our current moment of experience.

The 'fluid, ongoing process' of which Rogers writes is not confined to the individual. He saw individuals not simply as autonomous entities or members of various human social groupings but as an integral part of a much larger whole, as components of a web of nature, a nature which is constantly, creatively becoming. Rogers (1980/1995j) observed that the split between the rational mind and nature was at last being reconciled and looked forward to the day when we will all be 'ecologically minded' (p. 351) (see Chapter 3).

The therapeutic relationship, or, therapeutic relating

Rogers' ideas about the therapeutic relationship have remained influential in the education/training of therapists beyond programmes and courses that promote the person-centred framework. Unfortunately, the contribution of Rogers' (1957) original research and, more broadly, person-centred theory to such programmes is often limited to the presentation of only three of the six necessary and sufficient conditions as components of therapeutic technique, in spite of Rogers' warning that the therapist who employs them merely as technique is doomed to be unsuccessful. Thus, we take issue with the misrepresentation of these necessary and sufficient conditions as 'core conditions', for critiques and developments of which see Singh and Tudor (1997), Tudor (2000, 2011a), Embleton Tudor et al. (2004), Tudor and Worrall (2006), Rodgers et al. (2021), and, in this present work, Chapter 4 and Part 2. We should also note that, although we find it difficult to communicate without talking about our world as composed of 'things', including things called 'contact', 'incongruence', 'congruence', 'unconditional positive regard', 'empathy', and 'perception/reception', such language does not fully represent the universe as we now know it. The particles which were once perceived to be solid objects don't exist for long enough to be 'things'. The universe consists not of material substances but of connections between events—which makes a relational (re)conceptualisation of these relational 'conditions' or qualities even more important.

We can see a move towards this process view of the universe in the way Rogers (1980/1995i) talks about congruence in *A Way of Being*. Congruence is no longer to be thought of in terms of manifesting in our awareness and behaviour some sort of 'real self', as though the self has some fixed content, our awareness of which has been distorted by conditions of worth or whatever. When Rogers was first articulating his theory of congruence and its impact on healing, to some extent, he needed to accentuate the primacy of the individual and the individual (therapist's) experience of this. However, he later articulates a much broader understanding of congruence when he asks: 'Can we know... when we are in tune with the pulse beat of the world?' (Rogers, 1977/1995a, p. 313), which, we suggest, is as much about the first condition of contact—and, moreover, with our environment (see Chapter 5).

The image of 'the pulse beat of the world' is central to Rogers' cosmology. It reflects the concept of a living universe, and locates our individual process within the process of the whole. When Rogers (1963/1995e) describes his experience of therapy when he is 'at my best' he asserts that at such times his relationship with his client 'transcends itself and becomes part of something larger' (p. 129). The pulse beat of our individual experience from moment-to-moment is the pulse beat of the universe. Thus, our congruence from moment-to-moment is not merely the alignment of our personal experience, awareness, and behaviour, but the alignment of our whole being with living nature. We and our clients need to be congruent in our conscious and unconscious processes, or within our own organism: we need to be in harmony with the rhythms of nature.

If we are to avoid what Whitehead (1925/1997) calls 'the fallacy of misplaced concreteness' (p. 52) and acknowledge ourselves and our clients as process rather than substance, we have to revision not only our concept of contact and congruence but also those of unconditional positive regard and empathy (i.e., the therapist's 'conditions'), and, indeed, the therapeutic relationship itself. We cannot be either judgemental or non-judgemental of a self which has no substantial existence. The 'self' that the client brings to therapy is in the past, although their recollection of their (past) actions is in the present. However, even in observing our client in the present moment and in being present-centred, we are actually observing them in the past, as the light reflected from them and the sound they emit takes a finite time to reach us and further time to be processed in our brains before it reaches our awareness.

When Rogers (1963/1995e) defines unconditional positive regard as 'a positive, acceptant attitude to whatever the client *is* at that moment' (p. 116), he reminds us that we don't have to struggle to prize the client's self unconditionally as they have previously (and conditionally) experienced it. The past may have shaped 'whatever the client *is* at that moment', but it is only the present moment that matters (Stern, 2004). If we reflect that everything that comes to us through our senses is in the past, we must acknowledge that to be truly in the present with our client we must participate in the client's present moment, that is to say, in their subjective experience and experiencing.

When Rogers was theorising empathy in the 1950s, he emphasised that empathy involved perceiving the internal frame of reference of another person with accuracy *as if* one were the person. Empathy, as he understood it then, relied on observation and rational processing.

However, as early as 1961, he was acknowledging the influence of Martin Buber's ideas on his thinking:

> In these moments there is, to borrow Buber's phrase, a real 'I–Thou' relationship, a timeless living in the experience which is *between* the client and me. It is at the opposite pole from seeing myself or the client as an object. It is the height of personal subjectivity.
>
> (Rogers, 1955/1967d, p. 202)

This association of personal subjectivity with the I–Thou relationship is critical. Buber's thinking about the difference between I–Thou and I–It is often presented by those who have not read him as though an I–Thou relationship is simply a relationship in which the personhood of the other is properly acknowledged. For Buber this would simply be a nicer version of an I–It relationship. He insists that he is not writing about an I, a Thou, and an It who may be in relationship; he is writing about two kinds of relationship: an I–It one and an I–Thou one. In the former, there is a subject and an object; in the latter, subjectivity is shared. Empathy, as Rogers came to understand, is the experience of partaking in the moment-to-moment subjective experience of the other, of being in the 'between', outside the limitations of time and space. The height of personal subjectivity is not to be found in being an isolated individual with a full awareness of what one is individually experiencing; rather, it is found in the timeless living in the experience of relationship: it is in the *between*. In this sense, we suggest that the dash between 'I' and 'Thou'—or, as Schmid (2006) emphasises it, 'Thou' and 'I'—represents the liminality of the in between.

We know from theoretical physics that our notions of measurable, linear space and time don't represent 'reality' at all. They are merely our brain's way of surviving in the kind of universe we inhabit. We can legitimately talk of everything being contained in the present moment, and, we understand that in theoretical physics, there is an argument that 'there is only one electron' (Birch, 2008, p. 119). Gendlin and Lemke (1983) argue that, in a universe in which each item can only be measured in relation to other items, there can be no ultimate space and time. Without ultimate space and time, nothing can exist at a precise point of space and time. When Einstein stated that he was not prepared to believe in 'spooky actions at a distance' (quoted in Aczel, 2003, p. 70), Schrödinger pointed out that the evidence was against him. In the process conception of the universe which has its source in quantum physics, everything is connected: each momentary event involves the whole universe. Rogers (1980/1995j) is on the same page:

> There is a convergence of theoretical physics and mysticism—especially Eastern mysticism—a recognition that the whole universe, including ourselves, is

'a cosmic dance'. In this view, matter, time and space disappear as meaningful concepts; there exist only oscillations.

(p. 345)

In such a universe we should expect to find the boundaries we construct between us dissolving. Subjectivity can be shared. Messages don't have to pass through distance to go from one organism to the other. Often enough, the sense that someone dear to us is in pain or in trouble is registered in our body without having to pass between the space between us, and comes to our awareness through what we call intuition.

Intuition: A pre-condition or quality, and the next great frontier of learning

Intuition and phenomena such as remote sensing, thought transmission, clairvoyance, and synchronicity are exactly what we should expect to find in the kind of universe revealed by science, or, at least, the new science.

When Rogers writes positively about what are conventionally called parapsychological phenomena, it's a signal for some of his readers to decide that he is no longer to be taken seriously. They ignore the mountain of evidence, including that presented by Radin (1997, 2006) and Haule (2011) that demonstrates the— or a—reality of phenomena which, Rogers (1977/1995a) asserts, constitutes 'the next frontier of learning',

> the area in which we will be exploring exciting new possibilities, [which] is a region scarcely mentioned by hard-headed researchers. It is the area of the intuitive, the psychic, the vast inner space that looms before us… the area that currently seems illogical and irrational.
>
> (p. 312)

It is becoming increasingly clear that while logic and rationality have proved to be very useful instruments in predicting and controlling events in our everyday lives, they fall short when we use them to explore the universe beyond the reach of our senses.

Rogers (1977/1995a) asserts that to function fully as therapists 'we need to learn more about our intuitive abilities, our capacity for sensing with our whole organism' (p. 313). Like other theorists and practitioners (Charles, 2004; Hart, 2000; Haule, 2011; Vaughan, 1979), he sees intuition as a phenomenon of the same kind as remote sensing and mental telepathy. He suggests that such phenomena represented a capacity familiar to pre-scientific humans, a capacity which had atrophied through neglect in more so-called 'civilised' cultures. He argues, however, that it was possible to regain this capacity. In commenting on the 'undeveloped psychic powers' and the 'mysterious, unspoken communication' that he had witnessed in groups, Rogers' (1963/1995e) writing takes a transpersonal turn:

When I am at my best, as a group facilitator or as a therapist, I discover another characteristic. I find that when I am closest to my inner, intuitive self, when I am somehow in touch with the unknown in me, when perhaps I am in a state of slightly altered consciousness in the relationship, then whatever I do seems to be full of healing... Our relationship transcends itself and becomes a part of something larger. Profound growth and healing and energy are present.

(p. 129)

Rogers reflects a great deal on the nature of the 'something larger'. This included what he refers to as 'the good life'.

The good life

For Rogers (1957/1967h), 'the good life' involves the courage to be: 'It means launching oneself into the stream of life.' He continues: 'Yet the deeply exciting thing about human beings is that when the individual is inwardly free he [sic] chooses as the good life this process of becoming' (p. 196). If we are taking Rogers seriously, we need to acknowledge that in this brief statement he is being serious about several different ideas.

Firstly, he suggests that we must get rid of our egoic, heroic notion that we are isolated individuals who spend our lives making independent decisions, and let ourselves be carried along by the flow. Secondly, he tells us that he has found this flow to be in a positive direction. Thirdly, he observes that, in his experience, when people through therapy become free to move in any direction, they all seem to move in a similar direction, i.e., a positive one. Fourthly, he refers to 'becoming' as a process in which we participate. Finally, he suggests that letting ourselves be carried along by the flow of life is compatible with choosing freely. In the same book, he articulates a process conception of psychotherapy in which describes a movement from fixity to fluidity (Rogers, 1958/1967c), a concept that prefigures Csikszentmihalyi's (1990) work on flow.

When Rogers acknowledges that there is no possibility of a sharp line between organism and environment, and talks about launching oneself into the stream of life, he seems to suggest that we have little control over the direction we are taking. Yet he also declares that the fully functioning person is a separate, unique, self-governing individual. Surely, he is contradicting himself? We suggest that this is not lazy thinking. Rogers is following his intuition, backed by his experience, which tells him—and us—that this is not a contradiction, but a paradox. It is clear throughout his work that he doesn't believe that we can state incontrovertible facts about reality; rather, we are limited to stating perspectives. Both sides of this paradox represent some truth about the human condition, as does the tension between them. The issue of free choice and determinism is a critical one, and one that has been the focus of philosophers since human beings became capable of critical thought. It is clear enough in Rogers' writing that the conviction that our lives are embedded in a cosmic movement does not inhibit him from asserting and celebrating the reality of choice.

The holistic relationship between the organism and the cosmos may appear to imply loss of individuality and even loss of the capacity to choose, but Rogers (1963/1995e) does not see it this way: 'With greater self-awareness, a more informed choice is possible, a choice more free from introjects, a conscious choice which is even more in tune with the evolutionary flow… Consciousness is participating in this larger, creative formative tendency' (p. 127).

Rogers' philosophy proposes that the flow of life is not something that controls us but something into which we have creative input and

> To be at home in a world that consists only of vibrating energy, a world with no solid base, a world of process and change, a world in which the mind, in its larger sense, is both aware of, and creates, the new reality.
>
> (p. 352)

We learn something about Rogers' (1980/1995j) vision of the good life when we read his discussion of the world and person of tomorrow. His utopian vision is of a transformed world populated by people who are authentic, caring, open to experience, close to nature, distrustful of authority, sceptical, seeking intimacy, spiritual; aware that the one certainty of life is change. He imagines, with his confidence tempered by ambiguity, that this is where the flow of life is 'inevitably' taking us—'unless we blow ourselves up' (p. 355).

Conclusion

Even those of us who think that Rogers mainly got it right, and don't reject either his cosmology or the spiritual turn of his later writing, are challenged by the implications of ideas which Rogers himself took very seriously. We might believe that children will learn what they need to know if given the freedom to do so (Rogers, 1969, 1983), yet reserve the right to regulate them and maintain control of the process. We might believe ourselves to be committed to the PCA, yet imagine that it is our grasp of technique and/or the therapeutic relationship which is responsible for a positive outcome. We might place the actualising tendency at the centre of our understanding of what is happening in therapy, yet fail to wonder how an individual can have direction if this direction is not a manifestation of 'something larger'.

Some—both outside and within the PCA—are reluctant to take Rogers seriously when he starts talking about 'something larger'. They may think and/or feel that, if PCP is to maintain any credibility, we need to ignore or forget much of what Rogers was saying in his later writings and continue to practice within the mechanistic paradigm, after all, the half-truths of the mechanistic paradigm have served us well for some time. Despite its blind spots and its logical inconsistencies, it produces the measurable outcomes that our culture, or at least, health care managers and politicians, demand. We, however, argue that the half-truths of the organic paradigm help us understand the world in which we find ourselves. Rogers did not claim to have 'got it right' by doing his thinking within the organic paradigm, and it would be foolish for us or anyone else to make such a claim on his behalf. If we accept his epistemology, we have to limit our commitment to his conclusions, not least to avoid the fallacy of dogmatic finality, as, indeed, Rogers himself did, reserving the right to change his ideas as new evidence appeared.

Having set out some of the ways in which we take Rogers seriously, in the next two chapters we focus on the implications of (t)his ontology and epistemology for the mind and consciousness, and ego.

Note

1 All dates noted in this book are to Common Era (CE) or Before Common Era (BCE).

2 The mind of things

Introduction

In Chapter 1 we lay—or, depending on when you, the reader, are reading these present words, laid—out our view of Rogers as an organismic psychologist, implicitly drawing on process or process-relational philosophy. In this chapter, and drawing on the work of Jean Gebser, we consider the implication for a person-centred epistemology, that is, a theory of mind and consciousness.

Soul in Education (Bernie)

Some years ago, colleagues and I attended a conference on *Soul in Education* in Byron Bay—a beautiful subtropical location in northern New South Wales beloved by tourists, new agers, and hippies. Conference participants were delightfully diverse, ranging from alternative lifestyle types to academics from South Australia. There was a fair bit of magical consciousness around. The diversity of the participants' worldviews made for interesting and stimulating discussions.

The conference plenary sessions took place in the venue's refectory. Originally, the plan was to run these sessions in a large marquee on the grounds surrounded by a number of smaller tents where workshops were conducted. However, high winds on the first afternoon of the conference had collapsed the large marquee, and attempts by the conference organisers to persuade the contractor to set it up again had failed, to the extent that they had stopped the payment. On the last afternoon of the conference, I took part in a music workshop where we were experiencing the different sensibilities associated with the different scales on which ancient and medieval European music was based. We'd worked our way through the Ionian and Phrygian modes and the rest and came finally to the seventh and last mode, the Locrian. Our workshop leader explained that this mode was forbidden in churches in the Middle Ages. Because of its dissonance it was called the Devil's mode and people believed that if you played it the Devil himself would appear. Our leader declared that he would play it anyway and see what happened. As with all the others, he played it on his keyboard, and we listened and then hummed or sang it. The moment we finished, a truck roared up and a half a dozen men jumped out and started pulling down the tent, with what seemed

DOI: 10.4324/9781003397731-4

unnecessary violence. When we remonstrated they explained that it was because 'You haven't paid your money!' We sent them off to talk to the organisers and the matter was resolved.

Academics, like me, are inclined to pass off such events as amusing coincidences. Our rational consciousness does not allow such events to be meaningful. Yet, sitting in that tent with that group of people, there was no way to avoid a sense that the Devil's scale and roaring trucks were somehow connected.

Later that day we had a ritual to conclude the conference. Participants went off to the beach or the bush to find an object which 'called to us'. We brought them in and placed them in the centre of the room. The woman who was to choreograph the ritual asked us to form a human mandala, lying on the floor around the chosen objects, with our hands and feet touching. Those who were too slow or not sufficiently extroverted remained standing around the circle. As we lay on the floor, two indigenous women, tribal elders from northern Australia, ritually 'smoked' us with smouldering eucalyptus branches. Then we were told to start vocalising, making whatever sounds came naturally. Those outside the circle were invited to join in by vocalising or playing instruments. So, along with our voices there were guitars, a flute, a tambourine, a drum, and a couple of professional singers—Oscar and Marigold—who vocalised a sort of descant above the sound made by the rest of us. The whole performance was conducted with a turkey feather by a Native American elder who had been a central figure in the conference. It was all very nice and good fun. After a few minutes I got the sense that something strange was happening. The air felt electric, and there was a dull roar which didn't seem to be coming from us. Oscar and Marigold's singing was reaching higher and higher. Just as it reached its peak the room was struck by lightning, and the rain poured down.

My archaic mind felt the earth move.

My magical mind had no doubts about what it all meant. I felt in my bones that the ritual had 'worked'. We'd broken the drought. Many of my companions, the New Age types, were only too ready to confirm this: 'Of course our ritual has brought the lightning and rain. With all that psychic energy concentrated in one spot, what else would you expect?' Our Aboriginal elders were shaking their heads and saying, 'It's just as well we didn't use an eagle feather' and our Native American elder was saying 'We don't have turkeys like that in America!'

My mythical mind was caught between two ways of imagining our world. There was the conventional academic, scientific narrative within which I live my professional life, which says that such things don't happen, and a very different narrative, apparently shared by all my Byron Bay friends, in which such things happen all the time. They assured me that if I was a serious Jungian, as I seemed to be claiming, I should recognise synchronicity when I saw it.

My mental-rational mind could see that this was merely coincidence. This particular meteorological event had been building up in real time, and nothing that a group of people might be doing in this place at this time could possibly affect it. The preparations for this event took place some time ago when nobody could have foretold that we would be there at that time, in that room, making a noise.

My integral mind simply accepted the paradox.

Five-minded animals

When looking for the implications of 'five-mindedness' for therapy it is not historical or evolutionary development which interests us. Rather, it is the way these minds push and pull against each other in a therapeutic interaction, for, as Gebser (1949/1986) claimed, 'we must first of all remain cognizant that these structures are not merely past, but are in fact still present in more or less latent and acute form in each of us' (p. 42), or, as Jung (1977) wrote, 'We keep forgetting that we are primates and that we have to make allowances for these primitive layers in our psyche' (p. 119).

Within the mental structure of consciousness, dominant in Western societies since the Enlightenment, we see ourselves as individuals; consciousness as something which belongs to each of us separately. This was not Gebser's focus. He says little about individual psychology. In his discussion of the emergence of the structures of consciousness he does not find a place to mention Jean Piaget who was developing a theory of child development which paralleled Gebser's theory in significant ways. Piaget's (1936/1952) four stages of cognitive development—sensorimotor (infancy), pre-operational (early childhood), concrete operational (later childhood), and formal operational (adolescence and adulthood)—come close enough to Gebser's descriptions of archaic, magic, mythical, and mental-rational consciousness to have at least aroused his curiosity.

However, where Piaget's thinking was limited by his commitment to a hierarchical concept or taxonomy of stages of development, Gebser's idea of the different kinds of consciousness is not hierarchical. Some structures are more complex than others, but they are not an advance on them. The notion that they appear in sequence from most 'primitive' to most 'advanced' is a construction of our mental consciousness, which measures and calculates. Reality, for Gebser, is not constrained by our concepts of time and space. Everything is present in the present moment, though our mental-rational consciousness does not experience it in this way.

Kieran Egan's (1997) model of cognitive development echoes Piaget's, but, like Gebser, Egan is much more aware of the impact of culture on individual consciousness. In expounding his model of psychological development in the *Educated Mind*, Egan suggested that we are 'five-minded animals', explaining: 'We have, you might say, a fivefold mind, or, more dramatically, we are a five-minded animal in whom different kinds of understanding jostle together and fold on one another, to some degree remaining "somewhat distinct"' (p. 80).

The parallels between Egan's five minds and Gebser's structures of consciousness are obvious enough. Like Gebser, Egan lays them out in sequence: the somatic mind of infants, the magical mind of early childhood, the romantic mind of late childhood and early adolescence, the philosophic mind of late adolescence and early adulthood, and the ironic mind of the mature individual; and sees these minds as 'jostling together' rather than sequentially replacing one another. Similarly, Kegan (1983, 1998) distinguished five stages in psychological development, which he labelled the five 'orders of consciousness'. Both Egan and Kegan want us to understand that as we develop new ways of thinking and understanding through the course of childhood and adolescence, we don't outgrow and leave behind our earlier ways of understanding.

Gebser's focus on culture reminds us that we don't do our thinking as entirely autonomous individuals. We may be inclined to think of a culture as the aggregation of the thoughts, attitudes, assumptions, and behaviours of a particular group of individuals. We need to remember that group mind and group consciousness are not the sum of the minds or consciousness of the members of that particular group. On the contrary, individual consciousness has grown out of, and is grounded in, group consciousness.

Merlin Donald (1991, 2001) argues that, from the beginning, cognitive evolution has been tethered to culture. We may live more or less comfortably in what he calls 'the myth of the isolated mind'; yet it is the advantage of having a collective consciousness which has made us successful as a species. In his history of the evolution of cognition and culture, Donald points to three major transitions which changed the nature of human consciousness. The consciousness of our primate ancestors was episodic: they had awareness, sensitivity to events and the capacity to react to them, but no capacity for conscious, purposeful action. The first transition, a couple of million years ago, was to mimetic consciousness. Early humans had this new cognitive capacity which their primate ancestors had lacked, a capacity which involved body language, imitation, gesture, and intentional vocal sound. These enabled the development of a group mentality and a human culture. The second transition, to mythic consciousness, came with the emergence of *Homo sapiens* about 125,000 years ago. Spoken language produced oral culture, and ritual and spoken language held the clans and tribes together, giving them an advantage over competing subspecies. By Donald's reckoning, the third transition to theoretic consciousness came about 40,000 years ago with the emergence of technologies which made it increasingly possible to externalise memory. No longer did humans have to rely entirely on their brains to remember; no longer did they have to work out everything for themselves.

Both Piaget and Donald miss the crucial insight that is central to Gebser's work: that logical, rational thinking is not the most we can do. Our minds can handle paradox, irony, ambivalence, and mystery—and we live in a world where we need to use all of our minds. In the rest of this chapter, we describe and discuss Gebser's taxonomy of five minds as offering an epistemological basis for a person-centred theory of mind and, ultimately, for helping us to know, sense, and appreciate the mind of others (see Chapter 9).

Archaic mind

In archaic consciousness, the therapist and client do not inhabit separate worlds, nor are they separate from the planet and the cosmos. Gebser (1949/1986) compares it with 'the original state of biblical paradise: a time where the soul is yet dormant, a time of complete non-differentiation of man and the universe' (p. 43).

We slip back into our archaic unity-consciousness in deep sleep, or enter it voluntarily or involuntarily through trance, drugs, or certain kinds of meditation.

Our archaic minds have a dim awareness, which is bodily, pre-reflective, pre-lingual. A great deal of our behaviour, maybe most, is unconscious, even robotic. We experience the world and react to its stimuli without awareness. Our bodies are enmeshed in a physical world. For a few million years they functioned adequately in this world without the need for conscious attention. They continue to do so now, when our attention is absent.

We can, if we choose, change our ordinary state of consciousness to this less complex state through auto-suggestion, deep relaxation, or being put into trance by hypnosis; or by chanting, music, dancing, or drumming; or we can stop all mental activity for a time and let ourselves slip into a much simpler state of being. If we just sit, cease doing anything—with no thoughts, images, feelings, intentions—we may find that we can enter a state of trance in which our sense of our individual reflecting ego, and our sense of the boundary between our internal and external worlds, greatly diminish. We can enter a state in which we and the universe are comfortably one. In the language of developmental psychology or evolutionary psychology this simplest form of meditative trance is a regressive experience, a return to 'primitive' or intra-uterine experience through the shutting down of individual awareness. Through our pre-reflective, archaic consciousness we experience ourselves, however dimly, as continuous with the physical universe. There is no 'I'. There is no 'other'. There is no 'environment'. There is no reflection. There is only experience and instinct.

A dimly experienced oneness with the universe may seem to have little to do with therapy, but Gebser argues that the archaic structure of consciousness is the ground of all the others. Empathy is, for Gebser, utterly basic to the human condition, and the experience of oneness with the universe is the ground of our empathic experience of other people. We do not have separate lives, as individuals, groups, tribes, nations, or a species. The life in us is the life which is in everything. The relationship between therapist and client is based in an identity of being both with each other and with a universe in which time, space, and ego are illusions. We identify with the conscious mind through which we know ourselves as separate, autonomous, decision-making beings, but all the while we are connected to the universe through an archaic mind which is neither autonomous nor decision-making. Consciously we experience our own anxiety and, through empathy, the pain of those close to us. Unconsciously we experience the pain and stress of the planet.

Our connection with the universe is a physical one. For all the narrowness of its vision, behavioural psychology had one crucial insight: there is a level of human behaviour for which self-awareness is entirely irrelevant. Though we imagine ourselves to be self-aware beings, most of our behaviour is unconscious. We react to stimuli physically and emotionally; our awareness catches up after the event. There is evidence that even when we consciously choose to act, our body starts to move in the chosen direction before we are aware of making the choice. We are entirely entangled in our human and nonhuman world. Gebser suggests, more radically, that in our pre-reflective, archaic consciousness we do not have separate identities. We are parts of a bigger system in which we interact without awareness. It is our mental consciousness which constructs the arbitrary boundaries between self and other.

In describing therapy or, at least, his 'newer psychotherapy', Rogers' (1942) focus was on subjective experience, on the individual's capacity for choice. Not only does the therapist experience empathic understanding, the client must be aware of or, at some level, perceive this empathy. However, Carkhuff (1969a, 1969b) challenges Rogers' assumption that the therapeutic conditions are not effective unless they are communicated to the client, arguing that congruence, acceptance, and empathy are of themselves instrumental in effecting the client's healing, whether or not the client is aware of them being offered. Whether we think about therapeutic conditions à la Rogers or à la Carkhuff, we should consider that there is more than one mind in each of us, and that one of these minds works in just this way—with minimal awareness and no reflection. Our archaic minds are not dependent on verbal or visual communication. Our bodies may appear to be separate, but our embodied archaic minds are not, nor are they separate from the greater organism of which we are cells. From this perspective with regard to:

1. Psychological contact—we are already in contact with (what we might think of as) the other.
2. Client incongruence—we (as therapists) will also be experiencing or have experienced this form or aspect of discrepancy between experience and self-structure.
3. Our congruence or, rather, being congruent, genuine, or authentic in the relationship—this involves living as the kind of beings we are, at depth and breadth (i.e., in relationship or harmony with the universe).
4. Our unconditional positive regard, acceptance, or love, and to our empathic understanding or empathy—these don't have to leap across the space between us; they are present, or not.
5. The client's perception of the therapist's acceptance and understanding—again, it is not about being given or taking it/them, it is more about them being there in the in-between.

Whitehead (1925/1997, 1929/1978) argues that every 'drop of experience' of which the universe is constituted is dipolar—it has both a physical and a mental pole. In a molecule or a cell, the physical pole is dominant. In human experience, the mental pole is generally dominant. However, in our archaic consciousness, in those moments of experience where we lack awareness, it is the physical pole which dominates. The mental pole becomes dominant as we experience life through the more complex structures of consciousness.

Magical mind

Our archaic minds experience instinct and stimulus and act on them automatically. Our magical minds bring awareness and emotion to our impulse. We have no sense of individual selfhood, but experience 'the vegetative intertwining of all living things… in the egoless magic sphere of every human being' (Gebser, 1949/1986, p. 49). This sense of 'vegetative entwinement' is timeless, spaceless, and egoless.

Identity belongs to the group; we are one with the clan, bound to it by our emotions. It is this shared consciousness that Gebser labelled 'magical'. It may be the shared consciousness of the football (rugby) crowd, who collectively feel the fatigue, despair, and delight of the players and who engage in various rituals to ensure a propitious outcome. It may be the 'participation mystique' (Jung, 1921/1971; Lévy-Brühl, 1910/1985) of a mother and new-born child, the phenomenon of sympathetic illness or pregnancy, the uncanny coincidences in the experiences of twins. In such circumstances there can be an immediacy of communication through body-sense and emotion. Our magical mind does not have, and does not need, words. A rational, scientistic culture ignores this phenomenon, or labels it 'telepathy' and tries to find an explanation for it within the conventional communication paradigm. Pre-scientific cultures accept such phenomena as a matter of course, along with all the magical phenomena which we now label 'parapsychological'. For Gebser, these experiences are perfectly usual and normal.

Many therapists will admit to experiencing physical sensations, tensions, or pains while working with their clients, sensations which seem to belong to the client rather than themselves. The therapist may have an experience of fear, despair, or depression, and with it a sense that it is not their own response to something the client has said, but somehow a direct experience of what is going on in the client. This phenomenon has been reflected on much more within the analytic tradition than elsewhere and has been given labels by Freudian and Jungian writers such as 'projective identification' (Klein, 1952), 'syntonic countertransference' (Fordham, 1957), or 'reflected countertransference' and 'embodied countertransference' wherein 'the analyst's body is not entirely his or hers alone and what it says to him or her is not a message for him or her alone' (Samuels, 1989, p. 164). Within the person-centred tradition, Tudor (2011c) notes his use of the term 'visceral empathy' and Cooper (2001) refers to 'embodied empathy' to describe the therapist's embodied attunement, in which the therapist is resonating with 'the complex, gestalt-like mosaic of her client's embodied being… [in which] the whole of the therapist's body is alive in the interaction, moving and vibrating in tandem with the client's experiencing' (p. 223). Integrating neo-Reichian bodywork and PCP, Cameron (2000, 2002a, 2002b, 2004, 2015) raises our awareness of the embodied experience of the energy in the room, which challenges the notion of the separateness of our bodies.

Likewise, the client may have a direct experience of what is going on in the therapist, may feel in their body the therapist's stress or calm. Indeed, the therapist may be directing the client towards wellbeing through their non-verbal communication of their support for the client's actualising tendency. This does not have to be intentional on the part of the therapist, and it does not have to reach the client's awareness. Magical consciousness does not need and, indeed, does not have, words. If we drop our ego-centric assumptions, we can imagine a reality in which everything is connected, in which the shared somatic or imaginative experience of client and therapist are not transmitted from one to the other, but are, literally, co-incidental. This may not be the world as we rational, sophisticated people perceive it, but it is the—or a—real world nonetheless, and we usually experience it unconsciously.

Magical behaviour was quite adequate as a way of dealing with the world in the well-functioning tribal community and there are still aspects of our experience that we should attribute to magical consciousness. Our ability to heal ourselves by means of placebos, and the power of group religious ritual to heal and transform, attest to magical consciousness being a valid response to the world. Magical consciousness is found in therapies in which the healer is envisaged as a conduit for a transpersonal, palpable, healing energy (i.e., chi, reiki, orgone energy, or the Holy Spirit) rather than as someone whose personal intervention heals the patient, or even as someone who facilitates the patient's self-healing. It is found in traditional healing ceremonies where healer and patient enter a common psychic space through ritual.

Even conventional therapy is surrounded by ritual and 'magic'. The display of the therapist's qualifications on the office wall; the furniture; the way the therapist dresses: all are designed to influence the client. Labels such as 'Dr', 'psychologist', or 'registered psychotherapist' are used to predispose the client to a positive outcome. The exchange of money has ritual significance—the more expensive the consultation, the greater the expectation of healing or cure. In this, the individual client is, likely enough, not thinking about such things, rather, is carried along by the shared assumptions of their cultural group. We might (like to) think that person-centred therapists are less inclined to engage in these forms of ritual and magic than therapists of other persuasions, but magic is not easily avoided, even if that were totally desirable.

We cannot escape magic. We fill our lives with ritual: the morning cup of coffee, the favourite chair, the way we greet our clients: all function to keep us safe and to keep the world turning smoothly. We may have perfectly good, rational explanations about why we sit in a particular chair and decorate our consulting room in a particular way, but there is magic involved in all of this. Last time we did x, y happened; if we do x again, y will happen again. There may be perfectly sound theoretical reasons for doing x, but the magical mind simply bypasses them and does it because 'it works'. We may think that we are making our own decisions about our professional practice, but our actions are embedded in the ways of behaving in the particular professional clan to which we belong: 'This is the way we do things around here. If we do things differently something terrible will happen'. Those of us who take a more critical, political, and/or deconstructivist stance in and about therapy challenge the rationality of traditional explanations or ways of doing things (simply because Freud or Rogers did them); thinking about professional practice and, indeed, the professionalisation of practice; and embedded behaviour (see House, 2003, 2010; House & Totton, 1997; Tudor, 2017/2020).

Rogers found that if he constantly checked that he was understanding the client correctly, if he helped the client to find words for something felt but inadequately said, he got to understand what was going on in the client and was able to support them in their exploration. Somehow this was transformed into something called 'reflective listening' and, subsequently, therapists were trained in this 'technique'. Where the ritual reflection of content and feeling (or any other technique) is assumed to be therapeutically effective in and of itself, we are talking about magic.

It is not what Rogers had in mind. What he did have in mind was the healing power of the truly contactful, acceptant, and empathic relationship. In his theory lay the germ of the idea that relationship in and of itself is healing, because non-relationship is a toxic attack on the essence of who we are—and, ultimately, our existence.

Mythical mind

While the magical structure of consciousness is sensate, pre-rational, and pre-verbal; the mythical structure is imaginal, irrational, and verbal. It maintains the collective identity of the magical along with a limited sense of individuality. Mythical mind does not give me a direct experience of how you are and feel; rather, it enables me to imagine how you are and feel, and it enables this because our separate stories are a common story.

Mythical thinking is characterised by image and narrative. Its time is rhythmical or circular, a continuous reiteration of the basic narratives of our relationship to the world. Mythical empathy involves the therapist entering into the client's story, recognising its universality as well as its uniqueness, being in the story with the client. In our mythical consciousness we are both one and separate. I know your story by knowing my own; I know my story by knowing yours. The more intensely personal your story is, the more universal it is, and the more it is intensely mine. As Rogers (1961/1967i) notes: '*What is most personal is most general*' (p. 26, original emphasis). However, we do not assume, as we might in magical consciousness, that your story and my story are indistinguishable. Rather, the relationship is something which includes yet transcends these separate identities:

> In terms of the therapeutic situation, I think this feeling says to the client, I have a real hunger to know you, to experience your warmth, your expressivity—in whatever form it may take—to drink as deeply as I can from the experience of you in the closest, most naked relationship we can achieve. I do not want to change you to suit me; the real you and the real me are perfectly compatible ingredients of a potential relationship which transcends, but in no way violates, our separate identities.
>
> (Rogers, 1951, p. 164)

In our mythical consciousness, the thoughts we have are not strictly our own. We do our thinking within narratives into which we have been born or adopted to replace inherited narratives that we have found inadequate. Most of our beliefs and values are tribal. They have generally been absorbed at a young age from our culture: families, education, peers, the media, and so on, and accepted without reflection as 'the way the world is'. We do our thinking within the taken-for-granted, shared story about who we are and what sort of a world we live in.

Insofar as they are functioning at the level of what Kegan (1998) calls 'third order mind', both therapist and client, bring their respective myths to their interaction. The client lives within a narrative which defines appropriate roles, values, and behaviours. These may be taken completely for granted, or present as a tension with a different set of roles, values, and behaviours which belong to a different narrative and are currently forcing themselves on the client's attention. Therapists also come with a narrative which defines appropriate roles, values, and behaviour, both for themselves and for the client. As long as therapist and client continue to operate in third order/mythical consciousness, the only available outcomes are either confirmation of the client's old or emerging value-package (whichever best matches the therapist's narrative) or an unsuccessful attempt to shake the client free of a narrative which the therapist does not share.

Whereas magical mind works through emotion, mythical mind works through image. Construction of images is a right-brain activity. The right brain processes in image what the left brain can only process in words. Obviously the two often work together. However, a lot of what we call thinking might be better called imagining. It can be argued that all our language is based on metaphor, and that even the most sophisticated theories are grounded in our imagination. They are ways of imagining the world at least as much as there are ways of thinking about it (see Chapter 5).

Right-brain therapies such as Jungian active imagination and Assagioli's psychosynthesis depend on the ability to engage mythical consciousness. The therapist enters the imaginal world of the client and stays with the client's images, not interpreting, not rationalising, being an affirming presence in the imaginal world, helping the client to tell the story. Many person-centred therapists utilise the mythical structure when they cease reflecting and responding, and simply tune in to the client and wait for their felt sense to deliver an image.

Gendlin's concept of the 'felt sense' has been influential in the way many person-centred therapists go about their work. Gendlin (1981) suggests that we trust our somatic experience, and rest in this fuzzy, wordless 'felt sense', waiting for an image to emerge and patiently interrogating this image until we find words for our experience. The therapist can recommend this process to their client and guide them through it. More powerfully, therapist and client together can stop talking and start listening and rest in the felt sense of their being together in this transformational moment, allowing their (co-created and co-experienced) felt sense to deliver images which may help them articulate the meaning of their experience, each understanding that the images 'belong' to both of them.

For most of us, most of the time, our experience of the mythical world is diluted by reflection, abstraction, and pre-conception. The mythical world is far more unitary than the conceptualised world of mental-rational consciousness. It does not manifest the either/or of dualistic, rational thinking. Rather, its world is dipolar, taking the rational mind's oppositions—body/mind, conscious/unconscious, self/other, health/pathology, goodness/badness, subject/object, female/male, spirit/matter, one/many, even truth/falsehood—as complementary manifestations of a unitary reality. The mythical world is not a world of 'dead matter' like the world of rational, mechanistic science; it is ensouled, alive, replete with divinity (or divinities).

Jung (1964) refers to the sense of being in rational control of our lives (as epitomised in the motto 'Where's there's a will, there's a way') as 'the superstition of modern man' (p. 82). He states that:

> in order to sustain his creed, contemporary man pays the price in a remarkable lack of introspection. He is blind to the fact that, with all his rationality and efficiency, he is possessed by 'powers' that are beyond his control. His gods and demons have not disappeared at all; they have merely got new names. They keep him on the run with restlessness, vague apprehensions, psychological complications, [and] an insatiable need for pills, alcohol, tobacco, food—and, above all, a large array of neuroses.
>
> (p. 82)

From his examination of Homer's *Iliad* (8th century BCE), Julian Jaynes (1976) argues that, when these stories were first told, the ancient Greeks had no sense of being individuals who reflected on their situation and made decisions; they just did what the gods told them to do. He suggests that the ancient Greeks heard the gods' voices inside their heads and acted upon them. Their behaviour was governed by messages from the right cerebral hemisphere. However, by the time the stories in the *Odyssey* were first told (8th/7th century), they were able to reflect on their behaviour and make conscious, rational (left-brain) decisions. If Jaynes is right, the shift from right-brain dominance to left-brain dominance in the 7th century marks the breakdown of the mythical structure of consciousness in Greek culture and the emergence of the mental structure. Now we find them 'jostling together'.

Mental-rational mind

Our mythical mind allows us to live our lives within narratives which give meaning to what we do and meaning to whatever happens to us. However, we have a mental mind which enables us to check these narratives against the 'facts' of our experience. Our mental-rational consciousness is at work when we look at the world objectively, assess the facts, see connections, count, estimate, calculate, and plan. Mental consciousness is self-conscious, individualistic, and proactive.

In Rogers' early theorising about the nature of empathy, he was clearly concerned to develop a logical, systematic, and abstract way of explaining the phenomenon and its implications for therapy. He accepts the assumptions that therapist and client exist in separate, rational worlds; that one can look only from one direction at a time; and that, while the therapist knows the client's frame of reference, they don't experience any confusion of identity, or become engulfed in the client's experiencing. The therapist's value to the client depends on the latter's determination to maintain their distinct separateness. Rogers (1958) expresses this idea with some emphasis:

> Am I strong enough in my own separateness that I will not be downcast by his depression, downcast by his fear nor engulfed by his dependency? Is my

inner self hardy enough to realise that I am not destroyed by his anger, taken over by his need for dependence, nor enslaved by his love, but that I can exist separate from him with feelings and needs of my own? When I can freely feel this strength of being a separate person, then I can let myself go much more in understanding and accepting him.

(p. 15)

In *Client-Centered Therapy*, Rogers (1951) consciously and deliberately works within a mental-rational framework. Take his reflections on the proposition (VII): '*The best vantage point for understanding behaviour is from the internal frame of reference of the individual himself*' (p. 494). Here Rogers argues that human behaviour, no matter how bizarre it may appear to the observer, is always rational and purposive, 'in response to reality as it is perceived' (p. 494). He takes the perfectly rational view that, while it would be desirable to 'empathically experience all the sensory and visceral sensations of the individual' (p. 494), this is impossible. Admitting that a great deal of the client's experience of the phenomenal world is not brought to the conscious level, Rogers argues that, on the one hand, it is unsatisfactory to try to understand the client's unconscious experiencing through an external interpretative framework, and, on the other hand, to stay with the client's awareness gives us an incomplete picture. He acknowledges that the therapist's understanding of the client's phenomenal world will be at least partly derived by inferences from elements of that world that belong to the therapist and client's common experience or experiencing. Throughout (t)his discussion, the client's world is clearly the client's, and the therapist's world is clearly the therapist's; the contents of one can pass to the other only by communication and (less accurately) by observation.

Moreover, Rogers (1951) saw the aim of therapy as helping the client 'to perceive himself as the evaluator of experience, rather than regarding himself as existing in a world where the values are inherent in and attached to the object of his perception' (p. 139). He wants the client to move from the taken-for-granted world of third order consciousness to the critically observed world of fourth order consciousness: to emerge from the discomfort of living within a myth that does not match his experience, so that they can take responsibility for their own values and beliefs. In discussing this dynamic, Kegan uses the example of Rogers and Gloria, in the film *Three Approaches to Psychotherapy* (Shostrom, 1965). Towards the end of an interview in which Gloria has been unable to get Rogers to tell her what she should do, we find the following interaction:

GLORIA: [After a pause] I do feel that you have been saying to me—you are not giving me advice but I do feel like you are saying, 'You know what pattern you want to follow, Gloria, and go ahead and do it.' I sort of feel a backing up from you.
ROGERS: I guess the way I sense it, you've been telling me that you know what *you* want to do and yes, I do believe in backing up people in what *they* want to do. It's a little different slant than the way it seems to you.

(quoted in Kegan 1998, pp. 245–246)

When Gloria expresses confusion, Rogers points out that there is little point in her doing something that she has not actually chosen to do, and that what he has been trying to do is help her find out what her 'inner choices' are. Rogers' narrative involves the view that Gloria's 'actualising tendency' will enable her to move from the conditions of worth of third order/mythical mind to the independent action of fourth order/mental mind. Kegan does not appear to share this assumption, and argues that Gloria may (then, currently) be incapable of fourth order consciousness, in which case she will simply not be able to understand what he is talking about. She may not have attained the psychological development necessary to take on the role of 'author' of her own life, which is a function of mental consciousness.

The mental-rational mind seeks clarity, demanding a coherent theoretical framework within which to work and pursuing the fantasy that once we see clearly the causes and consequences of our self-destructive behaviour, we will cease to act in this way. Change comes through insight. In this context, empathy is essentially an act of intellection (i.e., the action or process of understand, as distinct from imagination). The therapist strives to understand what the world of the client is like. It has no necessary connection with feeling, and it is certainly not to be mistaken for sympathy. There is no losing of boundaries. What's yours is yours, what's mine is mine, and there must be no confusion. Nevertheless, like Jung, Rogers was 'beset by the all-too-human fear that consciousness—our Promethean conquest—may in the end not be able to serve us as well as nature' (Jung, 1931/1979, para. 750).

Our mental-rational minds imagine that self-actualisation is something we do, rather than something we allow to happen. In Rogers' (1963/1995e) thinking about both the actualising tendency and the formative tendency, he has no doubt that growth, by whatever name, is not our personal, Promethean achievement, but a consequence of our enmeshment in 'the directional trend which is evident in all organic and human life' (p. 351). In this he is on the same page as Jung who, when asked if individuation didn't always involve consciousness, replied that such a notion was an 'overvaluation of consciousness' (quoted in Sabini, 2002, p. 10), and explained that individuation is the natural process by which a human being becomes a human being, in the same process as that by which a tree becomes a tree.

Integral mind

In *Client-Centered Therapy*, Rogers (1951) points out that there is considerable agreement that therapeutic growth takes place as a result of experiences which have 'an emotional rather than an intellectual meaning for clients' (p. 165). He argues that the therapist must be touched by the experience of the client. Thus, the mental mind is not enough. Our capacity to be reasonable needs to be integrated with our (magical) emotions and our (mythical) imaginings and meanings.

Gebser argues that our contemporary consciousness is multi-structured or, to change the metaphor slightly, multi-layered. We may thank Freud and Jung for pointing out to us that, even when we are acting 'rationally', our magical and mythical consciousness is hard at work. The complexity of human behaviour comes out of the interplay of these several 'layers' or 'levels' of consciousness in whatever we do. Gebser suggests that the acknowledgement and appreciation of these discrete structures is a step towards their integration with the mental structure in a more transparent way of experiencing the world. Three elements stand out in Gebser's analysis of what he calls the *integral* structure of consciousness.

The first is *time-freedom*. Archaic and magical humanity seem to have had no sense of time, living in a continuous present. For mythical humanity, time was rhythmical, constantly returning to its beginning. For mental-rational humanity, time became continuous and sequential, and eventually mechanically quantifiable. What identifies an integral sense of time is the re-owning of pre-rational, magic, timelessness, and irrational, mythical, temporicity alongside mental, measured time. This 'makes possible the leap into arational time-freedom' (Gebser, 1949/1986, p. 289).

The integral structure of consciousness also has a new sense of *space*. Archaic and magical humanity lacked all spatial consciousness because it lacked a defined sense of a self as observer. Mythical humanity emerged from this enmeshment in nature, and became aware of an external world, but self-consciousness was still too weak to experience objective space. It is only in the beginnings of mental consciousness that human beings became able to locate events in objective space. Central to this experience was the discovery of perspective, which demands a point from which the world is viewed and an individual to view it. Mental mind sees reality from one position, gazing in one direction. In the emergent integral consciousness, it becomes possible to view the world without locating the viewer in a particular position in space. Reality can be observed from every direction and every position at once.

The third element is the *ego*. Archaic and magical consciousness were pre-egoic. Mythical consciousness holds only a dim sense of self as distinct from the tribe. Mental-rational consciousness allows the development of separate egoic identity. Integral consciousness is 'ego-free'. Similarly, Egan talked of the transition from 'philosophic' to 'ironic' understanding, wherein ironic understanding embraces the basic, sensorimotor, pre-lingual, somatic understanding that philosophical understanding manages to ignore. In our philosophic consciousness we value the clarity of our perceptions and thoughts. In our ironic mind we value the ambiguity and paradox we experience when our organic sense of reality turns up a different truth from our speculations or taken-for-granted narratives.

In Kegan's order of consciousness, fourth order, mental mind thinks about therapy within a framework which honours clear, left-brained thinking as the best way to find the truth; whereas fifth order, integral mind understands that this is only one way to find the truth and that, anyway, there are different kinds of truth. Where fourth order, mental mind thinks about therapy within a framework which sees the relationship as something created by two separate egos, fifth order, integral mind understands that the relationship creates the persons engaged in it. In this moment, the therapist is incomplete without this client, and the client is incomplete without this therapist. Where fourth order, mental mind sees the relationship simply as the context in which the client's healing may take place, fifth order, integral mind values the relationship itself as an opportunity to learn and to 'live out your multiplicity' (Kegan, 1998, p. 320).

Whereas mental mind is dominant in Rogers' early theorising of personality and therapy, he later acknowledges the impact of magical and mythical consciousness on the therapeutic process, incorporating them in a kind of experience which is highly 'aware'. Rogers (1955/1967d) set out his ideas on the nature of the therapeutic relationship, about which he states:

> I let myself go into the immediacy of the relationship where it is my total organism which takes other and is sensitive to the relationship, not simply my consciousness. I am not consciously responding in a planful or analytic way, but simply react in an unreflective way to the other individual, my reaction being based, (but not consciously) on my total organismic sensitivity to this other person.
>
> (p. 202)

In his focus on 'immediacy of the relationship' and 'total organismic sensitivity', Rogers echoes what Gebser has to say about integral consciousness, Kegan's understanding of fifth order mind, and Egan's sense that our complex ironic consciousness is grounded in our somatic experience. Yet, Rogers (1986a) is aware that within the mindset of modern materialistic science such experiences, such subjectivity simply does not exist. The rational mind has no way of dealing with them. Psychologically, the emergence of the aperspectival, arational, integral world demands disenchantment with a narrow rational consciousness and a re-owning of the earlier structures.

In the above passage, Rogers refers to an experience which he cannot justify rationally. We might be inclined to label it irrational. Yet, Rogers' (1986a) reflections are hardly those of someone who has abandoned rationality and slid into an 'immoderate and unmeasurable chaos'. Neither has he abandoned his sense of self; rather, he is able to hold the paradox of experiencing self-sense and transpersonal sense simultaneously.

What we loosely call 'the mystical' runs all the way from the dimly experienced unity-consciousness of archaic mind to the time-free, space-free, ego-free intense integral awareness of the ever-present origin. 'The mystical' may not be included in conventional scientific discourse, but it is certainly part of human experience.

Summary

Through the archaic structure of consciousness we simply experience our identity with 'all that is'. Through the magical structure we experience, still fairly dimly, our entanglement with the universe. Through the mythical structure we identify with our tribe and its stories. Through the mental structure we become aware of ourselves as individuals able to act on the world. Finally, the integral structure brings this mental awareness to our experience of unity, entanglement, and culture.

We are inclined to equate consciousness with the sense of self we experience at the mental level. Yet we constantly shift between this mental-rational consciousness and the older, simpler structures within which it is grounded. Jung (1977) disputes the artificial boundary which we set between ourselves and other more 'primitive' forms of life, frequently reminding his readers that 'we have to make allowances for these primitive layers in our Psyche' (p. 119).

Some would argue that these 'primitive layers' have limited value in the modern world. Others would claim that mythical thinking remains a very effective way of dealing with the world, and that it is our capacity for mythical, and even magical, thinking that enables us to find meaning in our lives and gives us a grounding in the concrete world which rational thinking seems bent on destroying. Magical and mythical consciousness can be either 'efficient' or 'deficient', but they are neither better nor worse than mental-rational consciousness. They are simply older and different.

Drawing on Stern's (1985, 1998) layered model of human development, we offer a similar presentation of Gebser's 'unfolding' or 'emergence' model of consciousness (Table 2.1).

Whilst this gives us a sense of the layers of consciousness, it doesn't give an accurate representation of the timeline, which, if expressed as a day, would be as follows: from just after midnight one day, the archaic structure; from two minutes past 11pm that day, the magic structure; from three minutes to midnight, the mythical structure; from 30 seconds to midnight, the mental-rational structure; and from .35 seconds to midnight, the integral structure! We offer this image as one which puts some context on the current privileging especially of mental-rational consciousness.

Coda: Mind(s) and brain(s)

Gebser warns us not to try to ground structures of consciousness theory in biological evolution. Nevertheless, there are some interesting parallels between his theory of five minds and more recent ideas as a result of research in neurobiology.

Neurophysiologist Paul MacLean (1990) and colleagues (MacLean et al., 1973) argue that we have not one brain but three. This 'triune brain' comprises our ancient reptilian brain (brainstem and cerebellum), paleo-mammalian brain (limbic system), and neo-mammalian brain (neo-cortex). Each has its own intelligence, subjectivity, sense of time and space, and memory. Each brain-layer has formed

Table 2.1 Gebser's model of layered consciousness

Timeline	Structures
From 20th century CE	integral structure
From c. 1,500 BCE	mental-rational structure
From c. 10,000 BCE	mythical structure
From c. 200,000 BCE	magic structure
From c. 5,000,000 BCE	archaic structure

upon the older layer beneath and before it, and is connected to the other two. The three brains tend to operate independently, so that we are like a car driven by three drivers—instinct, emotion, and cognition—each with its own steering wheel and its own idea of where it wants to go.

MacLean locates his three-brain model within the framework of biological evolution, seeing a sequential development from the most primitive to the most complex. It is now more acceptable to argue that even fish have the beginnings of a neo-cortex and a limbic system and not that they are 'lower' than horses and apes on some evolutionary ladder: they are highly evolved *as fish*; they just don't happen to be horses or apes or humans. McLean's picture of the brain has proved useful in helping us explain our behaviour, as long as we set aside the idea that each more 'advanced' brain grew out of the more 'primitive' brain on which it sits.

Expanding MacLean's three-brain model to include what we have learned from Jaynes' (1976) speculations about the 'bicameral brain' and more recent research into brain lateralisation (Dell, 2005; Ornstein, 1997), we suggest the following. Since the cortex and limbic system are split into two—a left brain which processes information atomistically and verbally, and a right brain which processes information holistically and imagistically—we may legitimately talk of four interconnected minds, even if the brains associated with them overlap somewhat. We can even speculate about integrating all four in a fifth—'integral' or 'whole-brain' thinking—and reach the conclusion that there is a neurological basis for the conceptualisation that there are all of five minds at work in each of us, which 'jostle together and fold on one another, to some degree remaining "somewhat distinct"' (Egan, 1997, p. 80).

While there is interest in mapping these models of mind against each other, it does not really matter whether they fit perfectly. What matters is the general concept that consciousness is complex and multi-layered; and that it ranges from the dim, somatic awareness that we share with lizards, through the emotional and imaginative experience that we share with mammals, through a capacity for abstraction that seems to be uniquely human, to what Gebser calls 'the transparency of the whole'. It takes no great stretch of the imagination to see the instinctual, pre-egoic self emerging from the brain stem, or our magical consciousness centred in the limbic system. We should note, however, that Gebser (1949/1986) warns us that the process he is talking about is not biological or historical. Consciousness is not determined by biology, and the mind (or minds) is not simply a function of brain (or brains).

That said, we acknowledge the contribution that neuroscience has made to our way of thinking about consciousness. We tend to overvalue our left-brain thinking and undervalue our other mental capacities. Our pre-frontal cortex is pretty useless when it has to read non-verbal or emotional communication. It is the limbic system which processes facial expression, vocal rhythms, scent, and posture and lets us know when someone is friendly, aggressive, or sexually attractive. Usually, we don't think this through; we 'just know'. It worked very well for us as infants and, if we don't ignore it, can work just as well for us as adults.

Finally, we hope that this chapter justifies the inclusion of these hypograms:

Psychology, so dedicated to awakening the human consciousness, needs to wake itself up to one of the most ancient human truths: We cannot be studied or cured apart from the planet.

(Hillman, 1995, p. xxii)

I wonder if butterflies can remember when they were caterpillars?

(B. Neville, personal communication, February 12, 2021)

3 We is

The ground of being

Gebser's theory of the mutations of consciousness (see Chapter 2), takes us from the emergence of archaic consciousness in pre-humans, through magic, mythical, and mental structures of consciousness to the integral consciousness he claims to see emerging in the mid-20th century. Gebser considers that the emergence of the different kinds of consciousness has a trajectory and, accordingly, it is possible for us to speculate credibly on what kind of human consciousness is in the process of emerging in the 21st century. A core dimension of consciousness is the sense of who we are and how we relate to the world. Gebser writes about this in terms of the ego—which, interestingly, in the context of our current argument, is often capitalised (thus, 'Ego'), and, thereby, reified. In the archaic consciousness of the earliest hominids there was no sense of ego or self: consciousness was cosmic or universal. The magical consciousness of the Stone Age was ego-less and earth-oriented. The mythical consciousness which emerged several thousand years ago was ego-less and we-oriented. The mental consciousness that emerged in the great classical civilisations was ego-centric—and, in the deficient, 'rational' form which has characterised European consciousness for the past 400 years, we would argue, obsessively so. Finally, the integral consciousness, as Gebser views it, is ego-free.

The notion that we have something called an ego is commonplace in our everyday discourse about what sort of beings we are. When we check dictionary definitions of the word, we find that it is used to indicate a person's sense of self-esteem, or the view that a person has of themselves, or a person's sense of superiority. We say that someone has a strong ego, a weak ego, a fragile ego, a conflicted ego, an over-inflated ego. Moreover, we think of the ego as something we *have*: a consciousness of who we *are*, an 'I', distinct from all the 'you's' and 'they's' around us.

The concept of the ego is usually attributed to Freud. Actually, we should credit Ernest Jones, Freud's translator. Freud wrote in German about 'das Ich', which simply means 'the I', but Jones thought it would sound more scientific if he used the Latin word ego, a move which Freud accepted and which helped shift 'das Ich' from being a subject to an object (and a reified one at that): a 'thing' we have as a component of our personality, alongside other components such as our id and superego.

DOI: 10.4324/9781003397731-5

Freud (1923/1984a) has no doubt that this reified and capitalised thing called the Ego has independent existence: 'Normally there is nothing of which we are more certain than the feeling of our self, of our own Ego. The Ego appears as something autonomous and unitary, marked off distinctly from everything else' (p. 14). Although, in his book *Civilization and its Discontents*, Freud (1930/1985) acknowledges that 'Our present ego-feeling is, therefore, only a shrunken residue of a much more inclusive—indeed, an all-embracing—feeling which corresponded to a more intimate bond between the ego and the world about it' (p. 255).

Conventional European science regards it as an undisputed fact that the universe is a vast machine consisting of multiple independent components connected by cause and effect relationships. Freud's theory fitted very well into the conventional scientific assumption that human beings are essentially machines consisting of a myriad of moving parts. We acknowledge that this is not a fact but a belief. When we use psychological language we make this same mistake of confusing facts and beliefs. If we think we have an ego (or Ego), we are thinking within the framework of a European psychology which has colonised the world. There are Asian, African, and indigenous psychologies whose languages do not include a word to denote the thing we call the ego, but the colonising powers have never taken them seriously. We should not assume that when we speak the psychological language of the colonisers that we are stating the facts, whilst people in other cultures are merely stating their beliefs.

Alfred North Whitehead was strongly influenced by the philosophies of Asia and he maintains that, for centuries, European philosophy has been haunted by the misconception that the entities of which the world is made have independent existence: 'There is no such mode of existence; every entity is to be understood in terms of the way it is interwoven with the rest of the universe' (Whitehead, 1948, p. 64). Whitehead was humble enough to propose this as a belief, rather than a demonstrable truth, arguing that there are no truths, only half truths. We have to balance the reality that we usually experience ourselves as being independent, egoic, subjects against the reality that we are not—and that both are 'half-truths'.

I, we, you, they, and it

Who am I? Who are we? Who are you? Who are they? Who or what is it? Within the Western intellectual tradition, including psychology, thinking tends to believe that it—life, being, and knowledge—starts with 'I', and that 'we' is simply a collection of 'I's. This is an assumption. We might equally suggest that 'I' starts with 'we' or even with 'it', a perspective represented in different, Eastern, and indigenous traditions.

Western thinking about humanity tends to divide it into 'we' and 'they'. In the context of this book, we (the authors) use the pronoun 'we' to refer to ourselves; however, sometimes we use 'we' to include 'you', the reader. Further, 'we' might include anyone who is interested in the PCA to therapy and in the interplay between psychotherapy, and its underlying psychology, and ecotherapy and ecopsychology (see Chapter 4). Further still and wider, given our identities as educators as well as therapists, 'we' might be intended and taken to include all psychotherapists and educators, even those who don't identify with or reject the PCA, because our 'we'ness is constituted of shared self-images, interests, and personal as well as professional responsibilities. We (the present and other authors) write 'we' because we also include a 'you' who shares these identities, images, interests, and responsibilities, and a 'they' who, by definition, do not.

This means that the boundaries of the 'we' are flexible. Our 'we' extends from the two of us (Bernie and Keith), to include only those with whom we share some identity (theoretical orientation, gender, ethnicity, nationality, etc.) or to all humanity. Whether a particular group of people are 'we' or 'they' depends on context. If Australians are talking about an international rugby match, New Zealanders will be 'they'. If, however, Australians are talking about Southern hemisphere rugby teams as distinct from Northern hemisphere teams, then Australians and New Zealanders become 'we', and, due to the current organisation of tournaments, might also include South Africa and Japan (albeit that the latter is in the Northern hemisphere). If we think about Southern theory (Connell, 2008), 'we' would include Australia, Aotearoa New Zealand, South Africa, and countries in South America; while 'the Global South' includes countries in Central and South America, Africa, and Asia (many of which are in the Northern hemisphere), as well as the South Pacific, but excludes Australia and Aotearoa New Zealand.

Many people exclude particular ethnic or cultural groups from their 'we', a position of which we (Bernie and Keith, and other, like-minded people) might be critical. However, when this we talk or write about 'people' or 'humanity', do we include terrorists, tyrants, and torturers? If we think about 'we' as a unified field, then that includes people who are totally opposed to us and to whom we like to think we are totally opposed. We (Bernie and Keith) find this perspective helpful in thinking about the social/political world. While we have and hold strong radical/socialist political perspectives, we also hold an interest in understanding the 74 million people who voted for Donald Trump in the 2020 US presidential election. While it is easy to demonise and dismiss Trump and his supporters, it is crucial that we understand him and their motivations, concerns, disenchantment, disenfranchisement, hatred, and so on.

Throughout history, colonists and other tribal aggressors have believed or, at least, presented the view that the people they conquered were not really human beings like themselves. Christian colonists justified their treatment of the indigenous people they were slaughtering or enslaving by arguing that they had no souls. They were not part of any 'we' of which they (who, of course, were their own 'we') were aware. We have not yet fully transcended this kind of thinking. Elsewhere Keith has discussed this with regard to what Berne (1972/1975b) referred to as a third-person life position (Tudor, 2016). Originally, Berne (1962) wrote that 'the subjects of all [life] positions are particulars of the polarity I–Others' (p.23), formulating 'I' as including 'we' and 'you' as including 'they.' Some ten years later, in his last book, *What Do You Say After You Say Hello?* Berne (1972/1975b) shifted by extrapolating 'they' as a third-person position, distinct from 'you'. Applying his concept of Okness (and not Okness), he identified eight life positions:

I + You + They +   which represents the position of a democratic community
I + You + They −   the prejudiced snob—or gang—position of a demagogue
I + You − They +   the position of the agitator or malcontent and sometimes missionaries
I + You − They −   the solitary, self-righteous critic position
I − You + They +   the self-punishing saint or masochist, the melancholic position
I − You + They −   the servile position
I − You − They +   the position of servile envy and sometimes of political action
I − You − They −   the pessimistic position of cynics or those who believe in predestination or original sin.

(Tudor, 2016, p. 165)

While Berne's model may be somewhat too positional for many person-centred practitioners, we think it catches or captures something of what happens between people and groups of people.

When we reflect on our sense of independent personal existence, we are inclined to see ourselves as separate, unique individuals. Yet even our 'I' is a 'we'. We tend to think of our bodies as independent entities, yet we know that they are inseparably connected to the whole ecosystem in which we exist. 'I am not a separate and enduring substance but an event in which the universe composes itself.' (Keller, 1986, p. 186).

Looking outward, we know that the boundary of our organism does not stop at our skin. In *Client-Centered Therapy*, Rogers (1951) balances his image of separate, unique, self-governing individuals with the acknowledgement that 'there is no possibility of a sharp line between organism and environment, and there is likewise no sharp limit between the experience of self and the experience of the outside world' (p. 497). If we shift our mindset from the image of a planet made of dead matter to that of a planet which is a living organism, we might hesitate to identify our self with (just) the bit(s) of us that thinks, feels, and moves, and may expand our sense of self to include our engagement with the organism of which we are a part.

Looking inward, we know from research into microbiota that we can legitimately claim only a fraction of the cells in our bodies as our own. Most of our bodies comprise independent organisms—bacteria, viruses, archaea, fungi—which seem to act with their own purposes. Indeed, some researchers argue that only 10 percent of the cells in our bodies are essentially our own human flesh. Others are more moderate in their claims, but agree that more than half the 37 trillion cells in our bodies are not our personal flesh and bone, but are the cells of separate organisms. So, 'we' are, in fact, more 'them' than 'us'! Moreover, if we take an 'I + You − They −' position, we end up as a solitary, self-righteous critic of our own bodies and human being. Some of these microorganisms just seem to find us a compatible environment in which to live their separate lives. Some of them have the potential to harm, even kill us. Some of them live in symbiotic relationship with our 'own' cells. We cannot live without them and they cannot live without us. They contribute to our health and sense of wellbeing. They are involved in all of our activity, including our thinking. Indeed, there appears to be direct communication between our brains and the microbiota in our gut. It is the condition of the microbiota in our gut which our brain interprets as stress, depression, or elation; and, there is an argument that it is the condition of these microorganisms which manifests itself in conditions such as Alzheimer's, autism, and depression.

The essence of our sense of identity is our subjective experience, which raises the question whether the microorganisms in our gut have any awareness. Is our personal experience of subjectivity actually the collective experience of millions of microorganisms? Surely, if these miniscule organisms were the size of cats or dogs we would see them behaving in purposeful ways and have no trouble assuming that they have experience, even awareness.

We may think about the microorganisms in our guts and brains as 'them' and indulge the idea that they are not 'me'—or, as we (Bernie and Keith) are generally being plural—'us'. We can even label our bodies as 'it(s)' and identify with our minds, or acknowledge that each of us is a collective, not an individual, and include the microbiota and their experience as my/our own 'I' and 'me' or, more accurately, 'we' and 'us'. However, we in the Western world and intellectual tradition, tend to accept the Cartesian separation of mind and body and imagine that it is a detached mind which says 'I' rather than our body and the bacteria, fungi, and archaea of which our organism is mainly composed.

Radical mechanistic psychology in the 20th century was driven by the notion that our experience of autonomy and choice is delusional, and that we react as machines to environmental stimuli. Likewise, exponents of psychoanalysis argue that our sense of being free, choosing beings is delusional: our behaviour is apt to be governed by unconscious dynamics. Jung goes further, arguing that our behaviour is embedded both in the personal unconsciousness and the collective unconscious, the Universal Psyche of which our personal psyche is merely an expression. In the establishment of the practice, profession, and discipline of therapy in the 20th century, it was Rogers and other humanistic psychologists who put subjectivity and choice at the centre of our experience and behaviour.

The self as subject: I and we

When Rogers (1951) put subjectivity at the centre of his theory of personality and therapy in *Client-Centered Therapy*, he took a step which was extremely radical in the context of North American psychology in the mid-20th century. For the previous 40 years, John Watson and colleagues had managed to establish behavioural psychology as an unchallengeable orthodoxy, declaring that 'the most complicated of our adult habits are explicable in terms of chains of simple conditioned responses' (Watson & MacDougall, 1929, p. 3). Rogers argues that this was an assumption rather than a scientifically credible conclusion and that only by dogmatically clinging to this assumption was it possible to avoid the conclusion that human beings have a capacity for choice, spontaneity, and creativity (see Rogers, 1968). Such a conclusion would run counter to the mechanistic mindset which had dominated European science for some 400 years.

In Rogers' understanding of therapy, clients must be treated not as objects to be advised or manipulated, but as autonomous subjects to be understood. While he writes at length about the self (the whole person, not merely the conscious part), he consistently avoids speaking of the ego. Moreover, in writing about the self, he avoids reifying it (as 'the Self'), referring instead to our 'awareness of being', 'perception of the self', 'the concept of the self', and 'self-experience' (Rogers, 1959, p. 245). We don't have a thing called a 'self', let alone a 'Self': we simply 'experience' a 'perception' and form a 'concept'. In his later writing, he moved beyond even this point in de-reifying the self and identifying it with our present moment of experience—which is why we are critical of the more recent emphasis within PCP on the self, and configurations of self (Mearns, 1996; Mearns & Cooper, 2005).

The primitive behaviourism of Watson and his colleagues may have dropped away, but cognitive behavioural therapy maintains its dominance in most places where the practice of psychotherapy has professional status (for a critique of which, see Dalal, 2018; Tudor, 2008/2018b). However, few therapists now see a problem in accepting Rogers' assertion that subjectivity is a core component of human behaviour. Without denying that in much of our behaviour we operate reactively without focusing awareness on what we are doing, we can accept without much argument Rogers' (1951) proposition (X) that '*Every individual exists in a continually changing world of experience of which he is the center*' (p. 483). This assertion is at the centre of Rogers' approach to psychotherapy as he envisaged it, at least, in 1951. In contrast to the mainstream theorists and practitioners at the time, Rogers put the radical argument that the data which best guide productive therapy are not generated by the therapist's accurate observation of the client's behaviour but by the therapist's accurate intuition of the client's internal experience, for, as he puts it, 'the best vantage point for understanding behaviour is from the internal frame of reference of the individual himself' (p. 494).

However, when he came to consider the desirable outcome of therapy, Rogers (1951) focuses on 'the fully functioning person' whom he describes as a 'separate, unique, self-governing individual' (p. 502). Such a person makes rational choices, free from domination by conditions of worth, social expectations, and defensive façades—apparently. Our personal existence may be totally insignificant in the context of the life of the cosmos, but we each have a sense that we are unique, experiencing individuals, and imagine that that must count for something. This is the point we start from when we seek therapy to improve the quality of our experience and lives.

With the development of artificial intelligence, we are now on the point of considering what once would have been unthinkable: that machines could be autonomous beings making choices of their own. We are faced with the real question that, if we are able to create a machine which is an accurate copy of a human being, doing everything a human can do, would it be human? If not, what is the difference? Is it the existence of something we can call a 'soul'? Is it the presence or absence of interior experience? Mainstream psychology in the 20th century relentlessly pursued the fantasy that we can entirely explain human behaviour without reference to such concepts. Interior experience, if we acknowledged its existence at all, was thought to be irrelevant. If human beings are indeed the machines that the behaviourist fantasy would have them be, there is no need to differentiate them from the humanoid machines of the post-industrial fantasy.

Rogers would have no doubt where he stood in all of this. Human beings are clearly not machines. On the contrary, they are organisms. We may sometimes behave like machines, and it may be quite useful to focus on our machine-like qualities (brain surgery comes to mind), but, essentially, we are organisms with subjective experience, interiority, and choice. Behaviour is not the response to stimulus, but 'is basically the goal-directed attempt of the organism to satisfy its needs in the field as perceived.... This perceptual field is, for the individual "reality"' (Rogers, 1951, p. 484). It is worth noting that Rogers goes on to point out that the perceptual field is not limited to the world that we perceive through our five senses and regularly refers to our sensory and visceral perceptions.

Rogers seems to be setting himself alongside the idealist philosophers in telling us that our subjective experience is all that of which we can be sure. Rogers' position is framed by the perceptual psychology expounded by Donald Snygg and Arthur Combs (1949), and we think that Rogers must have been aware of the philosophical implications. The American psychological science which was the cultural context of his theorising had totally embraced materialism, leaving it to the Europeans to carry on the arguments of Hegel, Schopenhauer, Pierce, and other idealist philosophers as to whether there was/is an objective reality independent of our perception.

When Snygg and Combs proposed perceptual psychology as a radical alternative to behaviourist psychology, they accepted the behaviourist assumption that all behaviour is reactive but, they assert, reactive to perceived experience, not solely to stimuli. Rogers didn't accept this assumption, but emphasises the human capacity for choice. When he came to consider the desirable outcome of therapy, he focuses on 'the complete and fully functioning human organism' (Rogers, 1959/1967f, p. 105), an organism which makes choices, free from domination by conditions of worth, social expectations, and defensive façades.

When Rogers talks about the self, distinguishing between the subjective 'I' and the observed, objective 'me', he doesn't grant the 'me' independent, objective reality. He sees the 'me' existing as part of the subject's perceptual/conceptual field, differentiated from the field as a whole and related to the 'I' in a special way. Furthermore, in his careful exposition of his personality theory, Rogers (1959) points out that what we reify as 'the self' is the product of our subjective experience and the subjective experience of others as it is communicated to us. He suggests that there is no objective, independent 'me' to be perceived by myself and those around me. On the contrary, my 'me' is constructed by my perceptions and my experience of the perceptions of others.

However, there is a logical problem here, which, by the time he wrote *On Becoming a Person* (in 1961), Rogers had realised. Perception involves the existence of something that one perceives. Idealist philosophers have exhausted themselves splitting this particular hair. Do we perceive things because they exist or do they exist because we perceive them—or, if not us, then is there a universal spirit that some of us call God? Are there subjects and objects or are there only subjects, or only one subject? Do you exist because I perceive you or do I perceive you because you exist, or both?

Rogers did not resolve this problem any better than anyone else. What he did was to find a way around the problem by adopting the process conception of reality which had been developed by Alfred North Whitehead and explored further by Charles Harteshorne and colleagues at the University of Chicago during Rogers' tenure. We should note that the Chicago philosophers were involved in a struggle with the philosophical establishment similar to Rogers' struggle with the psychological establishment. Process psychology had—and has—been marginalised in philosophy just as client—or PCP and therapy had and has been marginalised in psychology. Both were revolutionary in the 1940s and 1950s—and remain so.

Organic process: Us

Whitehead originally called his philosophy a philosophy of organism. However, his supporters at Chicago were more comfortable with the label process philosophy; a label that has stuck and sometimes modified to process relational philosophy. With or without this direct influence, in discussing human experience, Rogers uses both the language of organism—in *Client-Centered Therapy* (1951)—and process—in *On Becoming a Person*. It is difficult for us to imagine how radical it was in psychological theory of the 1940s and 1950s for Rogers to put organic process at the centre of his theory, suggesting that psychotherapy 'is a process by which man becomes his organism' (Rogers, 1953/1967g, p. 103) and, again, that 'clients seem to move toward more openly to being a process, a fluidity, a changing' (Rogers, 1960/1967j, p. 171).

We can see a Whiteheadian conception of reality behind Rogers' (1958/1967c) assertion that the person is 'a fluid process, not a fixed, static entity, a flowing river of change, not a block of solid material; a continually changing constellation of potentialities, not a fixed quantity of traits' (p. 151), and that 'The self is, subjectively, in the existential moment. It is not something one perceives' (p. 147).

Obviously, to call humans organisms made sense to a lot of his readers, but conventional philosophical and psychological thinking was still operating within the framework established by Descartes: that there are two kinds of entities—mind (spirit) and matter—and that they are entirely different. The fact that philosophers had failed to explain adequately how these entirely different kinds of being can influence each other had not weakened this assumption. To start talking about '*the organism*' was to bypass all the arguments around what was referred to as '*the mind/body problem*'. Through the influence of Rogers and other humanistic psychologists in the 1950s and 1960s, we have become comfortable talking about 'mindbody', 'bodymind', and 'embodied mind'. Recent research on the function of the vagus nerve has demonstrated the intricate connections between brain, mind, heart, and gut (Breit et al., 2018; Porges, 2009, 2011), but, in its time, it was an exciting new idea within North American psychology to propose that our bodies were somehow involved in our psychological wellbeing and that our 'I' was not identical with our consciousness.

Whitehead counters the proposition that there are two kinds of things—matter and spirit—by arguing that there aren't any 'things' at all. Whitehead was a mathematical physicist before he identified as a philosopher and it was the evidence from sub-atomic physics which inspired his theory. At the subatomic level, none of the particles of which we are constructed exist long enough to be things. There are only potentialities which fulfil themselves in a microsecond and disappear. Nothing exists—at the subatomic level, the human level, or the cosmic level—except these *actual entities*. Whitehead adopts William James' expression and labels them 'drops of experience'. Electrons, molecules, cells, human beings are successions of drops of experience. They are all embedded in the actual entities which constitute the organism we call the universe. Reality is constantly emerging. The world is a process, a process of becoming, and we are part of this becoming; hence, our belonging.

In this understanding, the difference between subject and object is a function of time. In one micro-moment, one drop of experience, we subjectively experience the world as it presents itself to us. This experience immediately becomes an object, a part of the world as we experience it in the next micro-moment. Each moment of experience incorporates two kinds of perception. On the one hand, we receive information about the world, more or less consciously, through our senses. On the other hand, all our past experiences feed into our organism, to be sensed in our gut, heart, and, more generally, through our body, without much awareness on our part; and, even though we may not be aware of all the past moments of experience, they nevertheless shape our present drop of experience.

In our moments of experience, we are purely subject. That particular moment of experience immediately becomes an object, an element in what we experience in the next moment. Our objective universe is constructed from the aggregation of our moments of experience. When we answer the question 'Who are you?', we are reflecting on our past moments of experience. Our subjective 'I' experiences our objective 'me'. Our 'me' is a selective amalgamation of all our recalled past moments of experience. Our momentary 'I' is shaped by the impact of all our past experiences of our organism and connection with all the other entities in the cosmos. We are connected to the total organism through 'prehension', a word which, for Whitehead, is roughly equivalent to 'feeling'. We are not independent subjects, observing other subjects and objects. On the contrary, it is our relations with the other subjects, including nonhuman and even non-conscious subjects, which make us what and who we are.

In Rogers' discussion of 'organic experience' and 'subception' in *Client-Centered Therapy*, he is clearly writing about the phenomenon which Whitehead (1929/1978) had labelled 'causal efficacy', that is, the prehension by the organism of data (in this case, threatening data) without conscious awareness. This is an important element in Rogers' understanding of neurosis. He argues that neurosis is often generated in the conflict between one's self-concept and one's organic experiencing, in an unsuccessful attempt to satisfy one's organic needs in ways which are consistent with one's self-concept. In successful therapy this conflict is overcome, as 'the person adds to ordinary experience the full and undistorted awareness of his [sic] experiencing—of his sensory and visceral reactions' (Rogers, 1953/1967g, p. 104).

In neurosis, as Rogers understands it, here is a clash between our awareness and our organic experiencing, between our experiencing 'I' and our experienced 'me'. It is the task of the therapist to assist the client to abandon the distorted 'me'—the self-concept, the conditions of worth, constructed by one's significant others and the broader culture—and live in a way which is congruent with our total organic experiencing. It is not surprising that Rogers found the notion of a fixed, reified ego (so much so that it is often capitalised, thus: 'Ego') incompatible with his understanding of what kind of beings we are.

Personal neurosis is matched by our collective neurosis. Collectively we cling to an identity as rational and powerful beings able to exploit the earth for our satisfaction and convenience, while our collective organic experiencing is of a planet in pain. Denial and distraction don't make the pain go away.

The living universe: It/us/we/I

In the universe as understood by Whitehead, life, subjectivity, and experience go 'all the way through'. Whitehead was convinced that the world experienced by human beings operates under the same rules of becoming, process, and indeterminacy as the world discovered by sub-atomic physics. Conversely, the micro (scopic) world operates under the same rules as the world of humans and other large organisms. If this is so, we must acknowledge the phenomena of subjectivity and experience in the micro world—and, likewise, in the macro world of the cosmos. For Whitehead, the cosmos is an organism. Organisms experience; experiences pre-suppose subjectivity; and there must be an 'I' to experience the 'it'. We note that experience is not the same as awareness. To say that quarks, leptons, and bosons (elementary particles) or, for that matter, our planet or the galaxy have experience is not to say that they have awareness. Maybe they do, but we have no way of proving it, just as we have no way of proving that they don't. Nevertheless, to cite Sheldrake (1990),

> As soon as we allow ourselves to think of the universe as alive, we realize that a part of us knew this all along... And we can begin to develop a richer understanding of human nature, shaped by tradition and collective memory, linked to the earth and the heavens, related to all forms of life, and consciously open to the creative power expressed in all evolution.
>
> (p. 188)

In the 1980s, Norwegian ecophilosopher, Arne Naess, gave voice to all those who intuitively felt that our 'we' must extend to all living things. He doesn't make the conventional distinction between living and non-living things, suggesting that rather than define certain beings as living and then extend our understanding to include beings conventionally thought of as non-living, we should 'conceive reality, or the world we live in, as alive in a wide, not easily defined, sense. There will then be no non-living beings to care for' (Naess, 1995, p. 235). He acknowledges the influence of both Buddhism and Gandhi on his thinking, concluding that:

> It seems to me that, in the future, more emphasis has to be given to the conditions under which we most naturally widen and deepen the 'self.' With a sufficiently wide and deep 'self,' Ego and alter as opposites are, stage by stage, eliminated. The distinction between Ego and alter is, in a way, transcended.
>
> (p. 236)

For Naess, our personal 'self-realisation' is a manifestation of the self-realisation of the whole system in which our personal selves are embedded. The universe has a self, and our personal selves are expressions of it. This is a concept which parallels Rogers' insight that the actualising tendency is a manifestation at the personal level of a directional tendency in the cosmos, a directional movement he calls 'the formative tendency'. When we accept Rogers' concept of the formative tendency, we are acknowledging that neither our personal 'I' nor our social 'we' drive the dynamics of our actualisation. The whole system in which we are embedded is becoming, evolving towards the realisation of its potentials, and our personal growth is an element in this becoming.

Rogers doesn't fall into the trap of imagining that, because our growth is driven by a force larger than ourselves, our sense of personal choice is delusional. On the contrary, the evolutionary flow in which our organisms are embedded is a flow towards consciousness, towards awareness, towards choice.

> With greater self-awareness, a more informed choice is possible, a choice more free from introjects, a *conscious* choice that is even more in tune with the evolutionary flow... The greater this awareness, the more surely the person will float in a direction consonant with the directional evolutionary follow... [and] Consciousness is participating in this larger, creative, formative tendency.
>
> (Rogers, 1963/1995e, pp. 127–128)

A key word in Rogers' description of the formative tendency is 'creative'. Our sense of personal subjectivity is not delusional. We are not controlled by a force larger than ourselves. Whether we think of the universe as creating itself, emerging, unfolding, or simply becoming, we must include our own subjectivity in this process. In process terms we make, in each microsecond of experience, a choice between becoming new and repeating ourselves. In this choice we make a positive or negative contribution to the cosmic creative process.

Whitehead realised that if he was correct in his understanding that what happens at the sub-atomic level, that is moments of experience fulfilling themselves in the emergence of objective reality, must be happening at the cosmic level, there must be a subject to experience and create it. He variously refers to the source of being as creativity, the creative Eros, and the divine Eros. Process theologians, such as John Cobb and Catherine Keller, find this an appropriate way of talking about God. For them, God is not outside the universe but part of it. The creative Eros is within us, urging us towards greater complexity, harmony, beauty, and peace. Process theologians and philosophers may argue about whether the creative

Eros is a blind force, having experience but not awareness, or whether God is a person as we understand it, thinking, choosing feeling joy and pain, but they are united in imagining God/god as 'both eternal and becoming... a living process of interaction' (Keller, 2008, p. 23). What is important to us here is that Rogers and Whitehead share the tentative conclusion that creativity is at the centre of life. For Rogers (1954/1967k), it is:

> the curative force in psychotherapy—*man's* [sic] *tendency to actualize himself, to become his potentialities*. By this I mean the directional trend which is evident in all organic life—the urge to expand, extend, develop, mature—the tendency to express and activate all the capacities of the organism, or the self.
> (p. 351)

When physicist David Bohm wanted to explain the connection between our everyday subjective experience and the cosmos, he used the analogy of a hologram. In a hologram the entire object is contained in each region of the hologram, enfolded by a pattern of waves (Bohm, 1980, 1996). He points out that 'relativity and quantum theory imply undivided wholeness, in which analysis and distinct and well-defined parts are no longer relevant' (Bohm, 1980, p. 144). We experience separate and independent entities, including the sense of an independent ego, because our experience is limited to the explicate order of reality, which is unfolded moment by moment from the implicate order where there is an unbroken relatedness of things. Bohm refers to this as mutual participation, arguing that no aspect of reality is exempt.

We like to imagine that when we think, feel, and act we are actually doing something for which we are individually responsible. However, this is not really how we generally experience thinking, feeling, and acting. Moment by moment thoughts come to us; we become aware of feelings; we find ourselves moving one way or another without having made a conscious choice to do so. In Bohm's understanding, thoughts, feelings, and actions 'unfold' from the implicate order: we make the choice between becoming new and repeating our past selves, and our thoughts, feelings, and actions are folded back into the implicate order to contribute to its transformation. Our thoughts, feelings, and actions impact on the creative advance of the universe. As Rogers points out, our experience of a subjective 'I' gives us conscious, creative participation in the evolutionary process.

Connection: The in-between

When process philosophers are called on to describe the universe in process terms, they occasionally go to Buddhism to borrow the image of Indra's net. Cook (1989) describes it thus:

> Far away in the heavenly dwelling of the great god Indra, there is a wonderful net which has been hung by some cunning artificer in such a manner that it stretches out infinitely in all directions. In accordance with the extravagant

tastes of deities, the artificer has hung a single glittering jewel in each 'eye' of the net, and since the net is infinite in dimension, the jewels are infinite in number. There hang the jewels, glittering like stars of the first magnitude, a wonderful sight to behold. If we now arbitrarily select one of these jewels for inspection and look closely at it, we will discover that in its polished surface there are reflected *all* the other jewels in the net, infinite in number. Not only that, but each of the jewels reflected in this one jewel is also reflecting all the other jewels, so that there is an infinite reflecting process occurring. The Hua-yen school [of Buddhism] has been fond of this image because it symbolizes a cosmos in which there is an infinitely repeated interrelationship among all the members of the cosmos. This relationship is said to be one of simultaneous *mutual identity* and *mutual intercausality*.

(p. 214)

Explicit in Whitehead's philosophy and implicit in Rogers' psychology is the view that we are all connected. Relationship is primary; personal identity is secondary. We are not autonomous individuals connected by relationships, but networks of relationships out of which our personal identities emerge.

Whitehead argues that, if we are to understand the universe exposed by quantum research, we must abandon 'the fallacy of simple location'; that is, the notion that the universe consists of independent things existing in different places. We are not separate beings, though we may often act as though we are. We are not even independent of things that we generally consider not to be alive, such as rocks, and mountains. Merleau-Ponty, a philosopher who strongly influenced the thinking of Rogers' colleague, Eugene Gendlin, argues that neither I, the perceiver, nor the object I perceive is wholly passive in the act of perception. We may like to think that when we see something that this is an action on our part, while the thing we see is simply there. However, this is an illusion. The light-energy travels from the object to us, not from us to the object. We could as readily say that the object is communicating with us as say that we are somehow seeing or grasping the object. Merleau-Ponty contends that participation is a defining attribute of perception. Perception is inherently interactive and participative. The world we participate in is a living world; we don't experience a split between an independent, subjective 'I' and an observed, objective 'it'. Scientistic propaganda may have persuaded us that it is so, but this is an illusion, and our organisms know better. Merleau-Ponty points out that there really is no boundary between self and other. We are part of 'the flesh of the world' a world which is a living being which both senses and is sensed. In Merleau-Ponty's (1968) words 'We are the world that thinks itself' (p. 136).

It is significant that, for Rogers, the height of personal subjectivity involves at least two people. It is a subject-to-subject relationship. This is not the subjectivity of an independent, self-governing person engaged in a relationship with another independent person. Even the relationship between a highly observant and accurately empathic therapist and a client who is the object of this empathic understanding does not qualify. The I–Thou relationship between client and therapist does not have a defining boundary. It transcends the subject/object distinction and demands a shared subjectivity (Clarkson, 1990, 1995; Schmid, 2006) or, more accurately, an intersubjectivity. Whitehead's insights about subject/object differentiation are useful here: subjects exist in the present; objects exist in the past. When I observe somebody or something, my subjective experience is in the present. The observed thing immediately moves into the past as an object of my experience. To put it differently, when we look at you or hear you, we are seeing or hearing your past self, because it takes a finite time for the information your body is sending us to reach our eyes and ears, to pass through our brain to our frontal lobes and to be processed there into our awareness(es) of what and who you are. We can only truly meet you in the present moment when we share our subjectivity, when we are sufficiently tuned in to each other to share this moment of experience, or, to put it another way, when we are no longer under the illusion that we—you (singular or plural) and I/we—are separate beings.

For Rogers, as for Buber, all true living is meeting. The sense of independent subjectivity is illusory. In Merleau-Ponty's (1968) words, we are not 'idle and inaccessible subjectivity' but, rather, 'all that I see', 'identical with my presence in the world', 'an intersubjective field' (p. 452).

In his book *Radical Knowing*, Christian de Quincey (2005) explores the concept of intersubjectivity. He distinguishes between three types of meaning:

- A weak meaning—'You and I agree about objective facts'.
- A weak-experiential meaning—'You and I are interacting with each other and our interaction influences the way we experience the world'.
- A strong-experiential meaning—'Our relationship creates our experience'.

It is this strong experiential view of intersubjectivity which is the foundation of both Rogers' and Buber's discussion of relationship. In accepting this understanding of intersubjectivity, de Quincey (2005) echoes Whitehead, Merleau-Ponty, and Bohm: 'All individuated subjects co-emerge, or co-arise as a result of a holistic "field" of relationships. The being of any one subject is thoroughly dependent on the being of all other subjects with which it is in relationship' (p. 281).

Buber argues that the essence of being human is relationship. The experience of being 'I' arises out of the 'between'. He writes: 'Spirit is not in the *I* but between *I* and *Thou*' (Buber, 1923/1937, p. 39). For Rogers, it is the acknowledgement and enhancement of the relationship between client and therapist which enables the actualising tendency, and it is the actualising tendency which enables creativity—or the fact that both tend to actualise (see Tudor & Worrall, 2006). This idea that it is in the 'between' that transformation happens has been taken up by Schmid and other theorists in the Rogerian tradition who write about relationship. Like Buber, they see dialogue as a key aspect of human existence. For Schmid (2006), 'dialogue is the authentic realization and acknowledgement of the underlying We' (p. 244); it is 'participation in the being of the other' (p. 244). Within the therapeutic relationship, client and therapist are co-creating themselves, participating in each other's becoming—and being, and belonging. More than that, in their 'betweenness', they are a moment in the universe's becoming.

Rogers (1963/1995e) notes the difference in his experience when he can be ego-free in the interaction with a client:

> When I can relax and be close to the transcendental core of me, then… it seems that my inner spirit has reached out and touched the inner spirit of the other. Our relationship transcends itself and becomes part of something larger.
>
> (p. 129)

Buber suggests that our capacity for I–Thou relationships with individuals and I–You relationships with the collective extends beyond our relationship with human beings. He understands that we can have an I–Thou relationship with an animal, tree, or mountain; that is to say, we can tune into their subjectivity. These days, many of us are inclined to acknowledge the subjectivity of animals, having long ago abandoned the Cartesian idea that they are simply machines that feel no pain when we torture them. There is increasing evidence to back up Whitehead's conviction that experience, and hence subjectivity, go all the way through nature. It has become possible to argue credibly from botanical science that plants can experience and communicate with one another (see Wohlleben, 2015/2016). We and the trees are intertwined parts of the same organism, an organism which is currently in pain; to cite Naess (1995): 'Human nature is such that with sufficient maturity we cannot avoid "identifying" our self with all living beings, beautiful or ugly, big or small, sentient or not' (p. 13). Furthermore, Naess takes pains to point out that our distinction between living and non-living beings may be misconceived. Whether or not this is so, we and the other living beings to which/whom we are most closely connected are currently in crisis.

Finding the way: All of us

In *Climate of the Heart*, Ian Mills (2019) argues that we must forget the idea of a separate self if we are to experience who we really are and deal with our current emergency. He cites Einstein's aphorism that: 'We can't solve our problems with the same thinking we used when we created them.' Like Dante, we find that the road we have been travelling has left us lost in a dark forest. We know that we must find another road if we want to escape.

The problems we face appear to be overwhelming. When we examine the road which has brought us to them, we may focus on science, technology, capitalism, communism, religion, or greed. In our view, we would do better to focus on the mindset, the taken-for-granted beliefs and corresponding behaviours which lurk behind the destructive elements in all of these. Gebser suggests that, on the one hand, we need to embrace and own the whole of human history in order to understand our situation, and, on the other hand, it is the deteriorating mental-rational consciousness of the past few centuries of Western culture and its colonies that has accelerated our journey towards catastrophe.

There are various ways of describing the kind of thinking which created our current problem. We can point to the deterministic materialism which had its origin in the thinking of Galileo and Newton and emerged in the late 16th century amid fierce debates about the nature of the world. It was founded on three basic dogmas: that everything in the universe is composed of tiny bits of matter; that these bits of matter don't have any subjectivity; and that they move according to fixed, mathematical laws. Descartes' contribution to this worldview was to explain that human beings were composed of bits of matter like everything else, and that their ability to think and feel came about because, unlike animals and plants, they possessed a mind, an entirely different kind of substance. Psychological thinking in Europe developed within this worldview, so that even human beings' sense of self became a thing among other things and eventually came to be labelled an Ego. Gebser points out that associated with this sense of an independent self is the experience of perspective, the ability to perceive the things of which the world consists from a specific time and direction. The sense of being independent, egocentric individuals is associated with the assumption that competition between individuals is the natural way of being, that power defines their relationships, and that patriarchy provides the normal structure of human affairs. This worldview has led to a commitment to controlling the natural world. On the one hand, it has enabled the blossoming of science and technology and major improvements in the quality of human life. On the other, it has provided a rationale for the dismantling of the world's ecosystems. We may, if we like, attribute global warming and the unsustainable exploitation of the earth's resources to human greed, but we must acknowledge that they are also the unforeseen consequences of initiatives designed to improve life on earth, initiatives which made a lot of sense within this all-pervading worldview.

Gebser, who was strongly influenced by the philosophies of China and India, saw the expression in 20th-century sciences and arts of a mindset which was in contrast to the deteriorating rationality which had been dominant for centuries. He saw the emergence in Europe of a mindset which no longer put an independent ego at the centre of our experience. The integral consciousness of which we are capable, and on which our survival depends, is 'Ego-free'. It is also able to hold in balance ideas which the modern, rational consciousness perceives as contradictory. We can perceive ourselves to be free, independent, choosing beings while at the same time acknowledging that we are simply momentary manifestations of 'the One' (however we or others conceptualise that). In integral consciousness, our experience is not of 'either/or' but of 'both/and'. Gebser's (1949/1986) analysis of the sources of the approaching catastrophe was written in the context of the Cold War (1947–1991). He sees two dysfunctional worldviews in competition: the capitalist worldview, which was characterised by 'perspectival attachment to the separated, individual Ego' (p. 4), and the communist worldview, which was characterised by 'unperspectival ties to the group or collective' (p. 4). Gebser (1949/1986) argues that we must tap new sources of thinking: 'the sources of the aperspectival world which can liberate us from the two exhausted and deficient forms which have become almost completely invalid' (p. 4).

Unfortunately, these two invalid, exhausted, and deficient forms linger on. The Soviet Union and China have converted to capitalism, and capitalism itself has embraced the extreme irrationalities of neo-liberalism. Communism may be largely in decline, but the 'unperspectival ties to the group and collective' are kept alive in tribalism and nationalism, even in the most capitalistic of nations. Gebser's aim was to provide evidence that a new consciousness and a new reality were emerging. There was no assumption that we would embrace this consciousness and reality, and consequently avoid the catastrophe. We may manage to do so, but we need first to acknowledge that we are involved in a new process which we can either embrace or deny.

Mills' (2019) conclusions are similar to Gebser's, though his language is different and his arguments are drawn from ancient rather than 20th-century sources, and from Asian rather than European sources. Like Dante, Mills argues that there is another road, an alternative way of thinking that does not need to be created from scratch. It is available to us in an alternative European intellectual tradition represented by Heraclitus, Dante (Alighieri), Spinoza, and Whitehead; and even more strongly expounded in Asian and Middle Eastern traditions, represented by the *Baghavad-Gita*, and the work of Zuangzi, Zenji, Rumi, and Ibn El Arabi.

For Dante and thinkers like him, and contemporary ecophilosophers like Naess, Mills, and Warwick Fox, the 'self' is identified with 'all that is', in a 'deep realisation that we and all other entities are aspects of a single unfolding reality' (Fox, 1990, p. 252). They are not speaking of an infantile sense of undifferentiated oneness with the world. Gebser was careful to distinguish between such a sense, which he identifies with the ego-less, archaic consciousness of the earliest hominoids and their mammalian cousins, and the integral consciousness which does not abandon rationality but transforms it (see Chapter 2). Neither is he speaking about the destruction of the 'I' as it occurs in mass movements, religious cults, and totalitarian collectivist regimes. It is neither egotist or ego-less; it is ego-free:

> Ego-freedom means freedom from the self: it is not a loss or denial of the 'I', not an Ego-cide but an overcoming of the Ego. Consciousness of self was the characteristic of the mental consciousness structure; freedom from the 'I' is the characteristic of the integral consciousness structure.
> (Gebser, 1949/1986, p. 532)

If human existence is not centred on the ego, where is it centred? For Mills, as for the philosophers from the East and the West to whom he refers, human existence is centred on relationship. The 'right way', which Dante and we must take if we are to find our way out of the dark wood and into an appreciation of the unity of all being, is love.

> Almost imperceptibly, an image of the person as a sovereign and potentially autonomous being has been receding in favour of an understanding that lives are inherently interwoven and interdependent and that relationship is at the core of life.
> (Barrett-Lennard, 2009, p. 91)

4 Person-centred psychology and therapy, ecopsychology and ecotherapy

Having considered some of the intellectual ground of our argument with regards to the embodied mind, consciousness, and identity, we now turn to considering PCP and its therapy in terms of ecopsychology and ecotherapy.

Introduction

There is increasing public and social/political interest in the environment and concern about issues such as: climate change (in particular, global warming); energy (the problem of the generation of energy, the burning of fossil fuels, and the issue of the use and abuse of nuclear energy); water (shortage and pollution); biodiversity and (unsustainable) land use; pollution (chemicals, toxics, heavy metals, water, air); waste management; the depletion of the ozone layer; overfishing; and deforestation (see Chapter 6). In this context, more and more therapists are becoming aware of the environment and environmental issues and concerns—an awareness informed by ecopsychology; that is, the study of human beings' relationship with the ecosystem of which we are a part, and finds expression in different forms of ecotherapy, that is, of the various applications of ecopsychology to therapeutic practice, including therapeutic practice about and with the ecosphere (for a scoping review of which see Key & Tudor, 2023).

Ecopsychology offers certain critiques of therapy and its traditional emphasis on the individual and the individual psyche; the ego (heroic or otherwise); the self (sometimes reified as 'the Self'); self-actualisation, especially when it manifests as at the expense of others or 'the other' (such as certain other groups or peoples, resources, the land, and so on); traditional therapeutic goals such as individual happiness, and autonomy; its general anthropocentrism; and the general lack of awareness on the part of therapists about the seriousness of the concerns noted above.

This chapter considers some of the theoretical and conceptual links between PCP and ecopsychology and their implications, adding to recent calls for a broader focus with the PCA and PCT to take into account environmental context and ecopsychological perspectives (Blair, 2011; Neville, 2012).

Although Rogers did not specifically discuss environmental issues as such, we know that his experience (from the age of 12) on his family's farm, and his initial studies in agriculture at the University of Wisconsin, influenced his empirical

DOI: 10.4324/9781003397731-6

approach to research and informed the images he used throughout his writing to illustrate his thinking about human psychology. For example, Rogers said:

> too many therapists think they can make something happen. Personally I like much better the approach of an agriculturalist or a farmer or a gardener: I can't make corn grow, but I can provide the right soil and plant it in the right area and see that it gets enough water; I can nurture it so that exciting things happen. I think that's the nature of therapy.
>
> (Rogers & Russell, 2002, p. 259)

If we are to promote, maintain, and even enhance philosophical congruence between the medium and the message, the language, images, and metaphors we use to describe concepts and to develop theories are significant. In bringing together the PCA and systems theory, Kriz (2008) makes the point that:

> we could use the process of growth in a deciduous tree to explain that the principle of 'growth' in humanistic psychology does not mean 'more and more' (as is in economics) but 'die and become' in adaptation to the changing environment (here: the seasons).
>
> (pp. 5–6)

Rogers (1980/1995j) does identify a benevolence towards nature as one of the characteristics he expects of people in the next generation: 'They feel a closeness to, and a caring for, elemental nature. They are ecologically minded, and they get their pleasure from an alliance with the forces of nature, rather than in the conquest of nature' (p. 351); and he wrote a paper on nuclear war (Rogers, 1982), a subject many people regard as the ultimate environmental issue.

Many person-centred and experiential writers have discussed the 'environment' in terms of the immediate therapeutic environment (the consulting room, the context and impact of therapeutic practice, such as working in General Practice, organisations, etc.); and of the client's context (family, social, cultural, etc.). However, few such writers, clinicians, and even activists have discussed the environment in terms of environmental/ecological concerns. Even a book specifically on politicising the PCA, with an agenda for social change (Proctor et al., 2006), contained only one contribution which refers to the ecological sense of environment (i.e., Wood, 2006). Those that do make a connection between PCP and the environment include: Amatuzzi (1984); Embleton Tudor et al. (2004); Barrett-Lennard (2005); Mountford (2006); Tudor and Worrall (2006); Wood (2006); Kriz (2008); Blair (2011); and Neville (2012), on all of whose work this chapter draws.

Within the ecological literature, as Neville (2012) points out, there has, with the exception of Fisher (2002), been little reference to Rogers or person-centred theory; and he suggests that 'a better understanding of person-centred theory and practice might give ecopsychologists an appropriate way of dealing, both theoretically and practically, with human psychopathology' (p. 59).

Person-centred psychology: Organismic and ecological

There are concepts in PCP particularly well-suited to a synthesis with ecopsychology. In a contemporary introduction to the PCA as an approach to life, which I (Keith) co-authored with others (Embleton Tudor et al., 2004), we devoted a whole chapter to environment, discussing and applying the concepts of organism and tendencies (formative and actualising), the necessary and sufficient conditions for growth and change, and the nondirective attitude to the environment and environmental issues, and provided a brief case study of the organisation Trees for Life (www.treesforlife.org.uk/) as an example of an active and engaged, nondirective attitude to the environment. Here we focus briefly on the organism; the view that organisms tend to *form* (see Tudor & Worrall, 2006); and the theory of conditionality, incongruence, and alienation as the foundation of a person-centred ecopsychology.

Organism

At the heart of the PCA and the theory and practice of PCT lies the organism, a pulsing biological entity and a significant and enduring image. The concept and image of the organism lies at the heart of Rogers' theory, his view of the authentic person, and the process and outcome of therapy. His use of the concept signifies both a unified concept of human motivation and a focus on all organisms, and in this sense it may be more accurate to talk about a people-centred or even species-centred approach to life and therapy (Tudor & Worrall, 2006). Rogers (1953/1967g) contends:

> one of the fundamental directions taken by the process of therapy is the free experiencing of the actual sensory and visceral reactions of the organism without too much of an attempt to relate these experiences to the self. This is usually accompanied by the conviction that this material does not belong to, and cannot be organized into, the self. The end point of this process is that the client discovers that he can be his experience, with all of its variety and surface contradiction; that he can formulate himself out of his experience, instead of trying to impose a formulation of self upon his experiences, denying to awareness those elements which do not fit.
>
> (p. 80)

The tradition of organismic psychology dates back to the work of Kantor (1924a, 1924b), and includes, notably, Goldstein (1934/1995), Wheeler (1940), Murphy (1947), and Werner (1948), all of whom were hugely influenced by the work of the philosopher, Alfred North Whitehead (see, especially, Whitehead, 1920, 1929/1978). These days, in the person-centred and experiential tradition, there is more talk and writing about the self, and human being as self, Self, selves, and configurations of selves (see Mearns, 1996; Mearns & Cooper, 2005; Schmid & Mearns, 2006). However, as the self is a differentiated portion of the greater perceptual field, i.e., the organism (Rogers, 1951), it follows that the organism is conceptually and developmentally prior to self (for further elaboration of which see Tudor and Worrall, 2006). As such, and given the qualities of the organism, which include being holistic, experiential, concrescent (growing together), differentiating, co-regulatory, interdependent, and directional, the image of organism appears to be a more accurate concept (than that of the self) for thinking about the world beyond individual human—and nonhuman—beings or organisms. As Kriz (2008) puts it: 'the distinction between the human organism—which is the total individual and the basis for the totality of experience (the phenomenal field)—and the self—which is a differentiated, structured portion of this field—is essential' (p. 13). This repositioning of the self is particularly significant for our current concern as it contributes to the challenge to individualistic notions of human beings and the relocation of us as beings living in a larger relational and ecological context (see Barrett-Lennard, 2005; Blair, 2011; Mountford, 2006; Neville, 2012).

Viewing the Earth as an organism, or a mega-organism, draws on ideas from Gaia theory (Lovelock, 1979/1987, 1988/1996, 1991a) and deep ecology (Naess, 1989), both of which appear entirely compatible with person-centred principles and practice. Lovelock (1991b) comments that 'The idea that the Earth is alive may be as old as humankind' (p. 11) and acknowledges the ancient Greeks' view of 'Earth' as a Goddess, Gaia. He traces the modern history of this view to James Hutton, the father of geology, who said in a lecture in the 1790s to the Royal Society of Edinburgh that he thought of the Earth as a superorganism—and that its proper study would be by physiology (see McIntyre, 1963).

In his own work, Lovelock (1979/1987) is clear that Gaia is a self-regulating system: 'it [is] not the biosphere alone that [does] the regulating but the whole thing, life, the air, the oceans, and the rocks. The entire surface of the Earth including life is a self-regulating entity' (p. ix). Interestingly, Andras Angyal (1941), the Hungarian American psychologist and psychiatrist on whose work Rogers drew, also refers to the biosphere, meaning the realm or sphere of life, in order to convey the holistic entity that includes both individual and environment, 'not as interacting parts, not as constituents which have independent existence, but as aspects of a single reality which can only be separated by abstraction' (p. 100). Reflecting on Gaia, Neville (2012) comments: 'The planet is not a machine but a living organism. We are cells of her body and have no existence apart from her' (p. 33).

There are a number of implications of this organismic view of life. Two that are particularly relevant to this present enquiry are radical holism and interdisciplinarity.

What we refer to as radical holism is the concept that everything and everybody is seen as an aspect of a single, interconnected existence (Levins & Lewontin, 1985). In the context of spirituality and the PCA, Bowen (1984) discusses interconnectedness in the universe and in psychotherapy. Barrett-Lennard (2005) discusses interconnectedness in terms of viewing persons in context and envisaging the multi-layered world of relation(s/ships), arguing that: 'Ultimately, we are members of the total life system of our planet, and issues around human impact on other species and the environment are a gradually increasing part of public consciousness' (p. 45) and suggesting that: 'Persons with highly developed ecological awareness may be very actively engaged on this system level' (p. 45). Such engagement is challenging. For example, Orr (1992) makes the link between the need to view things in their wholeness and sustainability or, perhaps more accurately, unsustainability:

> To see things in their wholeness is politically threatening. To understand that our manner of living, so comfortable for some, is linked to cancer rates in migrant laborers in California, the disappearance of tropical rain forests across the U.S.A., and the depletion of the ozone layer is to see the need for change in our way of life. To see things whole is to see the wounds we have inflicted on ourselves and on our children for no good reason.
>
> (p. 88)

In his 'Psychological Foreword' to Roszak et al.'s (1995) seminal work, *Ecopsychology: Restoring the Earth, Healing the Mind*, Hillman (1995) reviewed some 'basics' of psychological theory 'to show that the human subject has all along been implicated in the wider world of nature' (p. xix). He continues, rhetorically: 'How could it be otherwise, since the human subject is composed of the same nature as the world?' (Hillman, 1995, p. xix). This challenges the notion that 'we' are—or, more commonly, 'I' am—or my psyche is separate from 'nature'; rather, as Hillman posits: 'The most radical deconstruction of subjectivity... today would be re-placing the subject back into the world, or re-placing the subject altogether with the world' (p. xxi).

In his book, *Wild Therapy*, Totton (2011) comments on how human beings have not only been domesticated but have domesticated ourselves and, in being and doing so, have spilt ourselves off from the world. In this way, the world has become: 'our "environment", rather than the whole, of which we are an integral part... [and] by trying to control the world we have made it *other*, and therefore dangerous and frightening' (p. 2).

In economic systems based on division and competition, in cultures which promote individualism, and in psychologies which encourage us to think about ourselves (our selves), it is countercultural and ultimately subversive to think about 'us' and 'we' holistically—and even biospherically—and to develop a language of wholes as distinct from parts.

The second implication of an organismic approach for ecopsychology concerns interdisciplinarity. Separate disciplines are limited—and, as Lovelock (1991b) observed, fragmented—by and in their separateness. Although many of us live in a postmodern world in which interdisciplinarity is valued, intellectually, academically, and practically, we are still subject to the modernist division of certain disciplines. One of the contributions that the PCA has made is that it offers a certain framework, concepts, and principles, which are applicable to many aspects of life, including a principled way of being with/in the environment, across disciplines.

That organisms tend to form

Just as it makes sense to distinguish the self as a differentiated part of the organism, so it is important to understand the actualising tendency as a part of, or, more accurately, a manifestation of a broader tendency, that is to say, the formative tendency. Rogers (1963/1995e) defines this as 'the ever-operating trend toward increased order and inter-related complexity evident at both the inorganic and the organic level' (p. 126); in other words, a trend to 'syntropy' alongside entropy. For Rogers, the actualising and formative tendencies, taken together, are 'the foundation blocks of the person-centred approach' (p. 114).

Whilst the nature and relationship of these two tendencies has been the subject of some debate (Van Kalmthout, 1998), it is clear that they are different. Rogers describes the formative tendency as universal and evolutionary, and asserts that it tends towards greater order, complexity, and interrelatedness—or, as the word suggests, 'form'; whereas the actualising tendency tends towards maintaining, reproducing, and enhancing the health and wellbeing of the experiencing organism (see Rogers, 1963). Tudor and Worrall (2006) discuss the usefulness of clarifying both concepts by distinguishing their use(s) as nouns or verbs, arguing that it is more accurate to say that a person tends to actualise (rather than that they have an actualising tendency) and, similarly, that organisms tend—and, indeed, the Earth tends—to form. In his seminal paper on the actualising tendency in relation to motives and consciousness, reflecting on the resilience of a type of seaweed growing on coastline rocks, and citing research in biology, Rogers (1963) argues that life is an active, directional process towards wholeness and the actualisation of potentialities. This appears consistent with Gaia theory, which posits that the Earth is a self-regulating, complex system, involving all spheres: pedosphere (the outermost layer of the Earth), hydrospheres (water on, under, and over the planet), atmosphere, and biosphere. Neville (2012) comments that this tendency offers a non-anthropocentric base for theorising growth and change.

An important implication of this view of the world/Earth is an active, nondirective approach to the Earth; that is, we need to know the Earth and its directionality and to actively support it. Thus, in terms of sustainability, for instance with regard to mining resources, it makes ecological sense to plan not in terms of a fiscal quarter (of a year), or the lifetime of a particular parliament (usually between three and seven years), but, rather, for seven generations (i.e., over 200 years) as advocated by many North American First Nations' peoples. It is no accident that, worldwide, indigenous people are engaged in environmental issues and eco-governmentality (Ulloa, 2003).

Conditionality, incongruence, and alienation

In the same paper on the actualising tendency, Rogers (1963) also deals with what goes wrong; and poses:

> How is it that man is so frequently at war within himself? How do we account for the all too common rift which we observe between conscious aspects of

man and his organismic aspects? How do we account for what appears to be two conflicting motivational systems in man?

(p. 15)

Rogers responds to these rhetorical questions by summarising his theory that such rifts are the result of incongruence between self-perceptions held by the individual and their organismic experience; brought about by distorted perceptions of self and experience which, in turn, grow out of conditions of worth introjected from significant others (see Rogers, 1951, 1959). Bozarth (1998a) puts it succinctly: 'Conditionality is the bedrock of Rogers' theory of pathology' (p. 83). Whilst we agree, we think that the term 'alienation' gives more of a sense of the social origins of such conditionality and an analysis of the distortion, the 'distorted relations', which lie in oppressive forms of society and social organisation. Marx (1939/1973) conceptualises such alienation as comprising four basic social relations within capitalism: man's [sic] relation to his product—what he or she does or does not produce; to his productive capacity—the capacity or incapacity to produce; to other people; and to his species; to which Roy (1988) adds a fifth social relation: that of our relation with the Earth. We suggest that the concept of alienation from our relationship with the Earth—from littering to fracking, from the enclosure to the exploitation of land, from deforestation to dispossession, the latter which relies also on alienation from others through conquest and, usually, colonisation—is crucial to an understanding of ecopsychology and PCP. As Marx (1858/1964) puts it: 'Every self-estrangement of man from himself and nature is manifested in the relationship he sets up between other men and himself and nature' (p. 331).

A crucial implication of this view of psychology is an understanding of inauthenticity as incongruence, closedness to experience, psychological maladjustment, intensionality, and immaturity (see Rogers, 1959), and as a form of alienation, mediated by, for instance, 'environmental press' (Murray, 1938, p. 121), or pressure, that is, the significant determinants of behaviour in the external environment.

Having discussed some aspects of a synthesis between PCP and ecopsychology, we turn to the expression of this psychology in therapy.

Person-centred therapy: An ecotherapy

In this part of the chapter, we consider two aspects of PCT as an ecotherapy: Rogers' therapeutic conditions and encounter. This discussion offers a preview to Part 2 of this book which comprises chapters devoted to an elaboration of each condition.

Rogers' therapeutic conditions

On the basis of his previous research into what works in therapy, and in the context of developing his own theory of therapy, based on a conceptualisation of the nature of the human organism and its inherent, actualising tendency to develop all its capacities, Rogers (1959) identified six conditions which, he argues, were both necessary and sufficient to effect growth and, indeed, personality change. These conditions, their validity, necessity, and sufficiency, and application to fields other than therapy, have been the subject of much debate in the past 55 years. Nonetheless, we think most person-centred and experiential practitioners would agree that, fundamentally, the theory describes two (or more) people together, creating (or co-creating) certain conditions which are different from those conditions of worth which the person who is the client experienced previously and/or experiences elsewhere. It is this experience of a different 'climate', as Rogers often put it, that effects the growth and/or change in the client. Rogers' focus on what are, in effect, environmental conditions makes PCT literally an environmental therapy in the sense that it addresses the environmental conditions that surround the client (see Tudor & Worrall, 2006).

Rogers (1963/1995e) asserts that when we provide or create such a climate 'We are tapping into a tendency which permeates all organic life—a tendency to become all the complexity of which the organism is capable' (p. 134), and suggests that this organismic choice is 'guided by the evolutionary flow' (p. 127). As with the centrality to PCP of the concept of the organism, Rogers' theory of environmental conditions makes PCT particularly suited to being considered an ecotherapy even when thinking about therapy with individuals, precisely because we are working with their immediate environment: social, cultural, and ecological, past and present, and, arguably, future. The question then is whether these conditions are or can be the basis for developing a person-centred ecotherapy or, more accurately and globally, an eco-centred therapy, whether this is with an individual or individuals, a group, or with the environment and the Earth itself. We discuss this question with regard to each condition.

(1) That two persons are in contact

For this condition to be fulfilled, we would need to argue that the Earth itself has a consciousness or awareness and some conscious relationship with its inhabitants.

In the original article (Tudor, 2013b) on which this chapter is based, I (Keith) followed the argument I and others had made some ten years earlier (Embleton Tudor et al., 2004), that regarding our human relationship with the environment, this condition was not met, and that, the contact (or lack of contact) between a therapist and the Earth, was better explained in terms of other conditions. For example, in drawing the analogy between Rogers' theory of therapy and our understanding of the planet–human relationship, Blair (2011) 'include[s] empathic understanding within the domain of psychological contact' (p. 51). Nonetheless, I acknowledged that the concept of our contact with the natural world is an important one—see Louv (2005), Blair (2011), and Inguilli and Lindbloom (2013) who reported on a study which yielded a positive correlation between connectedness to nature and resilience.

However, and with the benefit of having listened and read more, and spent more time talking and thinking with Bernie and, specifically, thinking about the importance of 'connecting' (Neville, 2012; see also Tudor, 2022a), which I consider close to the concept of contact, I have changed my mind—that is, my mind-body!

We—that is, Bernie and now, I (Keith)—think firstly, that it is more useful to think about this condition in terms of contact (Rogers, 1959) rather than psychological contact (Rogers, 1957) as the former offers a wider conceptualisation of the concept. Organisms are in contact without thinking about it, and such contact is not dependent on being conscious or aware. In *The Hidden Life of Trees*, Wohlleben (2015/2016) describes the results in his work—and life—as a forester of paying more attention to trees:

> I began to notice bizarre root shapes, peculiar root patterns, and mossy cushions on bark. My love of Nature—something I've had since I was six years old—was reignited. Suddenly, I was aware of countless wonders I could hardly explain even to myself.
>
> (p. xiv)

Secondly, we need to extend our conceptualisation of this condition to contact between organisms. This is consistent with and supported by the work of Merleau-Ponty, a philosopher on whom both Bernie and I draw, and his identification of the subject, the experiencing 'self', with the bodily organism.

Taking these points into account makes it easier, thirdly, to think—and feel and sense—in terms of embodied minds being in contact (or not). In his work on perception and language in what he refers to as 'a more-than-human world', Abram (1997) emphasises the sensuous nature of the experiencing organism:

> To touch the coarse skin of a tree is thus, at the same time, to experience one's own tactility, to feel oneself touched *by* the tree... Clearly, a wholly immaterial mind could neither see things nor touch things—indeed, could not experience anything at all. *We* can experience things—can touch, hear, and taste things—only because, as bodies, we are ourselves included in the sensible field, and have our own textures, sounds, and tastes.
>
> (p. 68)

(2) That the first person... the client, is in a state of incongruence, being vulnerable, or anxious

On the basis of the same argument (as with the first condition) about *consciousness*, we consider that neither the environment nor the Earth (as client) is conscious of its own vulnerability or anxiety. However, as Embleton Tudor et al. (2004) note,

> the response of the environment [to some of the issues noted above and elsewhere in this book] may be viewed as an organismic expression of an incongruent relationship between humans and their total environment, including biosphere, atmosphere, oceans, rocks, flora and fauna.
>
> (p. 268)

This reading of the concepts of contact and incongruence require us to be more extensional in our understanding of experience. Thus, the experience of a tree, a wave, the wind, a parrot, etc., may not be as easily recognisable as the experience of a person—at least from a person's point of view or frame of reference. Nevertheless, without necessarily attributing consciousness to such organisms, we can—and both Bernie and I would say we *should*—acknowledge that such organisms have experience. The Earth experiences our activity and we experience the Earth's activity.

In terms of the analogy with the environment or the Earth being in therapy, as Samuels (1993) reflects wryly: 'the world has not shown up for its first session. The world is ambivalent about its therapy, suspicious of its political therapists, [and] reluctant to be a patient' (p. 30). Nevertheless, the concept and metaphor of an incongruent world, at odds with itself as an experiencing organism, differentiated into aspects of itself which are both positive and negative, is a useful one, and one which both invites and challenges us to evaluate the nature and extent of the world's presenting problems (see Chapter 6).

(3) That the second person... the therapist, is congruent in the relationship

Evaluating the state of the world has the benefit of bringing or keeping the ecotherapist in relationship with the world. Increased knowledge and 'ecological literacy' (Orr, 1992) can only heighten our awareness of environmental concerns and, as awareness is essential to congruence, this is a crucial quality of the ecotherapist. Congruence—or, we prefer, authenticity—is one of a cluster of related concepts identified by Rogers (1959) that describe the fully functioning person, including openness to experience, psychological adjustment, and extensionality.

- Openness to experience—an example relevant to our present interest is described by Naydler (1996): 'Contemplating... natural phenomena with alert senses and an open mind, is potentially a more powerful and exact instrument than any piece of specialized scientific equipment'.
- Psychological adjustment—according to Rogers (1959), is a state in which 'all experiences are or may be assimilated on a symbolic level into the gestalt of the self-structure' (p. 206), and which, in this context, involves an ability and a capacity to take in information about the environment, issues and concerns, and to adjust ourselves accordingly without being overwhelmed (and defeated) or underwhelmed (and in denial).
- Extensionality—a concept from the field of semantics describes a sense of differentiation, anchorage, multiplicity, and expansiveness—which, in this context, is summarised by the following from Merry (2002) when writing about the fully functioning person:I believe there are moments, either fleeting or sustained, when individual people experience that they are part of something larger than themselves. When we are free of distortion and denial, we open up the possibility of experiencing ourselves both as discreet and separate individuals and as significant participants in the continuation of life itself.

(pp. 34–35)

Person-centred and eco psychology 75

Like any other therapist, the ecotherapist will, of course, not always be congruent in the relationship. In his discussion of different spheres or levels of relation, Barrett-Lennard (2005) (who identified nine levels from the individual person to the whole of life system and habitat) argues that 'Not to appreciate this [total life system] sphere of relation leaves our own survival at risk… [but] to experience it strongly is to feel more connected in our world' (p. 45). Bernie refers to this as 'ecocentric congruence' (Neville, 2012, p. 53), and, in Chapter 7 explores congruent anxiety.

(4) That the therapist is experiencing unconditional positive regard toward the client

This describes the acceptance that the ecotherapist has for the environment, the Earth, and its formative tendency—or that it tends to form. It is the manifestation of the nondirective attitude and principle of PCP which, with regard to our present interest, is well summarised by Lao Tse (600 BCE/1973) in the *Te Tao Ching*:

> Do you think you can take over the universe and improve it? I do not believe it can be done.
> …
> The world is ruled by letting things take their course.
> It cannot be ruled by interfering.
>
> (Chapters 29 & 48)

As nondirectivity is sometimes equated with a kind of passivity, I prefer to put this condition and attitude more positively, thus: that the ecotherapist activity supports the formative tendency and inherent directionality and wisdom of the environment. In this book, Bernie and I develop this approach in Chapter 8.

(5) That the therapist is experiencing an empathic understanding of the client's internal frame of reference

As the term suggests, empathic understanding requires some understanding, i.e., knowledge and comprehension of, in this context, environmental issues, and perhaps more importantly, a sensitivity to ecological and even universal matters. There is a poignant example in the original first Star Wars film, *Episode IV: A New Hope* (Lucas, 1977), when, at the same time as the planet Alderaan is destroyed by the Empire's Death Star, the Jedi Master, Obiwan 'Ben' Kenobi, who is some light years away, clutches his side and says: 'I felt a great disturbance in the Force, as if millions of voices suddenly cried out in terror and were suddenly silenced. I fear something terrible has happened'. While some might find this example a little fanciful, many people feel the damage we are doing to the environment and the planet keenly and even viscerally. We would argue that such feeling and sensitivity comes from having authentic psychological and ecological contact with and empathy for the Earth. Wohlleben (2015/2016) puts this poignantly: 'When you know that trees experienced pain and have memories and the tree parents lived together with their children, then you can no longer just chop them down and disrupt the lives with large machines' (p. xiv).

One might also speculate that different people will have particular sensitivities to different spheres (pedosphere, hydrosphere, etc.), which may be reflected in their respective areas of understanding, interest, and activism. It is undoubtedly the case that many indigenous peoples have or have had a close relationship with the land and, whether or not currently living on their ancestral or tribal lands, often hold a keen sense of guardianship or custodianship of the land as distinct from ownership of the land. In the Māori language this guardianship or custodianship is referred to as kaitiakitanga. A 2010 survey conducted by Statistics New Zealand, which included questions about the state of the environment, found that 4 per cent of the total population of New Zealand expressed dissatisfaction with the state of native bush, forests, nature reserves, and open green spaces, but when this was analysed by ethnicity, amongst Māori this figure doubled to 8 per cent. A separate question regarding the state of lakes, rivers, harbours, oceans, and coastlines revealed similar differences: dissatisfaction amongst the total New Zealand population was 13 per cent; dissatisfaction amongst Māori was 23 per cent (Statistics New Zealand, 2012). We discuss the implications of this kind of empathy in the following section on encounter.

In terms of the application of this theory to the environment, Rogers' reference to the client's 'internal frame of reference' poses challenges to those noted with regard to conditions 1 and 2, challenges taken up by Bernie in Chapter 9.

(6) That the client perceives, at least to a minimal degree, conditions 4 and 5

As with the points made above (with regard to conditions 1 and 2), this condition is dependent either on a conscious (and, thereby, reified) Earth that perceives our acceptance and empathy for it, or, *the experiencing Earth*. Again, whilst not necessarily proposing this as a condition of a person-centred ecotherapy with the Earth itself, we think the idea that we might take account of any changes in the environment as a result of our therapeutic, environmental work is a useful one, and one we develop in Chapter 10.

Considering PCT as an ecotherapy with regard to Rogers' therapeutic conditions clarifies the ideas and raises further questions about this aspect of person-centred theory. It clarifies that, in terms of their application to restoring the Earth, the therapeutic conditions as a whole are neither necessary nor sufficient to effect or to frame environmental change, although the conditions of congruence and unconditional positive regard are the most clearly applicable to the environment as 'client'. Whilst the conditions offer a familiar framework for organising thinking about our relationship with the environment and the Earth, as a piece of theory it is, at least in my view, simply not the most appropriate for the subject or the purpose. In this we disagree with Mountford's (2006) application of the six conditions to the nonhuman world, although we appreciate his ecosophical perspective and the philosophical distinctions he has drawn between moral humanism, sentientism, vitalism, and ecosophy—and that, on the basis of these different traditions and their view of the Earth, one might apply the conditions differently. Nevertheless, the theory—and the conditions—do provide a useful framework for understanding the environmental context of the client and their capacity for contact; their incongruence or alienation or, as Neville (2012) expresses, our 'species anxiety' (p. 45); and their perception of positive regard (unconditional or otherwise), and empathy, all of which, arguably, are impacted by environment and ecology.

Encounter

The word encounter comes from the Latin *incontra*, meaning in front of (from in [in] + contra [against]); the Old French *encountrer* carries a sense of confront (ation); and, by the late 13th century the word was being used to refer to a meeting of adversaries; it is only a weakened sense and use of the word that it now commonly refers to casual meeting.

In a psychological context, encounter was first used in 1914 by Jacob Moreno in a series of poetic writings, and later developed as a concept in psychodrama; it was developed by Kurt Lewin in the 1940s in his training groups at the National Training Laboratory in Bethel, Maine, USA; from the late 1950s, it was used to describe the aggressive, confrontational style of groups in residential therapeutic communities for drug addicts such as Synanon; and, in the late 1960s, it was used by Will Schutz who developed the 'open encounter' model of group and groupwork. Rogers (1970/1973) develops the practice of encounter whereby the group facilitator takes a more participative (than directive) approach with/in the group.

Abram (1997), an ecologist and philosopher who draws on Merleau-Ponty's writings about encounter, notes:

> Our most immediate experience of things… is necessarily an experience of reciprocal encounter—of tension, communication, and comingling. From within the depths of this encounter, we know a thing or phenomenon only as our interlocutor—as a dynamic presence that confronts us and draws us into relation.
>
> (p. 56)

Within the person-centred and experiential tradition, encounter is associated with cross-cultural communication, often in large groups (Rogers, 1991; see also McIlduff & Coghlan, 1991, 1993; Moodley et al., 2004), and explored more recently in a bicultural context (Haenga-Collins et al., 2019; Rivers et al., 2022). We suggest that this cross-cultural and bi-cultural experience and thinking is useful as we propose shifting our thinking from people en-countering each other to people en-countering the planet.

We think the concept of encounter is a crucial one with which to describe a person-centred ecotherapeutic practice. As Schmid (1998) observes, the word 'points to the "against", indicating vis-à-vis [face-to-face]; as well as resistance' (p. 75). There are all too many examples of how we humans as a species have set ourselves against the Earth and are leaving unsustainable carbon footprints on the

Earth. The question here is whether we can face and encounter the Earth. Encounter involves allowing ourselves to be impacted by the other, in this case the Earth. In an early paper presented at the First International Forum of the Person-Centred Approach on the way of the approach, Amatuzzi (1984) talks about the jungle thus:

> The jungle is indomitable, unlimited, indefinite. It is impossible to contain it. But if you choose to live in it, it will also live in you... Now there is one thing. This is the conversation we are having here on the outside. But if we go inside, after walking for days on end, for moons and moons, then our conversation will change.
>
> (pp. 2–3)

This willingness to 'go inside' (ourselves, the jungle, the wild places), to allow the outside inside, and to be open to changing conversations is the kind of experiential knowledge that Rogers (1951) advocates with regard to culture, cultural setting, and influence as important preparation for the training therapist: 'A way that is the true way takes you into the jungle and makes you part of it. This is the explorer's strange reality. He may get lost in the jungle. But he feels the urge to go deep inside' (Amatuzzi, 1984, p. 8). It follows that if we are to develop ecological awareness and literacy, and to explore 'strange reality', we would advocate having some experiential knowledge of our environment. Barrett-Lennard (2005) argues:

> Effects of the world community on the total life system flow from the ways that the diverse human and constructed systems work and interact. As individuals, we may have particular animal friends, a wider sense of kinship with certain other species in the spectrum of life and/or a direct sense of connection, enjoyment or embrace in certain natural surroundings. All of these avenues entail some direct engagement with the wider system of life.
>
> (p. 45)

Again, such connection is not always enjoyable or comfortable. Whether gardening, walking with, or being in the wild with clients, we get our hands dirty, we get wet and cold, we fall over—and we pick ourselves up. Totton (2011/2012), a leading exponent of ecopsychology, has coined the term 'wild therapy' to point out 'the ever-present tension in human culture between the wild and the domesticated' (p. 153)—including the domesticated, professionalised, and regulated world of therapy. He proposes that we need more of 'wild mind' in order to reconnect with the world and with other beings that inhabit it—and to reclaim the political and spiritual practice of therapy.

Within the person-centred literature, there are few examples of ecotherapy, an ecological/systems therapy, or, with the exception of Amatuzzi (1984), wild therapy. A notable exception is the inspiring work of John K. Wood who, with his wife, Lucila Machado Assumpção, established an ecological reserve, Estância Jatobá, where they lived in Jaguarlúna/Holambra, Brazil (see Machado Assumpção & Wood, 2001). As Wood (2006) reflects:

> We began to see that we did not really take care of the land. We were a part of the land, the conscious part of the ecosystem taking care of itself. We extended the consciousness of Jequitibá and its rustling leaves… Most of all we championed the living Earth, the humus from which humans descended.
>
> (p. 280)

The other aspect of encounter that we suggest is significant for a person-centred ecotherapy is that it is a group encounter. Rogers (1970/1973) himself claims that the encounter group was one of the most successful of modern social inventions:

> the trend towards the intensive group experience is related to deep and significant issues having to do with change… in persons, in institutions, in our urban and cultural alienation, in racial tensions, in our international frictions… it is a profoundly significant movement.
>
> (p. 169)

The importance of the group, whether engaging in adventure therapy, outdoor experiential therapy, wilderness therapy, or other forms of encounter in and with the ecosphere, is precisely that it is a group. It thus helps us reconnect with ourselves as group (and political) animals, and experience ourselves as a group/community/tribe in relation to the land and Earth, and to taking action.

Conclusion

The chapter has suggested that certain fundamental concepts of PCP are useful in making links with ecopsychology and, similarly, that certain theories of PCT are helpful in contributing to the understanding and practice of ecotherapy. Building on previous work in and beyond the approach, the chapter advances the view that PCP has the potential to be developed into an ecopsychology; and that, as a vital and contemporary relational therapy, PCT has the potential to be developed as an ecotherapy for people and the planet, and, thus, may, more accurately and more radically, be reconceptualised as an eco-centred therapy.

Part 2

Conditions

Having established the intellectual ground on which this book is based in Part 1, in Part 2 we draw on Rogers' (1957, 1959) theory of the necessary and sufficient conditions of therapy to frame six discussions which, we hope, advance the 'conditions' of an ecotherapy that heals both person and planet.

As acknowledged in Chapter 4, Rogers' (1959) first therapeutic condition of *contact* or psychological contact (Rogers, 1957) is often viewed in terms of a one-person or one-and-a-half person psychology (Stark, 1999), whereas connection represents more of a two-person or even two-person-plus psychology (Tudor, 2011c). One problem with the theory of this particular condition is that it isn't taken very seriously, often being omitted, and, when included, more often than not being passed over lightly as an assumed pre-condition (for a critique of which, see Tudor, 2000, 2010, 2011a; Tudor & Worrall, 2006). It is only with the development of the theory and practice of contact reflections by Garry Prouty (1976, 1994), Marlis Pörtner (2000), and Dion Van Werde (2002) that the concept of contact has been taken more seriously as a condition of therapy (though, for the most part, this development also represents a one-person or one-and-a-half person psychology). In Chapter 5, we attempt to develop ideas about contact and, specifically, how we need the other in order to imagine and be in contact.

Rogers' second condition (also often ignored or discounted in representations of the theory) concerns the client's *incongruence* which Rogers (1951) defines as a discrepancy between (organismic) experiencing and self-structure (in effect, self-concept). We (Bernie and Keith) had some discussion about this chapter in terms of articulating the alienation a client or person might experience from their environment or nature, personally and transpersonally, locally and globally. However, we thought that it would be interesting to apply this 'condition' to the 'client' that is the environment/world/Earth/Gaia itself. Following Bernie's death—and as this was one of the two chapters we had not started—I (Keith) asked Len Gillman, a colleague and friend, and a Professor of Biogeography, to write a chapter on incongruence from this perspective. His contribution forms Chapter 6, for which I am grateful and which I consider adds another dimension to the theory and to the book.

DOI: 10.4324/9781003397731-7

Taking Rogers' condition of the therapist's *congruence*, Chapter 7 discusses the role of anxiety in people's lives—and in the theory of PCP—and clarifies some theoretical misunderstandings about anxiety, process, and personality. Somewhat confusingly, with regard to conditions two and three of his theory of conditions, Rogers uses the words incongruence (with regard to the client) and congruence (with the regard to the therapist) in two different ways: the first, to describe something about experience and self-structure with regard to personality, and the second, to describe a quality of being genuine or authentic (Tudor, 2011a). In Chapter 7 we refer to both, arguing (somewhat playfully) that, whilst being vulnerable or anxious may be a sign of incongruence (Rogers, 1957, 1959), we may also be anxiously congruent and congruently anxious.

Chapter 8 offers a discussion of Rogers' condition of the therapist's empathic understanding or empathy by means of returning to Gebser's work (see Chapter 2) and, specifically, his identification of five stages or mutations of consciousness, and articulating five kinds of empathy. This is followed by a further, briefer discussion of four modes of empathy which elaborates Stark's (1999) taxonomy of 'person psychology', with Keith's addition of a 'two-person-plus psychology' (Tudor, 2011c) that acknowledges the significance and importance of engagement with the world outside and beyond the clinic.

Chapter 9 offers a different kind of discussion of Rogers' fifth condition of the therapist's unconditional positive regard, which Rogers refers to variously as warmth, respect, prizing, and love. From research in and about psychotherapy, we know that hope is an important factor in the expectation of outcome (Lambert & Bergin, 1994; Larsen et al., 2007). What is less known or discussed is the reality of hopelessness and the importance of acknowledging and accepting this as part of a genuine acceptance of all feelings, processes, and states of being. Based on a paper I (Keith) presented at a person-centred conference (in Vienna in 2018), I dedicate this chapter to the memory of Peter Schmid, a great thinker and contributor to person-centred and experiential psychology, who was present when I read the paper—and complimented me on it. As this turned out to be one of the last exchanges I had with him before his untimely death in 2020, that exchange has a particular poignancy for me.

Rogers' sixth and final condition is that the client experiences or perceives (according to different formulations) the therapist's empathy and acceptance. This was the second chapter that remained unfinished at Bernie's death, though, as with Chapter 6, we had discussed what it might look like. Again, we wanted to take a creative approach and try to speak as it were from the point of view of the environment. Given the nature of this piece of writing, I am most grateful that Alisoun Neville, one of Bernie's daughters, was willing to step in as a co-author of this chapter, and thus complete this set of chapters and this Part of the book.

5 We cannot imagine without the other

Contact and difference in therapeutic relating

Introduction

Rogers' (1957) first condition of therapeutic personality change or therapeutic process (Rogers, 1959) is that the two (or more) people involved in the therapy are 'in contact'. As we note in Chapter 4, 'Organisms are in contact without thinking about it, and such contact is not dependent on being conscious or aware' (p. 65). In his 1957 text, Rogers catches the sense when he writes about psychological contact as when each person makes a perceived difference in the experiential field of the other, adding, we think, significantly, that 'probably it is sufficient if each makes some "subceived" difference [to the other], even though the individual may not be aware of this impact' (p. 96). We think that this concept of subception, which Rogers adopted from McCleary and Lazarus (1949), for whom it signified discrimination without awareness, helps us think about contact between organisms, and embodied minds. I (Keith) can certainly affirm having this experience as I was editing this book while Bernie was dying: a reality and process that certainly made a difference in my experiential field—and, I know, in Bernie's.

As we elaborated in Part I, human beings are interdependent: we can only say 'I am' because 'we are'. We are, therefore, subjective and intersubjective, and cannot imagine without the other. Thus, in any helping or therapeutic relationship, it is crucial to reflect on, process, understand, and evaluate how we relate, one with another, and with others. This is especially and particularly important when we are relating across differences. This chapter is an edited version of a paper originally given (by Keith) at the 2008 New Zealand Association of Psychotherapists' (NZAP) Annual Conference held in Waitangi, Northland, and later published in the NZAP's journal *Forum* (Tudor, 2008d). The theme of the conference was 'We cannot imagine without the other' and both the original paper and subsequent article were written to address this theme—which, from an organismic perspective, focuses on the importance of the other and the environment in co-creating contact. The view that the human being is an organism (which this whole book represents) connects the individual to their environment and to the significance of others, without which the individual cannot be understood. More recent research in neuroscience has confirmed that this psychological and, ultimately, political perspective has neurobiological foundations. On this basis, the

DOI: 10.4324/9781003397731-8

contact between client and therapist is crucial: from the initial contact before meeting, to the first face-to-face meeting, and throughout the therapeutic encounter. Drawing on the work of both Rogers and Stern, the chapter critiques the concept of 'the therapeutic relationship' as a fixed construct, and offers ideas about the importance of contactful 'ways-of-being' in therapeutic relat*ing*. We should say that when we refer to 'face-to-face', we include online contact, for a discussion of which with regard to Rogers' therapeutic condition, including contact, see Rodgers et al. (2021).

Interdependence, intersubjectivity, and imagining

Human beings are interdependent. The human infant is one of the most dependent born mammals and, of all mammals, has the longest period of dependency; hence the importance both of attachment and of social and psychological support for the mother or primary carer. However, when we look more closely, and particularly with the benefit of insights gained from recent research in the fields of developmental psychology and neuroscience, we see that the relationship between baby and mother is in fact one of mutual synchrony. This was encapsulated by Winnicott (1947/1957) who said: '"There's no such thing as a baby"—meaning that if you set out to describe a baby, you will find you are describing a *baby and someone*… A baby cannot exist alone, but is essentially part of a relationship' (p. 137). Most obviously, the baby is dependent on the mother. However, the mother is also 'dependent' on her baby, for instance, to stimulate oxytocin, a hormone produced when mother and baby interact in a mutually pleasurable way. Winnicott refers to the gleam in the new mother's eye, a perception supported by research which demonstrates the increase in the percentage of light in the mother's eye when she looks or gazes at her baby (see Schore, 1994). Also, if we consider the importance of regulation, we can think about ways in which the baby/infant/child both regulates—and dysregulates—the parents or carers, which is why it is so important that parents have space and support to reflect on what gets evoked by their children and by their own parenting.

There are wider, social understandings of interdependence. Marx and Engels (1848/1971) use the term in the *Manifesto of the Communist Party* when they describe the universal interdependence of nations, in comparison to the old systems based on local and national seclusion, isolationism, and self-sufficiency. Gandhi (1929) echoes this comparison:

> Interdependence is and ought to be as much the ideal of man as self-sufficiency. Man is a social being. Without interrelation with society he cannot realize his oneness with the universe or suppress his egotism. His social interdependence enables him to test his faith and to prove himself on the touchstone of reality.
>
> (quoted by Baldwin & Dekar, 2013, p. 220)

In 1945, American philosopher, Will Durant, drafted a *Declaration of Interdependence*, which aimed to promote human tolerance and fellowship through mutual consideration and respect (see Weyler, undated). Since then, a number of other such declarations have been drafted, most emphasising an ecological perspective (see the David Suzuki Foundation, 1992), one of which formed the basis and inspiration for a Symphony (no. 6 *Interdependence*) by the Finnish composer Pehr Henrik Nordgren (2001). (For a further psychopolitical analysis of interdependence, see Tudor, 2018a.)

Interdependence is a biological, neurological, developmental, relational, social, political, and environmental fact of life. It encapsulates a dynamic of being mutually responsible to and sharing a common set of principles with others. Some people, cultures, and societies advocate independence and freedom as an ultimate and abstract good; others advocate kinship, attachment, and loyalty to one's family, group, tribe, community, society, land, and earth. *Inter*dependence recognises the reality of each trend. This is encapsulated in the Nguni word *Ubuntu* which carries the sense that 'I am because we are'. In a similar vein, Lévinas argues that the self cannot exist, cannot have a concept of itself as self, without the other: 'I am defined as a subjectivity, as a singular person, as an "I" precisely because I am exposed to the other. It is my inescapable and incontrovertible answerability to the other that makes me an individual "I"' (Kearney, 1984, p. 62).

We think this is interesting in three respects.

1. Linguistic

We often think of 'I' as the starting point of the individual and identity. In fact, as infants, we say 'me' before 'I'. This personal pronoun represents the social self, that is, a self, defined by others, which we internalise in some way ('me want', 'me do', etc.). In terms of human development and the development of language, 'I' comes later, and represents a personal self. Language, of course, comes relatively late in an infant's development and, developmentally, before 'me' is, at least conceptually, 'us', a pronoun which represents the co-regulating 'mothering pair'. We suggest that 'us' is the fundamental life position on and from which we develop, through attachment and separation to individuation—but an individuation based *in relationship* and in connectedness (Tudor, 2016, 2022a); it is where we start and understand ourselves as an 'I', an 'us', and a 'self' or 'selves'. As Mihaka (2018) puts it: 'I am tangata whenua. I am not a people of this land; I *am* the land.'

2. Psychological

The second point of interest for us is Lévinas's use of the word 'exposed': we expose ourselves to the other; we put ourselves out; we lay ourselves open; we make ourselves vulnerable and known. Put in these terms, being ourselves may sound risky; yet, to live is to risk. Janet Rand (2010) in her poem, entitled '*Risk*' writes:

86 *Conditions*

> But risk must be taken because the greatest hazard in life is to risk nothing.
> The person who risks nothing, does nothing, has nothing, is nothing, and becomes nothing.
> They may avoid suffering and sorrow, but they cannot learn, feel, change, grow, love, live.
> Chained by their certitude, they are slaves, they have forfeited their freedom.
> Only a person who risks is truly free.[1]

We think this is particularly pertinent when dealing with difference, especially differences that we find difficult, which is why the concept and practice of encounter is so important and useful (see Chapter 4, and below).

3. Interpersonal

The third important point Lévinas makes is that we are individuals only because of the other or others, to whom we are answerable; that is to say: we have to answer to others in order to be ourselves. This makes sense to us. For example, at an interpersonal, social level, there is a sense that we, as authors are answerable to you, the reader for this chapter and book. Moreover, at an existential level, we need an answer from another (in this case, usually a review). The lack of an answer is the tragedy of Echo who, according to Greek mythology, could only repeat what the other said, and of Narcissus who was punished for not accepting Echo's love by being condemned to fall in love with himself. In this story there was—and is—no interdependence, no answerability, and no intersubjectivity. We refer to Narcissus as we think that one of the major psychological problems in Western society and, in some aspects, of the profession of psychotherapy is, as the American social commentator Christopher Lasch (1979) puts it, *The Culture of Narcissism*.

If we are interdependent and we define ourselves as 'a subjectivity', then it makes sense to think in terms of *inter*subjectivity. Atwood and Stolorow (1996) call this 'reciprocal mutual influence' and describe the implications of such reciprocity:

> from this perspective, the observer and their language are grasped as intrinsic to the observed, and the impact of the analyst and their organising activity on the unfolding of the therapeutic relationship itself becomes the focus of... investigation and reflection.
>
> (p. 181)

Rather than asking 'What's happening to you?' or 'What's happening to me?' we will, if we focus on the intersubjective world and the domain of intersubjective relatedness, tend to ask 'What is happening here between us?' Parlett (1991) suggests that: 'when two people converse or engage with one another in some way, something comes into existence which is a product of neither of them exclusively... there is a shared field, a common communicative home, which is mutually constructed' (p. 75), a perspective that inspired me (Keith) to write an article identifying certain qualities of co-creative therapeutic relating (Tudor, 2019). Thus, intersubjectivity supports what Stark (2000) refers to as a 'two-person' mode of therapeutic action. This perspective has its roots in psychoanalysis and its developments, such as Sullivan's (1953/1997) interpersonal theory of psychiatry and therapy. Whilst these origins of intersubjective and interpersonal, relational perspectives may be familiar to psychoanalytic therapists, what may be less familiar is that these perspectives also have their roots in humanistic psychotherapy, notably in Rogers' (1942) 'relationship therapy' and, more generally, in organismic psychology (see section below).

From a developmental perspective Stern (1985, 2000) writes about the interpersonal world of the infant, and suggests that, from nine months, along with other senses of self (emergent and core), the infant develops the sense of an intersubjective self:

> [This] quantum leap in the sense of self occurs when the infant discovers that he or she has a mind and that other people have minds as well. Between the seventh and ninth month of life, infants gradually come upon the momentous realization that inner subjective experiences, the 'subject matter' of the mind, are potentially shareable with someone else… This discovery amounts to the acquisition of a 'theory' of separate minds.
>
> (2000, p. 124)

Fonagy and colleagues (2002) refer to this as mentalisation, a preconscious or ego function that transforms basic somatic sensations and motor patterns through a linking activity. Assuming that others have minds enables us to work together. This is important both developmentally and in the present moment. It is also important for us as social/political beings; elsewhere I and a colleague have described the development of an active and engaged citizenship as involving the necessary movement from being 'a subject' to being an 'intersubject' by means of intersubjectivity (see Tudor & Hargaden, 2002).

So, how do we get to sharing? We think that we do this through imagining and empathising. Developmentally, the mutual synchrony and co-regulation of the mothering or caring pair is the basis for imagination and imagining: we cannot imagine—that is, to form and symbolise an image—without another, as we need another to reflect back our reflections, to regulate us, and help us make meaning of our world. The development of imagination is, thus, a co-creative process. To live, love, and work is to risk contact and, thereby, both attachment and loss. To risk contact is to risk exposing one's own subjectivity and to risk exposure to another's. To risk such intersubjectivity is to risk both imagining what it is to be that other, and to risk relating to the other.

In the context of our current interest, we should make it clear that the other with whom we are in contact perceived and/or subceived, is not confined to other homo sapiens. It could be a mountain, river, waka (canoe), rock, tree, animal, and so on.

Before discussing these aspects of life and of psychotherapeutic practice, we turn to organismic psychology, the theory which, for us, supports this view of interdependence and intersubjectivity.

Organismic psychology

The view that the human being is an organism connects the individual to their environment and to the significance of others, without which the individual cannot be understood. The biological entity that is the human organism, and its qualities, offer us a theoretical base for the interdependent life. It is central to organismic, gestalt, and PCP. Rogers was one of a number of psychologists who expounded organismic theory. Others include Kantor (1924a, 1924b), Brunswik (Tolman & Brunswik, 1935), Wheeler (1940), Murphy (1947), Werner (1948) and, more recently, Brown (1990). Rogers acknowledges his debt to Goldstein's (1934/1995) work on *The Organism* and to Angyal's (1941) *Foundations for a Science of Personality*. Thirty years ago, Hall and Lindzey (1978) recognised that Rogers adopted an organismic orientation in his theory and practice, a view also explored by Fernald (2000) who claims Rogers as a body-oriented therapist. Organismic psychology is, in our view, the lost tradition of the 20th century. In his excellent book on the conceptual domains of psychoanalysis, Pine (1990) discusses the domains of drive, ego, object, and self, a taxonomy which, we acknowledge, represents the development of Western psychotherapy in general. Pine, however, omits the domain of the organism. Drawing on this lost tradition, Tudor and Worrall (2006) elaborate the centrality of the organism specifically to PCAs to therapy.

According to Angyal (1941), the organism (from 'organ' meaning tool) refers to 'a system in which the parts are the instruments, the tools, of the whole' (p. 99). Feldenkrais (1981), the founder of a form and method of bodywork, defines it as consisting of 'the skeleton, the muscles, the nervous system, and all that goes to nourish, warm, activate, and rest the whole of it.' (pp. 21–22). In his foreword to the republication of Goldstein's work in 1995, Sacks traces a brief history of neurology, seeing Goldstein and others, including gestalt psychologists, as important in rebutting more modular and atomistic views of neural organisation and the human organism. Damasio (1994/1996) defines living organisms as 'changing continuously, assuming a succession of "states", each defined by varied patterns of ongoing activity in all its components' (p. 87). This understanding, as well as other more recent developments in neuroscience, supports the premise that the experiencing human organism tends to actualise, maintain, enhance, and reproduce itself. Tudor and Worrall (2006) elaborate that, as human beings, we are holistic, experiential, interdependent organisms; we are always in motion; we construe reality according to our perception of it; we differentiate, regulate, and behave according to need; and we have an internal, organismic valuing process.

There are a number of implications of this organismic perspective which are relevant to our present interest:

Firstly, Rogers' use of the term organism represents an holistic and experiential view of human beings.

As our mind, body, and spirit are inseparable, anything and everything we do is connected. Tom Waits notes: 'The way you do anything is the way you do everything' (reported by Kot, 1999). This was elaborated in the 1930s by Goldstein (1934/1995) in his studies of the organism, by the tradition of organismic psychology (for references to which, see Tudor & Worrall, 2006), and is confirmed by more recent developments in neuroscience. One of the implications is that we cannot separate our behaviour from who we are. Behaviour is, as Rogers (1951) puts it: '*basically the goal-directed attempt of the organism to satisfy its needs as experienced, in the field, as perceived*' (p. 491, original emphasis). Thus, we *are* our behaviour. This is challenging to theory and practice (predominantly cognitive and behavioural therapies) which seek to separate and compartmentalise behaviour from the person (see Tudor, 2008/2018b).

Secondly, as formulated in his theory of personality and behaviour, Rogers (1951) asserts that the human species, as with other species, has one basic tendency and striving: 'to actualize, maintain, and enhance the experiencing organism' (p. 487).

Whilst this is useful, it tends to get collapsed into the notion of an actualising tendency seeking self-actualisation and autonomy. By contrast, Angyal (1941) sees the organism as having *two* related tendencies or trends: one towards increased *autonomy* and another towards increased *homonomy*. He defines the organism as autonomous in the sense that it is 'to a large extent, a *self-governing* entity' (p. 23), and homonomous in the sense that it longs 'to be in harmony with superindividual units, the social group, nature, God, ethical world order, or whatever the person's formulation of it may be' (p. 172). As Panksepp (1998) puts it: 'Homologies at the neural level give us solid assurance of common evolutionary origins and designs' (p. 14). Human beings live autonomously and homonomously in a world that is heteronomous or other. Most practitioners trained in psychotherapeutic theories and methods which draw on Western psychology will be familiar with the concept of autonomy, for instance, as an ethical principle or a political aspiration or demand. We may be less familiar with the concept of homonomy, although when the NZAP (2018) talks in terms of 'interdependence', describing it as 'a commitment to maintain relationships of reciprocity and respect with all living things' (p. 1), it is expressing a trend to homonomy. Interestingly and significantly for our present enquiry, the NZAP includes in its reference to all living things, the natural environment.

Thirdly, as organisms, human beings are interdependent with our environment, and cannot be understood outside of that environmental context.

Perls (1947/1969) states: 'No organism is self-sufficient. It requires the world for the gratification of its needs... there is always an inter-dependency of the organism and its environment' (p. 38). Recent research on brain development confirms the importance of the environment and the dynamic relationship between the environment and the mental phenomena of the organism. Damasio (1994/1996), for example, suggests that:

mental phenomena can be fully understood only in the context of an organism's interacting in an environment. That the environment is, in part, a product of the organism's activity itself, merely underscores the complexity of interactions we must take into account.

(p. xix)

Again, Angyal (1941) provides us with a useful term, the 'biosphere', by which he means the realm or sphere of life, and by which he conveys the concept of an holistic entity which includes both individual and environment 'as aspects of a single reality which can be separated only by abstraction' (p. 100). Thus, Angyal concludes: 'The subject-matter of our considerations are [sic] not organic processes and environmental influences, but biospheric occurrences in their integral reality' (p. 100). This is a remarkable statement and one which supports a genuinely *integral* individual/environmental approach to psychotherapy (as distinct from 'integrative psychotherapy'). In this sense, it may be more accurate to talk about a *people*-centred, or life-oriented approach to therapy, and to life. To extend Stark's (2000) taxonomy, this makes the PCA—or, in the context of Aotearoa New Zealand and Te Tiriti o Waitangi (Treaty of Waitangi), a 'partnership-centred approach' to psychotherapy—a 'two-person-plus' psychology (see Tudor & Worrall, 2006; Tudor, 2011c; and Chapter 8).

Fourthly, as we grow and develop through differentiation, we are inherently diverse.

Rogers (1959) states that 'a portion of the individual's experience becomes differentiated and symbolized in an *awareness* of being, *awareness* of functioning' (p. 223). 'Such awareness', he says, 'may be described as *self-experience*' (p. 223). Recent research in the fields of neuroscience, infant development, and human communication points to the fact that infants are capable of differentiating themselves, their bodies, faces, and hands from those of their mothers and, therefore, in some sense, knowing themselves. This offers us an experiential basis for understanding and appreciating personal difference and diversity and, ultimately, social and cultural diversity. Angyal's (1941) reference to *heteronomy* is useful here: 'The organism lives in a world in which things happen according to laws which are heteronomous from the point of view of the organism' (p. 33). In this sense, *anyone* else or other is different, and thus, as human organisms, we know what it is to be different and, thereby, to relate to difference. I would argue that this is a more human and relational basis for working and struggling with difference than that, for instance, imposed by an 'equal opportunities' agenda. Such agendas often impose forms of contact with the other which, we argue, often creates a distance, and we know that, for example, racism is often fuelled by projections onto the racial other, precisely in order to demonise and marginalise. In *Humankind: A Hopeful History* Bregman (2020) writes about the soldiers in the Battle of Makin in the Pacific during the second world war who would not shoot. If we are actually in contact with a person or an object, and we see that person and/or object as a living process, it is easier to empathise with them/it, and harder to oppress or kill them/it. As a colleague and mentor of Keith's put it succinctly and directly: 'If people thought of Papatūānuku [Mother Earth], as their own mother, it would be harder to exploit and rape her' (H. Kohu-Morgan, personal communication, 9th February, 2021).

Finally, human beings develop an organismic valuing process, which Rogers (1959) defines as: 'an ongoing process in which values are never fixed or rigid, but experiences are being accurately symbolized and continually and freshly valued' (p. 210).

This speaks of an open, reflective, and fluid process of being, *and of a being in contact and process with its environment.* Stinckens et al. (2002) argue that: 'Inborn, intuitive experiencing should enter into a continuous dialectical relationship with the laws of social reality for the valuing process to correspond with the social embeddedness of the individual' (p. 48). In other words, a person's internal, organismic valuing process doesn't lead to rank individuality or individualism; rather it takes into account others, especially those in partnership, and the environment in trust. In this sense, a hurt to one is a hurt to all and, perhaps more importantly, a hurt to all, especially when 'other', is a hurt to one. Equally, if we are thinking more ecologically and ecopsychologically, a hurt to a person is a hurt to the land, and a hurt to the land is a hurt to the people.

It is our contention, then, that an organismic perspective transforms our view of life and of psychotherapy from an individualistic, reactionary paradigm to one which is social if not radical, and relational if not collective.

Contact/encounter, relating, and imagining

In the last part, we turn to the implications of these perspectives for clinical practice and, specifically, when, as psychotherapists, we are working and struggling with contact and difference. We discuss this with regard to contact in encounter, relating, and imagining.

Contact in encounter

For Rogers (1957, 1959), contact or psychological contact is the first condition—or pre- condition—of therapy. Others since have developed this concept and an approach to 'pre-therapy' with clients who have some impairment in their ability to make and maintain contact, for example, people with learning impairments or diagnoses of schizophrenia, autism, and dementia, (see Morton, 1999; Pörtner, 2000; Prouty, 1976, 1994; Prouty et al., 2002). Contact through greeting, seating, and meeting is the beginning of genuine encounter. Rogers (1962) describes therapy as 'relationship encounter' (p. 185). The English word 'encounter' comes from the Latin *contra* meaning 'against'; and so 'encounter' carries both a sense of 'face-to-face' meeting *and* of difference. In *I and Thou* Buber (1923/1937) describes 'being counter' as the foundation for meeting: to be opposite to the other offers the possibility to face and to acknowledge them; as he puts it: 'All real life is encounter' (p. 18), and encounter is where dialogue takes place. Guardini (1955) suggests that encounter means we are touched by the essence of the opposite. Tillich (1956) goes further and argues that the person only emerges through resistance: 'it is through the resistance of the other that the person is born' (p. 208). This is important on developmental and interpersonal levels, and social and cultural levels. On this basis, contact, certainly on the part of the therapist, becomes a much more engaged and engaging concept and activity. We think of this view and experience of contact and encounter as embodying our commonality, connectedness, and sense of community (the trend to homonomy) and, at the same time, our difference, resistance, and sense of our differentiated selves (the trend to autonomy). This kind of contact in encounter is also true of our relationship and contact with the environment, whether it is feeling embraced and loved by mother Earth as Archie Roach (2016a) describes in his song 'Get back to the land', or challenged by climbing a mountain, and losing our way.

This perspective gives us, we think, a basis for a positive approach to struggle. To contend resolutely, to resist, to make efforts to escape from constraint, to strive, to make progress with difficulty, in other words, to struggle, is not a problem; it is a developmental, relational, and social necessity. Struggle is not a problem; it is the problem that we make of struggle that is the problem—and, unfortunately, the history of psychotherapy includes theories and practice which pathologise struggle, resistance, being critical and, for that matter, being radical (Schwartz, 1999). We think it is important to reclaim the importance of struggle in contact/encounter and in dialogue; the importance of difference; and the importance of not knowing. As Lévinas (1983) contends: 'Encountering a human being means being kept awake by an enigma' (p. 120).

Relating

It is widely accepted in the psychological therapies that the therapeutic relationship is a key factor in the outcome of therapy and it has become the subject of considerable study within and beyond different theoretical orientations. However, this relationship is not fixed and, in our view, is better described in the language of both Rogers (1958/1967a, 1980/1995i), and, more recently, Stern (2000), as 'ways of being with' or ways of relating. This verbal form—'therapeutic *relating*'—emphasises therapy as an activity between two (or more), interactive and intersubjective human beings or, extending this, between client, therapist, and environment. Furthermore, if we take an intersubjective approach, we must also view these ways of relating as co-created. Thus, I think it more useful to describe transference and counter-transference (nouns) as 'co-transference', as Sapriel (1998) does or, better, as 'co-transferential *relating*' (Summers & Tudor, 2000). This acknowledges that the therapist is also involved, and enters into and/or maintains a present-centred or past-centred, transferential way of relating, rather than attributing their feelings solely to the client. We would argue that, if we have a view of people as beings in process and of therapy itself as being a process, then it is more congruent to use process language to describe both the person and activity of therapy (see Tudor, 2008c).

We say 'present-centred' as we are interested in working with the present moment (see Stern, 2004). The fact that, according to Stern (1985, 2000), our senses of self develop in parallel throughout adult life supports working therapeutically in and with the present, and supports present-centred development, with the *neopsyche* (or, in transactional analytic terms, the Adult ego state), which represents an elaborative system connected to the mental-emotional analysis of the here-and-now (see Berne, 1961/1975a; Tudor, 2003). In other words, we are interested in what is happening now, between us: between therapist and client, supervisor and therapist, trainer and student, speaker or author and audience *and the environment*. If these are viewed as complementary concepts, then the relationships they describe are complementary. Our focus on the present is not to say that how we relate in the present is not influenced by the past. As Ritchie (2008) puts it (in the context of working in Aotearoa New Zealand): 'Everything that is bicultural is available to you in the present moment... all you have to do is to be open to this experience'. It is to say that history and story are available to us in the present, and that we can change our history, herstory, or narrative about the past. It *is* too late to have a happy childhood; it is not too late to acknowledge how unhappy that childhood was, and to have a different experience/perception of the present—and of the past. One of the epigrams in King's (2003) *History of New Zealand* is from the French historian Ernest Renan who says that: 'A nation is bound together not by the past, but by the *stories* of the past that we tell one another in the present' (p. 8). So, in terms of relating to the environment, the issue or questions are: what's happening now between us and our environments? How does our practice relate to the environment? What do we know about our clients' relationships to their environments?

In terms of the theme of struggle, we are interested, as we relate to another, in what, if any, struggle there is between us and how that reflects the story of the past for them, for me, and, over time, for *us*: that is, the co-created and co-creative relating that is therapy-in-context. Moreover, given what we've said about contact and encounter, we are also—and perhaps particularly—interested if there isn't a struggle!

Imagining

When I (Keith) first saw the literature for the 2008 Conference, I was particularly struck by the elaboration of the theme on the NZAP (2008) website: 'Psychotherapy aims at the development of an imaginative partnership that can acknowledge difference and replace ignorance and intolerance with recognition, reciprocity, and respect'.

In this chapter we propose ways in which that imaginative partnership is created, co-created, and developed through recognising that we are interdependent and intersubjective—and that this extends to include the environment. The expansion in the nature of their sensed self, and their capacity for relatedness, catapults the infant into the domain of intersubjective relatedness—which is the basis for and the beginning of recognition, reciprocity, and respect. This is not an easy process either for the infant and their parent(s), or for two adults communicating, for example, across cultures. There may be little shared framework of meaning; gestures, postures, and facial expressions may be misunderstood and misinterpreted across differences of race, culture, gender, sexuality, and/or class. Nevertheless, Stern's theory of selves, and their respective domains of relatedness, offers a framework for communication as it explains the development of empathy. It is precisely as we develop a sense of intersubjectivity that we experience the *process* of empathy.

Rogers (1959) says that empathic understanding means: 'to perceive the internal frame of reference of another with accuracy, and with the emotional components and meanings which pertain thereto, as if one were the other person, but without ever losing the "as if" condition' (p. 210). In this sense, empathic understanding stands in a tradition of a psychology that seeks to understand rather than to explain, a distinction which underpins the concept of empathic understanding in PCT, and distinguishes this therapy from therapies which seek to analyse, interpret, or explain. Extending our understanding of empathy, we would argue that the 'as if' attitude supports I–Thou relating but that this can distance the relationship from the relational, which we think is better described as a 'Thou–I' encounter (Schmid, 2006). We also suggest that the 'Thou' presented by the client can and does include their environment, and that when the therapist ('I') is in genuine contact with the 'Thou', the therapist will see the Thou-in-context. Furthermore, empathy requires imagination and identification. Elsewhere, Keith has written about imagination and imagining as being a quality of the *neopsyche*:

> Free from the contaminations of archaic fixated and introjected material, the mature organism/person is curious, open to contact and relationship—not only with people but also with things, through ideas, aesthetics and the arts. It/he/she is playful and sensual. Just as this is the ego state of pure Reason, it is also the location of sheer intuition… Alongside its reflective and critical consciousness lies the state of unconsciousness, re-membered through dreams and the imagination.
>
> (Tudor, 2003, p. 219)

So, psychotherapists need to imagine—to imagine what it is to be 'as if' another; what it is to be different from ourselves in terms of ability, education, opportunity, and privilege; what it is to struggle; what it is to be repressed and oppressed; and what it is to have land, language, and identity taken away—and to imagine what it is like for the other if we (as therapists, healers, or helpers) are associated with that past history and, indeed, with present realities. I (Keith) come from a country (England, Britain, United Kingdom) that has a long history of conquest, domination, and of dispossessing the other and live in a country (Aotearoa New Zealand) which is still coming to terms with its history and in which I inhabit a privileged position. We (Bernie and Keith) consider that, as citizens, we are implicated in and, thereby, involved with others in this history and its manifestation in the present. Thus, we, as therapists and citizens, are—or should be—engaged in continuous and necessary struggle. It is how we approach that struggle, how we listen and learn, and how we repair the inevitable ruptures which occur when relating with others that marks us as effective and active therapists and citizens.

Note

1 This poem has also been attributed to the academic and poet Leo Buscaglia.

6 Crying for the loss of nature
Incongruence and alienation

Len Gillman

Introduction

I grew up within a forest in Titirangi on the shores of Manukau harbour in a time when Titirangi was a rural locality on the outskirts of Auckland, Aotearoa New Zealand. The indigenous Māori people of Aotearoa identify with a mountain and a river. I don't have a mountain or a river, but I identify with the whole mountain spine of this land and the rivers shed from this spine. They are not 'my' mountains, but I feel that I belong to them—and the tears they weep. It is important to Māori to belong: to a mountain, to a river, to a people. In te Ao Māori (the Māori world) and te Ao Pākehā (the non-Māori world), and beyond these mountains, rivers, forest, and shores, there is a widespread feeling that our modern civilisation has lost something vital. Perhaps it is this sense of belonging to the land and the nature it cradles that has been lost for most people and is declining for the rest?

In this chapter, I start with a discussion about the nature of evolution, the biosphere, and our place within it. I then review the major wounds that humans are inflicting on Earth. Lastly, I discuss potential losses due to alienation from nature.

Nature

The nature of evolution

Humans, and all other species, are the culmination of 4.2 billion years of fierce and ruthless competition among individuals. There has never been any benevolent direction to this evolution. For every individual plant or animal, survival to reproduce has been at the expense and death of countless other individuals. For instance, on average just two out of approximately 50 ducklings produced by a pair of ducks survive. The vast majority of all ducklings that have ever hatched have been eaten while still cute and fluffy. Despite this, biological altruism, where individuals help a relative to survive to reproduction and thereby enable shared genes to be passed on to the next generation, evolved. For example, among honeybees, the workers never reproduce but instead work to enable their queen to do so. It is altruism that has enabled humans to act in a way that benefits society as a whole. In *Humankind*, Bregman (2020) argues that cooperation, trust, and

DOI: 10.4324/9781003397731-9

kindness all have an evolutionary basis that can be traced back to the beginning of our species. However, despite the altruism and cooperation that is embedded in our DNA, we are destroying nature on Earth at an ever-increasing rate in the full knowledge that human civilisation will suffer.

The nature of nature

Nature has never been in balance—it has always gone through cycles of collapse and change. However, we, *Homo sapiens,* along with the vast majority of extant life on Earth, are dependent on a biosphere (air, water, land, and all living organisms) that has changed relatively slowly during the evolution of our species. Most extant species have existed for less than one million years—a mere blink in time relative to the more than four billion-year history of life. However, the rate of extinction now is thought to be exceeding the rate of the catastrophic extinction event of the late cretaceous age, some 65 million years ago, when the majority of animal species on Earth disappeared.

There is a substantial body of research that shows that species act and respond to the environment in an individualistic manner. Communities do not remain the same over time, acting as cohesive units, nor do they simply migrate in unison according to environmental changes. As the climate has moved through cycles of warm and cold periods unique communities have assembled each time in a manner that indicates that communities are simply the result of individualist dynamics by species and populations within species (see Coats et al., 2008; Taper et al., 1995).

Nonetheless, the biosphere can be viewed as one ecosystem encompassing an uncountable number of interactions and interdependencies. The interactions among individuals, among species, and among ecosystems are extensive and complex. Disruption to any component of an ecosystem will often have unpredictable and far-reaching effects on other components of the ecosystem. Some species within these systems are more important than others and regarded as keystone species (Paine, 1969). A keystone species is likened to a stone in an arch of an old building that is key or critical to the integrity of the arch and, therefore, to the whole building—if a keystone is removed the building will collapse. Keystone species are those that are critical to many other species in the community and thereby critical to the integrity of the ecosystem in which they belong. The loss of a keystone species from an ecosystem may either result in an abrupt transformation to a dramatically different ecosystem or in the complete loss of the ecosystem.

Although many components of the biosphere are buffered, such that they are resilient to change from external pressure, there are tipping points when external forces exceed a critical level, and the particular component of the system becomes destabilised and often irrevocably changed. Scientists have been warning against human activity breaching important tipping points for many decades (for recent examples, see Ripple et al., 2017; Steffen et al., 2018). Like cracks appearing in a dam, the imminent breach is frightening to those looking up at them.

In the following sections I discuss the major assaults on nature that humans are inflicting. Most of these involve tipping points and the loss of keystone species that precipitate catastrophic change. They all involve aesthetic challenges and are likely deeply impacting our collective wellbeing.

Climate change

Climate change in the past

Climate change on Earth is not new. One hundred million years ago, when our planet had a very different climate to that which we encounter today, diverse forest with trees up to 40-metres high and 1-metre in diameter grew at 85° S (almost at the South Pole) and forest trees up to 70-centimetres diameter grew to within 11° of the North Pole (Pointing et al., 2015). (Note that land extended much closer to the North Pole at that time than it does now.) However, this was approximately 100 million years before we evolved, and life on Earth was vastly different. Nonetheless, significant climate changes have occurred in our species' lifetime, i.e., 400,000–700,000 years (Stringer, 2016), with the climate oscillating in and out of glacial periods every 100,000 years or so (Crucifix, 2012)—the last glacial maximum was 20,000–26,000 years ago (Clark et al., 2009) when global temperatures were on average 3–8° C colder than now (Rehfeld et al., 2018).

Climate tipping points

The Earth's climate is changing, and we know this is due to human activity. Just how much warmer the Earth will get is uncertain. The critical question is at what point in time will positive feedback loops take over and accelerate warming even if we stop adding climate forcing gasses to the atmosphere? This point in time is referred to as a tipping point. An example of one of the known several climate forcing feedback loops is the melting of permafrost. As temperatures rise the permafrost melts releasing vast quantities of methane, a potent climate forcing gas, which will further increase temperatures. The resultant increase in temperature will melt more permafrost perpetuating the feedback loop. Steffen et al. (2018) predict that irreversible tipping points will occur when preindustrial warming exceeds 1.5–2.0° C, leading to a hothouse Earth, even if we stop all carbon emissions, with temperatures approximately 5–6° C warmer. Current international pledges for emission reductions, if they are met, will lock in 3° C of temperature rise (Lenton et al., 2019)—well above the threshold for this predicted tipping point.

Climate change threat to humanity

The difference between past climate change experienced by humans and the current change is the time span over which it is occurring. We are now expecting a climate change of a similar magnitude to that which occurred over the last 20,000 years to occur within a single human lifespan. Moreover, largely because land will warm faster than water, the mean temperature increase that humans (and our agricultural systems) will face is predicted to be 2.3 times that of average temperature rise. Thus, global warming will affect human health, livelihoods, food security, and water supply. The majority of humans currently live within climates with average temperatures of between 11 and 15° C. Under current projections, almost 20 per cent of Earth and 3.5 billion people will be subject to average temperatures of more than 29° C, similar to conditions now found in the Sahara desert (Xu et al., 2020), conditions that are not survivable without external inputs. Estimates of the number of people that will be displaced by sea level rise vary greatly from 88 million to 1.4 billion (Hauer et al., 2020).

Climate change threat to biodiversity

In tropical land areas, where diversity and primary productivity is greatest (Gillman et al., 2015), such as the Amazon, Indian subcontinent, and Indo-Pacific regions, the biota (the living organisms of a particular region) is most at risk from warming (Trisos et al., 2020). If greenhouse gas emissions are not reduced, more than 90 per cent of species in the latter two areas will face temperatures outside their known tolerance before the end of the century. In the Amazon, 100 per cent of species are likely to suffer temperatures outside their known tolerance in less than 30 years. These temperature thresholds will occur abruptly with the majority of species exposed simultaneously. In tropical oceans such as the coral triangle (between the Pacific and Indian oceans) and parts of the Caribbean, temperature thresholds across assemblages are probably already being exceeded (Trisos et al., 2020). The implication is the likely extinction of entire ecosystems in the most diverse areas of the world. Averting catastrophic collapse of these ecosystems requires massive and rapid reductions in greenhouse gas emissions (Trisos et al., 2020).

Species declines and extinctions

Species are connected to each other via ecological interactions; therefore, the loss of any one species reverberates through ecosystems. Likewise, loss or depletion of populations within species (that are not close to extinction) can nonetheless have widespread impacts on other species and on ecosystem composition and function, both on land and in the oceans (Johnson et al., 2017).

Our genus *Homo* has been associated with extinctions (two-thirds of large mammal species) throughout its 2 million years of existence. Between 100,000 and 500,000 years ago, 140 genera of mammals (10 per cent of the total at the time) became extinct. These extinctions are associated with the arrival of *Homo sapiens* in a region rather than with climate change, indicating that we were the culprits of such genocide (Johnson et al., 2017). In the last 500,000 years, 363 vertebrate extinctions have been documented and an additional 279 species have either become extinct in the wild or have been listed as possibly extinct (Ceballos et al., 2015; Johnson et al., 2017). Accurate numbers for plants and invertebrate extinctions are lacking but vertebrates act as a good proxy for what is happening in other taxa (units of biological classification). This current human-induced extinction event is occurring at a rate that is at least 100 times higher than the long-term background rate of extinction. If less well documented but highly probable extinctions are included, the rate is more than 1,000 times higher (World Resources Institute, 2005). It is an extinction event not seen on Earth since the last mass extinction 65 million years ago. Furthermore, in the near future, the rate of extinction is expected to increase by a factor of five (Johnson et al., 2017).

The main causes of recent extinctions are loss of habitat and overexploitation. However, invasive species, disease, and climate change are increasingly the cause of ecosystem disruption and of growing importance as causes of extinction (Johnson et al., 2017).

Humans have dramatically changed virtually all ecosystems on Earth. In 2005, a Millennium Ecosystem Assessment examined 14 global biomes (large, naturally occurring communities of flora and fauna) and found that 20–50 per cent had been converted to human use. Three quarters of temperate grasslands had been converted to cultivation; 20 per cent of coral reefs destroyed; and, between 1995 and 2005, 35 per cent of mangrove forests had been lost (World Resources Institute, 2005).

Habitat loss on land has both a direct impact on the species populations that are extinguished and indirect impacts as a result of increased nutrient runoff into rivers and dewatering of rivers for irrigation. Increases in nitrogen, phosphorus, and sulphur runoff have emerged as one of the most important drivers of ecosystem degradation in terrestrial, freshwater, and coastal ecosystems. Aerial deposition of nitrogen into natural grassland and forest ecosystems has reduced plant diversity. Habitat loss also occurs in coastal and marine systems due to trawling of the seabed, and coral reefs are particularly vulnerable to destructive fishing, coastal development, and warming sea temperatures. Overexploitation has been the dominant driver of degradation in marine systems. The biomass of fish targeted in fisheries has been reduced in most areas by 90 per cent relative to levels prior to the onset of industrial fishing. Just 3 per cent of the world's ecosystems remain intact and only 11 per cent of the functionally intact areas exist within protected areas (Plumptre et al., 2021).

Forest loss

Earth's biodiversity on land is concentrated within wet tropical rainforests (Gillman et al., 2015) where up to 265 different tree species can occur in a tiny 1000 m^2 plot (approximately ¼ acre) (Gentry, 1988). By contrast, in temperate climates, such as New Zealand, an equivalent area typically contains fewer than 11 tree species (unpublished data) and the entire diversity of trees native to the UK is only 32 (Wikipedia, 2021). The massively diverse tropical forests are where forest loss is greatest. Wet tropical forest experiences twice as much loss as temperate or boreal forests (Leberger et al., 2020). Over the last decade, 38.3 million hectares (Mha) of primary (largely unmodified) wet tropical forest has disappeared. This is an area larger than Germany (34.9 Mha). Furthermore, the annual rate of loss increased from 2.7 Mha in 2002 to 4.2

Mha in 2020 (an equivalent area to Denmark). The main causes of loss are due to demand for timber and conversion to agricultural land, and fire (Global Forest Watch, 2022).

Plastic pollution in the oceans

For many people, going to the beach is an opportunity to be free from our artificial environments—a place where we can feel wind and salt spray on our skin, and embrace the natural world. However, whenever we go to the beach, we see plastic litter. Plastic has become a ubiquitous part of the mosaic of tidal debris; there are approximately 580,000 pieces of plastic in every square kilometre of ocean and this pollution is increasing exponentially (Wilcox et al., 2015). Plastic pollution is not confined to the oceans, but, in this environment, it is particularly obvious and perhaps of greatest danger to wildlife. Almost 60 per cent of seabird species studied have ingested plastic, and, of those species that ingested plastic, it is estimated that 90 per cent of individual members of that species have done so. Furthermore, it is predicted that plastics ingestion will increase to 99 per cent of all species by 2050 (Wilcox et al., 2015).

The only up-side of plastic pollution is that it is easy for people to pick up bits and remove them from the environment—and the very act of doing something to contribute to protecting the planet then helps us to feel better, even if our efforts are just a drop out of the ocean of plastic.

Invasive pest species

Few ecosystems on Earth are free of introduced pest species, and an increasing proportion of biomes, ecosystems, and habitats are becoming dominated by them (Pyšek & Richardson, 2010). Invasive species have negative effects on biotic communities by reducing indigenous species diversity and populations. In a global meta-analysis of publications on invasive species, average losses in species richness recorded due to animal pests were 21 per cent in aquatic habitats and 27 per cent in terrestrial habitats. Birds suffered the greatest decline in species richness (41 per cent) (Mollot et al., 2017). Invasive species have significant impacts on ecosystems, ecological processes, and economies and can substantially disrupt the composition, structure, or function of native ecosystems. Their impacts may occur directly or indirectly at the genetic, organism, population, community, and ecosystem levels (Poland et al., 2021). For example, invasive insects and pathogens in forests can cause tree mortality, gaps in the canopy, stem thinning, and loss of emergent trees. In turn, these can alter microenvironments and hydrologic or biogeochemical cycling regimes. These changes can shift the overall species composition and structure of the biotic community, including components of terrestrial and aquatic fauna.

Invasive species also degrade ecosystem diversity through a process termed biotic homogenisation (Smart et al., 2006). The concept of 'ecosystem diversity' is one that reflects the importance of the unique nature of species assemblages in different parts of the world. Ecosystems across the globe, especially those associated with human occupation, are becoming dominated by species introduced from other places and the increasing abundance of these invaders is leading to an ever-increasing similarity among ecosystems. The unique biotic character relating to location is being diminished and replaced by assemblages of species that could represent any part of the world. The distinct character of ecosystems is being lost by the introduced species that either spread on their own account or are deliberately introduced by planting or release. This is both an ecological and an aesthetic issue.

Expanding built environment

As humans we once sensed the world as much through our feet and skin as we do now through our hands and eyes (see Chapter 2). The soft damp of mud or sand on the soles of our feet, the brush of grass or shrubs against our legs, the cold breath of air against our skin as the wind shifts quarter—these conveyed critical information to us about our environment. For the majority of humanity and for the majority of our two million years of *Homo* evolution, our visual landscape was dominated by greens with irregular, mostly soft margins; our olfactory landscape was likely dominated by humic vapours from fermenting leaf litter on forest floors. Between each sound there was space for a silence we can only now imagine. Our world today mostly consists of hard flat surfaces that we are shielded from by clothes and shoes. Our visual landscape is dominated by hard straight lines and penetrating blue light from our screens. Our offices and homes hum and the tissue of our bones vibrate from millions of vehicle miles per minute on a constant unrelenting timeframe. There is a need to escape from the built environment but, alas, even forest tracks in wilderness reserves are being progressively 'upgraded' to flat gravelled and stepped paths that hold us hostage to the ever-expanding built environment. To escape we must go to ever increasing extremes, but even the summits of mountains have handrails and signs to avoid the discomfort of any uncertainty about our balance and location. This progress, designed to ensure that everyone can enjoy the outdoors, is ever pushing back the probability of any one of us encountering wilderness.

Catastrophic collapse of ecosystems

I have outlined above some of the key mechanisms *Homo sapiens* are using to destroy life on Earth. Since the evolution of our genus, we have inflicted extinctions on other species but the rate at which we are doing so has increased, such that it is now 100 to 1000 times greater than the background extinction rates recorded over the last 65 million years. Historically we have caused extinctions mainly by overexploitation, but we are now fuelling the fire that is ripping through biodiversity by adding out of control forest loss, pollution (especially of the oceans), distribution of invasive pests, and climate change. Concurrently, we are ever increasing the imposition of our built environment on the landscape. There is precious little left on Earth unsoiled by our presence.

Alienation and incongruence

Our modern civilisation has lost something vital—we have lost a sense of belonging to the land and the nature it cradles. Having grown up in forest, building huts, scrambling on sea cliffs, and navigating wilderness, I find it hard to imagine what it would have been like to grow up in a city among endless acres of paving. Yet, an increasingly high proportion of the world's population is being concentrated into artificial environments, comprising concrete, dust, noise, plastic grass, and water from plastic bottles—if they are wealthy enough to have access to unpolluted water at all. When I was in my early twenties, I worked for a few weeks in Sydney on a building site shovelling rocks next to men on jackhammers. For those several weeks, my colour-scape was a mixture of greys and harsh light; my ears rang constantly. I flatted in a townhouse in the city centre within a row of decrepit buildings that had no gardens and smelt of stale tobacco. I eventually escaped to the Blue Mountains for a weekend. When the train entered the forest, I felt a strange sensation sweep over me. Being surrounded by the green of forest trees gave me an immediate sense of relief: a home-coming. I had left an alien planet and returned to Earth. The men on the building site never escaped. Their life was one of perpetually shaking bones and brain tissue, rattled into numbness on the end of the jackhammers.

Today people in their early twenties face an additional attack on their senses, and a shaking of their sense of future and, therefore, of self: they are constantly bombarded by news about the ecological collapse of Earth systems I have discussed above. People who are open to this, who care, and who understand may be worse off than those who ignore the news and stumble along in blissful ignorance. However, I can't help but suspect that even those who ignore or deny the reality of climate change are subconsciously suffering from the uncertainty of our future, a future we are experimenting with like a child pushing at a sandcastle. What will the outcome be?

I fear for the future of our young people and I fear for the fear they face. It's not just that humans have destroyed so much of the Earth; it's that every year the rate of destruction increases and there's nothing that individuals can do about it. The loss of nature and, for those that are aware of the loss, a lack of power to change the way society interacts with nature, are both, in my opinion, serious losses of freedom. Some people attempt to make a difference, by opting for a vegetarian diet or cycling to work, but, for the most part, these actions appear futile in the face of the dynamic global economy that makes every resource disposable on ever decreasing time frames. The response? Amongst those who care in the older generation, guilt is the usual response I have witnessed—and I certainly feel it. But guilt has never been useful in solving social issues. Hardin's (1968) essay on the tragedy of the commons and discussion of guilt, is evermore true today. Guilt only punishes those who care while those following self-interest continue to benefit and exacerbate the dilemma. In young people who grasp the enormity of the global decline, I have witnessed a combination of anger and a sense of hopelessness. For some there is oscillation between the two. It appears to me that the lack of any clear path to reversing the decline leads many into a state of apathetic alienation.

I believe the plants and animals that make a particular environment unique are important to people beyond aesthetic reasons—they offer a sense of place and belonging. The biota in partnership with the land provide a place to anchor ourselves. Our sense of place, our sense of belonging, our sense of equilibrium within the world around us, and our contentedness, can all be influenced by the relationship we develop with the biodiversity that is unique to the place where we live.

However, there is a phenomenon whereby loss of knowledge about our environment and its decline occurs with each passing generation. Each generation accepts what they find as normal and hardly notices what has disappeared over one lifetime let alone what has disappeared among lifetimes. The accumulated losses cannot be experienced—they can be researched and documented but people don't feel them because they have not 'known' that which has been previously lost. Likewise, for those who have never engaged with wilderness, who might at best have looked on from a place of comfort, there may be a lack of any awareness of alienation or incongruence because they cannot miss that which they have not known. People may have little sense of place, or connection to the landscape, because their whole lives have been alienated from nature. Perhaps many feel there is something missing but don't know what it is. Others lament in the knowledge of how much is disappearing.

A brief return to evolution

The evolution of conceptual abstract thought and the ability to make predictions based on accumulated knowledge about patterns is not unique to humans but perhaps we are the species in which this capacity is most developed. African wild dogs can predict that if half their pack hides in the long grass and the other half circles around behind their prey, their pray will run into the path of their kin resulting in food for the entire pack. However, when food is short in supply the stronger members will consume all the food leaving the weaker members to starve to death. Humans can measure the pattern of species extinction and predict the collapse of the biosphere. Through the products of cultural evolution, humans have the means to instigate change to prevent this self-destructive trajectory. However, to do so requires us to overcome the competitive instinct that has enabled each and every one of us to be alive today and, instead, act collectively in a way that might inconvenience us as individuals but will have long-term benefit to our kindred fellows and generations to come. In essence, we must overcome the tragedy of the commons that Hardin (1968) talked about over 50 years ago.

> Whatungarongaro te tangata, toitū te whenua | As people disappear from sight, the land remains.
>
> (A Māori whakataukī [proverb])

7 Being anxiously congruent, and congruently anxious

Rogers suggests that one of the conditions for therapeutic growth and, indeed, personality change, is that the client is anxious or at least vulnerable to anxiety. What he did not say is that the outcome of successful therapy is the absence of anxiety. Just as he avoided writing of self-actualisation as an end-state, preferring to theorise about the actualising tendency, he writes about becoming 'that self which one truly is' (Rogers, 1960/1967j, p. 163), not in terms of achievement but in terms of process: the process of 'being one of the most widely sensitive, responsive and creative creatures on this planet' (Rogers, 1961/1967j, p. 178). Becoming congruent, for both therapists and clients, is a continuous process. We don't reach a point where we have achieved optimal congruence, or a point where we are totally free from anxiety. Indeed—and one of the main arguments of this chapter is that—an integrated awareness of our anxiety may best be thought of both as an example and an aspect of congruence.

We tend to imagine anxiety to be a personal thing. A client is anxious about a relationship, a job, the future, their health. However, we argue, as the existentialist philosophers have done, that anxiety comes with being human. They argue not only that we should be anxious, but that we *are* anxious, no matter what strategies we use to deny it. If that is so, then congruence involves embracing that anxiety and finding ways to live with it. By contrast, incongruence involves the denial, conscious or unconscious, of who we really are. We also suggest that anxiety is over-determined. Our individual, personal anxiety is not grounded merely in the circumstances of our personal, relational lives. We are anxious because of the kind of universe in which our lives are embedded. We are anxious because we are faced with the inevitability of death and responsibility for making choices in a universe which we cannot demonstrate to be meaningful. We are anxious because we belong to a species which is destroying its home and itself. We are anxious because we are cells of a suffering planet. We might argue that the anxieties which arise from our inability to deal creatively with the peculiar circumstances of our lives have their source in these deeper layers of anxiety which we share with our culture and our species. As long as we fail to acknowledge that this is our experience of life we are incongruent.

DOI: 10.4324/9781003397731-10

Being in the universe

In *The Hidden Heart of the Cosmos*, Swimme (1996) suggests that if we want to get a sense of ourselves in the universe we need to get away from urban pollution and find somewhere where we can lie on our backs, look up at the night sky, and gaze into the Milky Way. When our earliest ancestors did this they probably felt awe as we do, but their sense of themselves was different from ours. In the first place they knew that they were in a container bounded by the earth below them and the sky above them. The earth was clearly flat, more or less, and the sky was a saucer-shaped disk over which the sun and moon and specks of light moved in a more or less regular fashion. Our species spent millions of years evolving and adapting to such a world. Our brains are wired to have us look at the stars and imagine that we are standing on firm, unmoving ground and the stars are moving 'up in the sky'. Even after Aristarchus of Samos (c. 310–c. 230 BCE) went on record to say that the earth is round, and Ptolemy (c. 100–170 CE) insisted that the sphere of the earth is the centre of the universe surrounded by seven rotating spheres—the still point in a turning universe—we kept imagining that we were looking 'up' at the sky. We know of course that when we look at the sky we are not looking 'up' at all. Lie on the grass and gaze at the stars and realise that you are looking 'down' into the three hundred billion stars of the Milky Way. We hover in space, only stuck to the Earth by gravity—whatever that is! We know now that the earth is not a still point but is spinning on its axis while spinning around the sun. Neither is the sun a still point. Our idea of 'up' has no relation to the reality of a spinning earth, circling a spinning sun, at the centre of a solar system which is spinning round the outer edge of our galaxy at 290 kilometres a second, while the Milky Way itself is gliding through space like a giant mantra ray. No still point here. Yet we are biologically adapted to looking 'up' at the sky, standing on solid ground in a stable and predictable universe.

When you are gazing at the night sky you may be able to pick out a faint blur of light in the Andromeda constellation. Edward Hubble discovered in the 1920s that this faint blur is not a star but a galaxy, a twin to the Milky Way, and that these two galaxies, with all their smaller satellite galaxies, constantly wheel around each other. And this cluster of galaxies is but one of thousands of clusters revolving around what is known as the Virgo cluster, some 53 million light years away. And this whole supercluster is only one of the millions of superclusters hurtling away from each other in an expanding universe. In the 19th century we could at least hang on to the concept that the universe was fixed and stable. In the 20th century we had to acknowledge that it isn't so. Even Einstein fought against the idea that the universe was expanding until Hubble persuaded him otherwise. At least in the 20th century we could hang on to some notion of stability through our knowledge that the pace of expansion was slowing down, drawn back towards a fixed point by gravity. We don't know that anymore. Now we know that space is expanding at an accelerating pace, which goes contrary to our experience of what happens when we throw things.

Our common sense is assaulted when we find that everything in the universe is rushing away from us—which places us at the centre of the universe. We might say that this puts us back where we started, were it not for the fact that an intelligent being on another speck of cosmic dust millions of light years away—provided the same or better technology is available—would find the same thing. Every point in the universe is at its centre. And all these centres are rushing away from each other as the space between them expands faster and faster. It makes no sense to us and only the mathematicians have a language to describe it. Each of us is the centre of an explosion; and the universe—or the multiverse—seems to be limitless and unpredictable. We evolved to think that we are individual, separate beings, living in a world of things. Astronomy and physics tell us that it isn't true. Nothing holds us in existence but connectedness and process. The cosmos appears less and less to be the stable and predictable machine that we once thought it to be. No wonder we are anxious. The tension between who we are and who we have evolved to think we are is uncomfortable. Schneider (2004) suggests that it is our relation to the cosmos—our relation to infinity—which is the ground of our deep anxiety. We can't cope with the mystery of being. When we lie on the ground and look down into the universe, we don't fall off the earth. But the earth is falling, the solar system is falling, the galaxy is falling. The universe is falling—in every direction. We humans are entirely embedded in this phenomenon. To use Schneider's expression, we are in 'free fall'. In our lives this manifests in the free fall of addiction, compulsion, depression, rage. How we cope and help our clients to cope is the focus of existential psychotherapy. The human tendency is to defend against it through denial. The authentic response is to confront it, to live congruently in the awareness of our cosmic anxiety.

Coping with existence

Søren Kierkegaard did not have the understanding of the cosmos available to us, but he did get close to the idea of free fall when he described our dilemma: how to live a meaningful life on the edge of the abyss. We are overwhelmed by too much possibility. We are accountable for not living up to our possibilities, yet we know that we cannot live up to them. We look into the abyss and feel giddy. We have to let ourselves experience our anxiety, let go of our illusions, and admit that we are lost and helpless. Only then are we able 'to be that self which one truly is' (Kierkegaard, 1941, p. 29). Only then are we congruent, capable of authentic being and able to stand up against the pressures to conform. If we're *not* anxious, we're in a bad way.

Kierkegaard (1985) proposes that it is our capacity for anxiety that makes us human. It is an indication of our capacity to be more than we currently are. As long as we are not all that we can be, we are anxious, whether we are aware of it or not. There is no final escape from insecurity and uncertainty. Schopenhauer (1994) was convinced that the ground of our anxiety is our fear of death. We can try to avoid death as much as we like but the anxiety won't be controllable until we accept that death is the purpose of life. We must accept our anxiety and realise that our will to live is 'perverted' because, obsessed with our individual survival, we identify with our individual will. We need to let go. Life goes on without us. To be congruent is to live and act in the awareness that our fear of death is a front for our perverted desire to be individually immortal.

Heidegger (1927/1978) argues that awareness of death is fundamental to the human condition. We cannot really live a full life unless we are aware of death. However, it is not death which arouses our anxiety, but freedom. We are thrown into the world and confronted with choice and a limited time to make our choices. If we are authentically ourselves, we will stay aware of the temporary character of our being and avoid living a mediocre life. Contemporary existential psychotherapists explore the same themes. We are terrified of having to live as an isolated individual, of being separated from the whole. Yet we also fear the loss of our individuality in death. We are tossed between these fears all our life, which accounts for the fact that we are inherently anxious, and our anxiety is too complex to be easily confronted. We know objectively that we will die. This makes us anxious, so we find ways to deny it. The favoured way to deal with it is delusion. We delude ourselves into imagining that we are immortal. We do this by identifying with a tribe or nation so that we share in its ongoing life. We find an ideology or religion which promises us immortality. We imagine that we can achieve immortality through art, wealth, possessions, children, reputation. These delusions are supported by our culture, even by therapy. Irving Yalom argues that the central aim of existential therapy is to dissolve the illusions we have constructed to avoid facing the realities of existence. We must deal with the conflict that, as Yalom (1980) describes, 'flows from the individual's confrontation with the givens of existence: death, isolation, freedom, and meaninglessness' (p. 8).

Confrontation with our existential situation may bring despair, yet acceptance of our existential situation 'is painful but ultimately healing' (Yalom, 1980, p. 14). Being congruent involves becoming aware of our situation. This is not comfortable, but this discomfort and vulnerability is a blessing as it may stir us to become more of what we can be. Our dissatisfaction may be transformed into a decision to change and we may begin to take responsibility for our life. Viktor Frankl (1969) wrote of the existential vacuum which comes with the collapse of universal values. We live in a world where values and meanings are relativised, where rationality is suspect, where exchange has taken the place of substance. There appears to be no generally accepted ground on which to stand. We no longer agree about what we must do, or even what we should do. We may not even know what we want. When there is no such thing as a universal meaning, we have only the unique meanings of individual situations. Yet the will to meaning is at the core of our being. We don't know where to find it so we pursue sex, power, and money instead.

Being congruent in the world as the existentialist philosophers and psychologists describe it is to live in awareness of the reality of human existence—variously depicted as absurd, meaningless, or tragic. Even those like Kierkegaard and Frankl who don't believe that human life is meaningless acknowledge that it is not possible for us to find meaning through observation and logic. Meaning is to be found through faith, and faith is irrational. In *Reinventing the Sacred*, Kauffman

(2008) suggests that the existentialist focus on meaninglessness is a consequence of adopting the reductionist assumptions of mainstream science, yet mainstream science does not have all the answers.

The existentialist insistence that we make our meaning in a meaningless universe by our choices and actions was a response to reductionism, in which the universe is meaningless. But life is part of the universe. In a newly envisioned universe, biosphere, and human culture of unending creativity, where life, agency, meaning, value, doing, and consciousness have emerged, and that we can create, we can now see ourselves, meaning-laden, as integral parts of emergent nature (Kauffman, 2008).

Coping with catastrophe

Even without our existential anxiety we have reason enough to be anxious. The world is not in a good way. When we stop thinking about the global financial crisis we are still confronted with the threat of global catastrophe. We have strategies for remaining in denial, but we are nevertheless anxious. Our techniques of denial and distraction enable us to separate our awareness from our experience, but denial only increases our stress. At the beginning of the 21st century we have a dozen reasons to conclude that human society is on the edge of destruction: environmental degradation, over-population, a deepening abyss between the rich and poor, a collapsing financial system, the exhaustion of non-renewable sources of energy, the greenhouse effect, holes in the ozone layer, extreme weather events, the starvation of millions, global warming, melting ice-caps, rising sea-levels, disappearing biodiversity, tribal conflict, uncontrollable pandemics, an ongoing and increasingly destructive arms race, the global slave trade, the displacement of populations, the global drug trade, pre-emptive wars, the engineering of hate and fear, epidemic mental illness. We find human alienation and frustration on a vast scale and ecological, financial, political, and psychological feedback loops which seem to be rushing us towards catastrophe. The sense of impending disaster is not new. We have been living with it for half a century. For decades we feared the imminent nuclear winter. We took a moment to draw breath at the beginning of the 1990s and then fell once again into deep anxiety, this time about the imminence of global heating. Whatever it is that we choose to worry about, we have evidence enough that we are currently in the midst of an era of ecological crisis and psychological incoherence.

On top of all this, the explosion of information and communications technology means that we can no longer escape knowledge of incompetence and corruption among the leaders we depend on to avert the catastrophe. One aspect of this psychological incoherence is our unwillingness to see that in a complex, dynamic organic system such as the one of which we are part, all the elements—economic, political, cultural, social, environmental, psychological—are interconnected. The paradox in all of this is that, though we are well aware of these dangers, we do almost nothing to confront them. We have known for decades that the resources of the planet are running out, yet this information has minimal impact on behaviour. We do little in our daily lives to address the crisis, and attempts to confront it at a global level meet with staunch resistance. Indeed, our political masters keep expressing their delight at rising production and consumption, when that is what is killing us. We are caught in the growth trap. Keep growing and we die. Stop growing and we die. Even if we could stop growing; suddenly stop polluting our soil, air, and water; stop the emission of greenhouse gases; stop consuming more of the planet's resources than we can replace, would it save us? Lovelock (2009) argues that the best we can do is learn to adapt to a changed planet.

Why are we so unaffected by the prospect of catastrophe? Why are we so incongruent, denying both our intuitions and the evidence of our senses? Why, to quote Rogers (1957), is there 'a fundamental discrepancy between the experienced meaning of [our] situation as it registers in [our] organism and the symbolic representation of that experience in awareness' (p. 222)? Why do we do nothing, or at least so little that it will make no difference? The stresses on our planet and our personal and collective pathology are deeply connected. We are crippled by an anxiety of which we pretend to be unaware. Evolutionary adaptation has prepared us to respond to threat instinctively by fighting, fleeing, or freezing. It worked for us in the Stone Age but it doesn't work now. Our response to crisis appears to be largely reactive. Confusion is simplified and identity sustained by collectively employing our psychological defences: denial, projection, fixation, displacement, dissociation, splitting, and psychic numbing. These defences may help us to avoid being traumatised by the horror of our situation, but they only make the crisis worse. When we experience the anxiety aroused by an uncertain future, we are as likely to engage in 'retail therapy' as in environmental activism. We may tell ourselves we are not anxious, but deep down we know better. We suggest that a great deal of what our clients bring to us is a symptom, and that patching up symptoms is not what person-centred therapists do. We may listen with deep empathy and find that our clients' 'presenting problems' are but a surface manifestation of their discomfort with their current way of being. Many of them are under the impression that there is something wrong with them which needs to be fixed. Maybe what needs to be fixed is the culture in which they feel uncomfortable. James Hillman's (1982) comment is pertinent here:

> I find today that patients are more sensitive than the worlds they live in... I mean that the distortions of communication, the sense of harassment and alienation, the deprivation of intimacy with the immediate environment, the feelings of false values and inner worthlessness experienced relentlessly in the world of our common habitation are genuine realistic appraisals and not merely apperceptions of our intra-subjective selves. My practice tells me that I can no longer distinguish clearly between neuroses of self and neuroses of world.
>
> (p. 72)

Unfortunately, there are many who have no sense of anxiety at living in a toxic culture. To quote R. D. Laing (1967): 'Only by the most outrageous violation of ourselves have we achieved our capacity to live in relative adjustment to a civilization driven to its own destruction' (p. 64). If the conditions of worth imposed by society support adjustment to a toxic and self-destructive culture, we need to broaden our concept of congruence in our discussions of the process and outcomes of therapy. Congruence—for our clients and for us—requires opening ourselves to the fullness of our experience and being aware of the dissonance between our experience and both our personal and cultural conditions of worth.

Organismic anxiety

In *A Way of Being* Carl Rogers (1980/1995i) argues that our becoming is not only individual but is an element in the becoming of the universe. Such a view fits within the picture of an organic, emerging universe—a picture being taken more and more seriously by science. Rogers observed the materialistic–mechanistic–reductionist paradigm of the clockwork universe being challenged by the paradigm of the organic universe, a challenge in which he was happy to join. His formulation of the formative tendency was not an isolated or odd idea. It belongs to a worldview which has an honourable history and a complex contemporary expression. Earlier in his career, he had been acknowledged (by Hall & Lindzey, 1970) as an organismic theorist; in 1980 he was taking his place in a group of key intellectuals who were reviving the view of an organic universe, a concept which had been suppressed by conventional science. Rogers could find plenty of support in contemporary science and philosophy for the view that the universe is not a machine but an organism of which we are a part (see Birch & Cobb, 1981; Capra, 1983; Lovelock, 1979/1987; Naess, 1973; Prigogine, 1980; Sheldrake, 1981). Rogers was seriously committed to the view that human beings are living, growing, and choosing—a perspective that is either totally obvious or totally incredible according to our view of what kind of universe this is. Behind his observation of a *directional* tendency (Rogers, 1959) is an understanding of a universe which is alive and directional. 'Becoming' is not just a characteristic of human beings or, indeed, of all human life, rather it is a feature of the universe as a whole. There is, Rogers asserts, 'a formative tendency at work in the universe, which can be observed at every level' (p. 124). Our personal growth is to be seen within the context of this larger, universal formative tendency: 'a tendency which pervades all organic life—a tendency to become all the complexity of which the organism is capable' (Rogers, 1963/1995e, p. 134).

The emergence of the PCA within the individualistic culture of North America ensured that in its conventional expressions person-centred theory has maintained an individualistic notion of the self. More recently (in the history of psychology), critical psychologists have pointed out that this narrow definition of the self has produced a narrow definition of mental health (Hepburn & Jackson, 2009; Parker, 1997; Teo, 2009). We might add that a consequence, in person-centred theory, is a narrow definition of congruence. It goes to the heart of our understanding of what it means to 'be that self which one truly is'. In *On Becoming a Person*, Rogers (1959/1967f) refers to the therapist's 'accurate matching of experience with awareness' (p. 282) and in *A Way of Being* he writes of 'a close matching... between what is being experienced at the gut level, what is present in awareness, and what is expressed to the client' (Rogers, 1963/1995e, p. 116). When we read this statement in the context of the book in which it occurs, it is clear that 'what is experienced at gut level' is not limited to the organism's response to information received through the senses. On the one hand, he affirms the reality of the non-sensory connections between individuals which are apparent in such phenomena as premonition and remote sensing. On the other hand, he points to evidence that in certain circumstances 'persons feel they are in touch with, and grasp the meaning of, this evolutionary flow. They experience it as tending towards the transcending experience of unity. The person feels at one with the cosmos' and refers to their own experiences as a therapist when 'our relationship transcends itself and becomes a part of something larger' (p. 129). Norwegian ecophilosopher, Naess (1995), argues that we have too restricted a notion of the self: 'Human nature is such that with sufficient all-sided maturity we cannot avoid "identifying" our self with all living beings, beautiful and ugly, big or small, sentient or not' (p. 13).

For Naess, self-realisation is the broadening and deepening of the notion of 'self' to achieve as wide an identification with the world as possible. The same thinking is echoed in the writing of many ecopsychologists (Fisher, 2002; Greenway, 1995; Kidner, 2001; Roszak, 1992), ecophilosophers (Abram, 1997; de Quincey, 2005; Mathews, 1991), and complexity theorists (Kauffman, 2008; Laszlo, 2003) all of whom argue that human beings are so entirely entangled in the world that the sense of individuality is illusional—and, indeed, may well be considered delusional. They variously acknowledge the influence on their thinking of Spinoza, Einstein, Bateson, Schopenhauer, Heidegger, Merleau-Ponty, and Whitehead, and, more often than not, refer to Buddhist philosophy. For example, Heidegger's (1927/1978) ideas challenge the assumptions on which most therapy is based; he argues that the 'self' as we commonly understand it is a fallacious idea and considers 'being-in-the-world' as a unitary phenomenon. Thus, there is no meaningful distinction that can be made between self and the world: self-world is one concept, one reality.

Ecophilosophers such as Naess have challenged the individualistic and anthropocentric assumptions on which most therapies are based. They don't perceive a boundary of 'difference' between humans and the rest of the planet. In such a perspective, adequate human functioning demands a congruence not just between one's behaviour and one's self-concept, or between one's self-concept and one's 'real self', but between one's way of being and nature. The planet is a living organism of which we are a part. Our self-realisation is the self-realisation of a larger self. Rogers makes it clear in *A Way of Being* that his thinking about the PCA needs to be put in a broader context. Behind his observation of a 'directional tendency' is a particular understanding of the universe. He places his formulation of the actualising tendency within the context of a universe which is organic, alive, emergent, and directional. If we accept this notion, we might consider that we participate in the 'creative advance' (Whitehead's expression) of the universe, and experience, with or without awareness, the collective anxiety of all living beings, all organic life.

Rollo May (1977) follows Kierkegaard in proposing that our existential anxiety arises from the struggle between actuality and potentiality in our personal experience:

> There is anxiety in any actualising of possibility. To Kierkegaard, the more possibility (creativity) an individual has, the more potential anxiety he has at the same time. Possibility ('I can') passes over into actuality, but the intermediate determinant is anxiety.
>
> (p. 27)

We might argue that our species is involved in the same struggle between potentiality and actuality and that our vulnerability to the collective anxiety of humanity is the consequence. Kierkegaard argues that our capacity for anxiety is a blessing. Those who have no awareness of their anxiety are stuck in it, and being stuck in it is misery. The therapist's awareness of their own enmeshment in the collective anxiety of humanity reflects the condition of their clients' insight into their own anxiety, an insight which Kierkegaard suggests is necessary if they are to cease wasting their lives.

'To be that self which one truly is'

In Rogers' later writings, becoming 'that self which one truly is', an expression he borrowed from Kierkegaard, is not something we *do*, not even something that *happens to us* as individuals. It is an evolutionary process in which our being and becoming are embedded, i.e., a belonging. Originally, it made sense for Rogers to theorise about the process of therapy from the perspective of the individual's experience, subjectivity, and self-actualisation. In his essay on Ellen West, Rogers (1977/1995c) comments on the suffering which is a consequence of the tension between our attempts to live up to other people's expectations and our experience—our deep, and maybe inarticulate, sense of who we are, for: 'the experiencing organism senses one meaning in experience, but the conscious self clings rigidly to another, since that is the way it has found love and acceptance from others' (p. 165).

Here Rogers is thinking of the individual trying vainly to live up to 'conditions of worth' imposed by family and social context, conditions which are antagonistic to the 'self' which is trying to actualise. However, if we take Rogers seriously in his theorising of the formative tendency and his understanding of 'self' as process, congruence becomes more than the integration of experience, awareness, and communication in an individual. Both we and our clients need to be congruent not only in thinking and feeling and behaviour, and within our own organism. We need also to be congruent with what we call the 'natural world'. The 'person who we truly are' is in an intimate relationship with all living beings. If our relationship with the natural world, experienced in our organismic felt sense, is denied to an awareness shaped by an individualistic culture, we are 'anxious or vulnerable to anxiety'. 'Becoming' is a central element in Rogers' understanding of congruence, but has no place in a mechanistic paradigm. It belongs in the organic paradigm which was the ultimate ground of Rogers' theorising. For Rogers (1963/1995e), the basis of all motivation is 'the organismic tendency toward fulfilment' (p. 123); 'the universe', he says, 'is always building and creating as well is deteriorating. This process is evident in human beings, too' (p. 127). Congruence, then, involves openness to one's own becoming, not simply to one's current state of being. It involves openness to process, creativity, emergence, the evolutionary flow. The fully functioning person, that is to say the congruent person, is aware of: 'The ongoing flow of feelings, emotions, and physiological reactions that he or she senses from within. The greater this awareness, the more surely the person will float in a direction consonant with the directional evolutionary flow' (p. 127), and, in sense is integrated.

Schopenhauer (1844/1958) argues that self-centredness is a prison to be avoided at all costs. We need to commune with the collective spirit and thus be released from the unending cycle which is always wanting more. For Schopenhauer, our sense of individuality is an illusion. There are no things in themselves, only a single thing in itself. From this perspective, the 'natural' way to live is to feel and show real empathy for others, since this is the only way to free oneself from the sufferings that arise from self-preoccupation. Not that it makes much difference to anything. The flow of Schopenhauer's universe is blind, purposeless, and uncontrollable. This is clearly not how Rogers imagines the universe. For Rogers (1963/1995e), human creativity has its source in the creative evolution of the universe. As individuals and as a species we are potentially moving 'in the direction of wholeness, integration, a unified life… in this larger, creative, formative tendency' (p. 128) or, as Kauffman (2008) puts it, collectively 'living with the creativity in the universe that we partially co-create' (p. 232).

Ecocentric congruence

We are ready enough to accept that the separation of mind and body is pathological. We need to be equally aware of the deep pathology that has come from the modernist separation of culture and nature. The incongruence between who we as individuals have learned that we are and who our total organisms know that we are can be understood as a manifestation of the incongruence between our culture and nature. Rogers (1980/1995j) suggests that 'persons of tomorrow'—presumably excluding incongruent persons of tomorrow—feel 'a closeness to, and a caring for, elemental nature. They are ecologically minded, and they get their pleasure from an alliance with the forces of nature, rather than in the conquest of nature' (p. 351). We can set this view next to Wilson's (1984) 'biophilia hypothesis'. In *Biophilia*, Wilson argues that we have evolved to feel kinship not only with other humans but with all organic life. To distance ourselves from nature is to act in a way contrary to what evolutionary process has long ago made essential to our humanity. Wilson suggests that:

> to explore and affiliate with life is a deepened complicated process in mental development. To an extent still undervalued in philosophy and religion, our existence depends on this propensity, our spirit is woven from it, hope arises from its currents.
>
> (p. 1)

Wilson was writing from the perspective of an evolutionary biologist. However, support for his argument is provided by a wealth of recent research on the association between contact with nature and psychological well-being (Chalquist, 2007; Kaplan & Kaplan, 1989; Kidner, 2001; Maller et al., 2005; Snell, 2012). An argument first proposed by Roszak (1992) and often repeated in the ecopsychological literature would have it that urbanisation, which represents the split between subjective experience and nature, is environmentally destructive and contrary to our evolutionary context. Beneath our surface adaptation to modern life is a biological and psychological discomfort. We might imagine an ideal world in which there is no conflict between the actualising tendency of the individual, the conditions of worth imposed by the culture, and the maintenance of the total ecological system of which both the individual and the cultural group are elements. Unfortunately, in the world which shapes our introjected conditions of worth there are aspects of culture which are impediments to the individual's proper relationship to the planet. In such a world, the ecologically sensitive therapist pursues the point of discomfort in the client's subjective experience on the understanding that as the nature of the client's incongruence comes into their awareness and as they find the feelings which are congruent with their organismic experiencing, they will be reborn as the person they 'naturally' are, someone whose freedom and autonomy are totally compatible with the nature of the larger world. Within an acceptant, empathic, non-judgemental relationship the client becomes increasingly congruent as they find a balance between conditions of worth and organismic experiencing. This implies avoiding on the one hand the loss of their individual identity, and on the other hand the loss of their connection with nature in a deluded sense of individuality.

Conclusion

Client-centred therapy works at the client's point of discomfort, the point of incongruence between the client's organismic experiencing and their symbolisation of this experiencing. Moving towards congruence starts with allowing this sense of discomfort to come into awareness. What we hear clients saying when they articulate their discomfort is shaped by the perspective we bring to the interaction. When a client complains about their partner's dominating behaviour and illustrates it with an anecdote about their insistence on how and where they live, we may hear it either as a statement about their relationship or as a statement about their unease at being unable to find a satisfying connection with the natural world. When a client expresses concern about committing their mother to a nursing home against her objections, we may hear it as a statement of their filial guilt or as an expression of their existential fear of death and dying. When a client expresses how depressed they are we can hear this not simply as a personal statement about dissatisfaction with their life but as an indication of their sensitivity the collective, barely articulated struggle of our species to match our performance with our potential. The adolescent's self-harm, suicidal fantasies, or psychic numbing may have their source in the ecological or political, rather than the personal, dimensions of existence. The deeply congruent therapist will be listening.

We have suggested that congruence involves experiencing who we really are. If we are congruent, authentically ourselves, we will be creatively anxious, sensitive to the human situation, and stirred to move onward. We have suggested that if we deny our experience of who we really are we will be incongruently anxious. There is no escape from anxiety. We should acknowledge Kierkegaard's insight that experience of anxiety is integral to being human and it is this experience which prompts us to move towards becoming all that we can be and doing what we need to do. It was clear enough to Rogers that both the means and end of therapy is congruence, not contentment. If we and our clients allow ourselves to experience and acknowledge the discomfort of rigidly denying who we are, we will be able to move from incongruent anxiety to congruent anxiety and begin to experience the full complexity of our being.

8 Accepting hopelessness as a hopeful process

In this chapter, we argue that accepting hopelessness is an important aspect of facilitating authentic hope, and, indeed, that one of the important personal and societal challenges we face today is precisely to be able to accept as well as to empathise with people's feelings of anxiety, hopelessness, and despair as part of the process of changing from fixity to fluidity (Rogers, 1958/1967c). This is particularly important at a time when many people are experiencing such feelings about the state of the world as well as their own lives. Drawing on the framework of Rogerian theory, with illustrations from clinical practice and our own lives, as well as from the social/political world, we examine firstly, the extent to which hopelessness—and helplessness—are aspects of congruence (in terms of awareness and communication) as well as incongruence (in terms of Rogerian personality theory); secondly, how acceptance of both is part of a therapeutic process—in this sense, this chapter stands as something of a meditation on acceptance; and, thirdly, how this perspective can help address what has been referred to as 'ecological anxiety disorder'. Drawing on poetry, myths, and spiritual traditions, as well as psychological sources, this chapter explores both hopelessness and hope in terms of their origins, and discusses them in terms of philosophical and psychological ideas about essence, existence, and experience. As the chapter is based on an original paper delivered to a conference—the 13th World Conference for Person-Centered & Experiential Psychotherapy & Counseling (PCE2018)—it makes reference to that conference and its theme.

Hope and hopelessness: Personal, societal, and theoretical challenges

We have an issue with the word hope. Indeed, when I (Keith) first saw the theme of the PCE2018 Conference 'Facilitating hope', I had two responses: one of interest, and the other of disappointment. My interest was drawn to the subtitle: 'Personal and *societal* challenges' (my emphasis); my disappointment was to do with hope. It seemed—and seems—too optimistic; too future-oriented; and, in some way, too fixed. In our global predicament, feelings of hope are fragile. To talk authentically about our experience of hope, we suggest that we need to balance hope with felt experiences of hopelessness and its close cousin, helplessness. In separating these two, we draw on Schamle's (1964) distinction between helplessness as a loss of autonomy—in his original theory, the loss of ego autonomy due to inability to receive a desired gratification from another—and hopelessness as a similar loss but due to one's own inability to provide this gratification. Thus, helplessness is a more helpless position in that 'You can't always get what you want'—from the other—'But', as Richards and Jagger (1969) suggest 'if you try sometime you'll find | You get what you need'. In other words, we might need to accept and understand that we won't or can't be gratified or, staying with the Rolling Stones, get 'no satisfaction' in order that we experience some self-gratification, which may include hopelessness as a transition to hope. Drawing on Klein's (1957/1975) formulation of hope, Akhtar (2015) states: 'real hope emerges only after false (i.e., idealized) hope has been given up and when love predominates over hate in the internal psychic economy of the child. In other words, a certain "normal" hopelessness is essential for psychic growth' (p. 11).

This is important if we are to avoid false or idealised hope (Klein, 1957/1975) and relentless hope (Stark, 2017); to be more present-centred; and to acknowledge that both hope and hopelessness are and involve a process or processes rather than being fixed states. This desire to balance hope with hopelessness is part of a broader project both to reclaim humanistic psychology as a critical psychology, and to critique aspects of that psychology, including its lack of engagement with the more difficult and what might be viewed as 'dirty' aspects of life, including evil (see Greening et al., 1986). In this chapter, we discuss hope and hopelessness with reference to different modes of psychology as identified and developed by Martha Stark (1999), and articulate a number of personal, societal, and theoretical challenges. This kind of development of theory based on experience is very much in line with Rogers' methodology as his theories and views were theories and views about experience; as Van Belle (1990) says: 'They discover order *in* experience' (p. 33).

Hope springs eternal

The English noun 'hope' comes from the late Old English *hopa* which means 'confidence in the future', and carried a sense of this confidence being placed in God or Christ as the basis for hope. As St Paul puts it: 'For now we see in a mirror, darkly; but then face to face; now I shall know even as also I have been known. But now abideth faith, hope, love, these three; and the greatest of these is love' (II Corinthians 13:13). From the 13th century hope also referred to an 'expectation of something desired' and 'trust, confidence; [and] wishful desire'. From the 14th century, hope became personified (*Online Etymology Dictionary*, 2021); hence the images of Hope as one of the three Christian virtues, alongside Faith and Charity (see Figure 1).

The English verb 'to hope' is often used to describe having hope (i.e., the qualities of the noun), though some have suggested a connection with the word hop in the sense of 'leaping in expectation' (*Online Etymology Dictionary*, 2021), a meaning that is significant in giving a sense of movement and, therefore, process and fluidity (see Rogers, 1958/1967c). This sense of hope as involving movement is found in other languages such as Welsh (gobaith) and Italian (speranza).

Accepting hopelessness as a hopeful process 119

Figure 8.1 Hope, Charity, and Faith—Stained glass windows by Sir Edward Burne-Jones (1887), in the Lady Chapel, All Saints' Church, Leek, UK
Source: Photo—Michael Critchlow, reproduced with permission and acknowledgements to the *Victorian Web* https://victorianweb.org/painting/bj/glass/67.html.

As a subject and a concept, hope has been discussed more by philosophers and poets than psychologists. It has been referred to as 'a waking dream' (attributed variously to Pindar, Plato, and Aristotle), while Alexander Pope (1732/2007) coined the phrase 'hopes springs eternal'. Hope is important in psychotherapy. In the psychoanalytic tradition, while Bion (1967) suggests approaching the patient without preconceived aspirations, both Loewald (1960) and Hoffman (1992) advocate the importance of the analyst's optimism with regard to treatment. Lambert's (1992) research found that a psychotherapist's optimism, confidence, and sense of hope makes a difference to the outcome of psychotherapy; and, more recently, Timulak (2007) reveals that clients identify hope as a core category of positive events in psychotherapy. However, it wasn't until Snyder's work in the 1980s that hope began to be studied in any detail, and it has remained under-theorised. Like Schmid (2019), we have searched the indexes of Rogers' books and found no entries on hope; and there have been no articles on hope—or hopelessness—in 16 years of the journal *Person-Centered & Experiential Psychotherapies* (*PCEP*);

and, in nearly 60 years of the *Journal of Humanistic Psychology*, there has been only one: on hope-healing communities (Nwoye, 2002). By contrast, a search of the Psychoanalytic Electronic Publishing database reveals 11 titles on hopelessness (which may not be surprising), and 116 titles on hope (which we found pleasantly surprising). At the PCE2018, while there were 44 presentations on hope, only four mentioned hopelessness at least in the title or abstract of the presentation; three articles on hope were subsequently published in a special section on hope in *PCEP* (Volume *18*, Number 2) (Murphy et al., 2019).

While hope is important, we contend that hopelessness is equally, if not more, important for two reasons:

1 For therapists, in attuning ourselves to this aspect of the human condition and, therefore, being more helpful to those clients who feel hopeless (see, for instance, Semel, 1990).
2 In avoiding false hope and its manifestation as a kind of reassuring hopefulness.

The phrase 'hope springs eternal' comes from a poem titled '*An Essay on Man*' by Pope (1732/2007), the 18th-century English poet and essayist. Pope's philosophical poem is an attempt 'to vindicate the ways of God to Man' and an affirmative poem of faith in which human beings are viewed as having limited intelligence and grasp of the whole, ordered world or universe and, thus, that 'man' must rely on hope, which leads to faith. In more common usage, the phrase 'hope springs eternal' means that people hope for the best, even in the face of adversity. The idea that hope springs at all prompts reflection about the origins and location of hope and the subsequent implications: in effect, the whence, thence, and hence of hope (see Table 8.1), which summarises the challenges offered in the chapter (based on those identified in the theme of the original conference).

This question of the location of hope is important in that, if we think it is internal then we are, in effect, proposing it as an essence of our being, our self, and our humanity, whether through nature and/or nurture. If we think it is external, then it is something to be achieved or grasped, or to which we might aspire, and, conversely, something we may 'instil' in others. These represent, we would say, a one-person and a one-and-a-half person psychology (Stark, 1999), respectively. In this chapter, we explore what these and two other modes of psychology have to offer us in thinking about hope and its challenges.

Essence, experience, engagement—and environment

In elaborating the question of the nature and what we are referring to as the location of hope and hopelessness and how to work therapeutically with these phenomena, we draw on Martha Stark's (1999) taxonomy of psychologies by which she distinguishes between three different, although mutually enhancing modes of therapeutic action; though we note that Stark advocates that the therapist could and should be able to move between all three modes. We introduce these modes and

Table 8.1 The whence, thence, and hence of hope, and the challenges of hope

	One-person psychology	One-and-a-half person psychology	Two-person psychology	Two-person-plus psychology
The origins of hope (whence hope)	Essence	Experience	Engagement	Environment
The location of hope (thence hope)	Hope springs *internal* (in the person/client)	Hope springs from one person (i.e., the therapist) to the other	Hope springs in the relationship	Hope springs *external* (in and in relationship with the environment)
The implications of hope (in terms of time) (hence hope)	Past	Past	Present	Present
Challenges				
Theoretical	Challenge 1		Challenge 4	
Personal/Societal (political, therapeutic)	Challenge 2			Challenge 5
Personal (therapeutic)		Challenge 3		

Keith's own addition (Tudor, 2011c), and discuss hope and hopelessness in this context, also with reference to Stark's (2017) work on *Relentless Hope* which she frames in terms of her three modes of therapeutic action.

One-person psychology

In this mode, Stark (1999) suggests that 'the goal is strengthening of the client's ego through insight facilitated primarily through the therapist's interpretations' (p. xv). The therapist is not a participant in a relationship but, according to Stark (1999), an 'objective observer of the patient' (p. xvi). She continues: 'The therapist conceives of her position as outside the therapeutic field and of herself as a blank screen onto which the patient casts shadows that the therapist then interprets' (Stark, 1999, p. xvi). This mode is more often associated with the interpretive model of classical psychoanalysis and ways in which empathy is used to interpret, evoke, and inquire, whether from a hermeneutic perspective or not, so as to keep the therapist as a distant 'as if' figure (see Keil, 1996). However, many cognitive behavioural therapists, as well as humanistic therapists, also use empathy in this way, or, perhaps more accurately, their empathy reflects a one-person psychology. When we say to a client, 'You look sad', we are, in effect and in essence, offering an interpretation based on some observation—usually of their eyes, face, and posture—as well as the content and tone of what the person is saying. Furthermore, there is at least one form of empathy—hermeneutic empathy, as described by Keil (1996)—that describes the situation when the therapist understands more than the client and differs from the client in what they understand. In this context, we were interested to read Finke's (2018) article in which he acknowledges Rogers' use of interpretation. Thinking about empathy with regard to this mode of psychology, we suggest that the following quotation from Rogers (1974/1995f) reflects this well: 'I and my colleagues realized that this empathic listening provided one of the least clouded windows into the workings of the human psyche, in all its complex mystery' (p. 50). The only recorded example of Rogers working with hopelessness is in his interview with Gloria:

> C30 Right. (Long Pause) (Sighs, then speaks in a slower, somber way.) Well, I have a hopeless feeling. (T: Mhm) I mean, these are all the things that I sort of feel myself, and I feel uh—OK, now what?
>
> T30 Mhm. You feel this is the conflict and it's just insoluble, and therefore it is hopeless, and here you look to me and I don't seem to give you any help…

Gloria's sense of defeat and hopelessness is both verbally and non-verbally expressed. 'Now what?' she asks plaintively. For his part, Rogers makes no effort to lighten her burden, or express how he feels, a clear example of PCT as a one-person psychology.

In one-person psychology, hope—and hopelessness—is viewed as *in* the human psyche if not as essence, and thus we might say 'hope springs *internal*'. Synder's work on hope as a way of thinking is such an example. In this mode of psychology, we might think about relentless hope and hopelessness as forms of incongruence, i.e., a vulnerability or anxiety that is an expression of a discrepancy between self and experience. In this sense, if we think of ourselves as positive, optimistic people (self-concept), and we then feel hopeless, we are likely to feel incongruent or discrepant. The traditional therapeutic work of this mode of psychology is insight, whether through interpretation or empathy, which leads to knowledge that Stark (1999) views as rendering the defence less adaptive.

Herein lies the first, theoretical challenge (see Table 8.1, challenge 1). In person-centred theory, anxiety is viewed as a description of incongruence (Rogers, 1957, 1959), which, some years earlier, Rogers (1951) had elaborated in terms of personality theory. What this denies, however, is that anxiety that is congruent, i. e., in which our experience is consistent with our self-concept or, if not entirely consistent is, at least, not a threat (see Chapter 7). I (Keith) have a personal example of this with regard to having emigrated, some 14 years ago, from the United Kingdom to Aotearoa New Zealand.

> Before I emigrated, I did not experience myself as particularly anxious or an 'anxious person'; however, following my emigration/immigration, and especially in the first couple of years of living in my new homeland, I felt anxious about certain aspects of my life and experiences. The issue was not so much that I felt anxious—which took the form of feeling new, strange, dislocated, embarrassed, ignorant, small, disempowered, etc.—but that feeling anxious was new and at times uncomfortable. In this sense, Rogerian personality theory, with its concepts of vulnerability, anxiety, threat, defense, distortion

(of experience), denial (of awareness), and intensionality, is useful in describing such experience. However, while it refers to incongruence as creating or exacerbating psychological disorganisation, it doesn't allow for the potential of incongruence as creating or helping to develop greater psychological *organisation*. In my own case, I would say that my anxiety—*and my acceptance of that anxiety*—has made me stronger.

Stark's reference to relentless hope brings us to a second challenge (see Table 8.1) which is a personal and societal/political one. During the 2020 New Zealand general election campaign, Jacinda Ardern, leader of the Labour Party (and now Prime Minister), described herself as 'relentlessly positive'. Whilst, in the context of a campaign in which she wanted to challenge negative politics, this was broadly welcomed, we were curious about what room there was for her own negative or less than positive feelings, especially as there was something somewhat insistent, tiring, and off-putting about her relentless positivity. The challenge, as we see it, is for politicians to show more vulnerability by acknowledging their own uncertainties, ignorance, limitations, failings, etc., as well as demonstrating less guarded or circumscribed ways-of-being-with each other. Interestingly, and perhaps unsurprising, in the four years between 2018 (the year of the conference) and 2022 (when we finished this chapter), Ardern has lost her relentless positivity, especially towards those who opposed her policies on mandatory vaccinations.

One-and-a-half-person psychology

Stark (1999) introduces what she refers to as the second mode of psychology by means of brief history of the shift in the aetiology of psychopathology from nature to nurture, a shift influenced by object relations and self psychology. Stark argues, 'The locus of therapeutic action shifted from insight by way of interpretation to a corrective experience by way of the real [therapeutic] relationship' (p. xvii). However, as the therapist uses a part of themselves to provide what Alexander (1946) refers to as a 'corrective emotional experience' (p. 66); this, according to Stark (1999) makes it 'more of an "I–It" relationship than an "I–Thou"… relationship and hence the designation of this mode as a "one-and-a-half-person" psychology' (p. xviii). In this mode, empathy—and, for that matter, acceptance— may be viewed and experienced as a way of being on the part of the therapist by means of which the client may emerge with greater self-understanding of themselves, others, and the world. The classical Rogerian empathic listening, together with reflection, would be seen as an example of this mode if the intention is that the therapist's empathy is curative; and, indeed, Stark classifies Rogers (1961/1967c) as a therapist in this mode or model.

In this sense and mode, both hope—and hopelessness—spring *from one to the other*. An example may be found in the most famous story about hope, at least in the Western intellectual tradition, that of Pandora's box. It is part of the creation story in Greek mythology in which a box or a jar was given to Pandora, the first woman, who had been made by Hephaestus, the God of crafts, from water and earth. Other Gods had given her gifts of clothes (Athena), beauty (Aphrodite), music (Apollo), and speech (Hermes), but, after Prometheus had stolen fire from Olympus and given it to mankind, Zeus punished Pandora by giving her to Prometheus' brother, Epimetheus, and giving her the famous receptacle which contained all the evils in the world including death—and, lastly, hope. In moral philosophy and theology this story is an example of theodicy, i.e., an attempt to answer the question why a good God permits the manifestation of evil, and in this explanation, both evil and good—in the form of hope—are given and exist in the external world. Thinking about this in terms of modes of psychology, it appears (at least to us) that the myth presents hope as the corrective gift from the gods for the experience of humans—and also, and significantly for our argument, that hope is the last thing to be released.

In the therapeutic field, the instillation of hope is one of Yalom's (1995) curative factors in group therapy, in which the group itself becomes the corrective or curative experience. Given Rogers' philosophy and methodology, we would say that PCE therapists generally don't operate on the basis of a one-and-a-half person psychology, or, at least, not deliberately so. It's one thing for unconditional positive regard and empathic understanding to be experienced and/or perceived by the client, the sixth of Rogers' (1957, 1959) necessary and sufficient conditions of therapy (see Chapters 4 and 10), it's another thing for the therapist to offer a corrective experience (emotional or otherwise) intentionally. If they were to do so, it would certainly represent a high level of interventiveness in the taxonomy outlined by Warner (2000), and in this context we agree with what Schmid (2019) and Keys (2018) say about not 'giving' hope—and we recognise that this may also be a third and personal challenge (see Table 8.1).

Two-person psychology

The third mode of psychology identified by Stark (1999) conceives of therapy as 'interactive engagement with an authentic other' (p. xix). In other words, what heals is the therapeutic relationship itself, facilitated by empathic attunement and resonance. In this mode, client and therapist create and co-create an interactive dyad in which each affects the other—and each recognises that they affect the other. This is sometimes referred to as a person-to-person relationship or, following Buber (1923/1937), an I–Thou relationship. In this mode, more attention is paid to the processing of inevitable empathic failure and mis-attunement on the part of the therapist, e.g., 'I think I missed you there', as well as ruptures in the relationship. This is reflected in the person-centred literature that has an interactional orientation (see van Kessel & van der Linden, 1993) and focuses on empathy as an aspect of 'the between' or the interpersonal encounter (see Barrett-Lennard, 1997; Myers, 1999; Schmid, 2006), perspectives that highlight the reflective and co-creative nature of empathy. Schmid (2006), in particular, makes an important contribution to the development of a dialogical PCT, pointing out that as it is the other who calls the 'I' into service, this relationship is more accurately described as a 'Thou–I' relationship, which, of course, also reflects a focus or centredness on the client. In this mode, both hope and hopelessness spring (intersubjectivity) *between* us.

> I (Keith, writing in 2018) have a personal interest in hopelessness, which derives from my personal experience in relation to a family member who, for various reasons, I have found difficult and extremely challenging and, after some particularly difficult years, lost a sense of hope both for them and for our relationship. I have felt hopeless and helpless—and then bad about feeling those feelings. Part of my personal journey has been to feel hopeless; to allow such feelings, as well as other feelings of frustration, rage, bitterness, discomfort, etc.—and to accept such feelings. In working through this I found it useful to distinguish between helplessness and hopelessness and to move from one to the other. I also experienced and appreciated acceptance and understanding from my wife, Louise, close friends, including Bernie, and colleagues (especially a therapist and two supervisors), and the environment, especially the sea near where I live as another element of the hopeful in-between.

In this sense and mode we would say that anxiety, hopelessness, and despair are all part of life, and, therefore, that both hopelessness and hope may be experienced and understood as part of a two-person psychology, which, as Stark (1999) summarises, is concerned about engagement in relationship. In this sense we can advocate and attend 'Hope—beyond hopelessness' (Slochower, 1984, p. 237).

Working with what is between the therapist and a client requires the therapist's empathic attunement; such attunement requires the therapist to 'tune in to' or resonate with the client. O'Leary's (1993) description of empathy caught something of this when he likens empathy to two tuning forks tuned in the same key: 'When one is struck the other picks up the sound emitted by the first while losing nothing of its own essential nature. Empathy is tuning into the wavelength of the client. Therapists must attune themselves to that particular wavelength' (p. 113). Shakespeare (1608/1998) captures this sense of attunement when he writes: 'Yet hope, succeeding from so fair a tree | As your fair self, doth tune us otherwise' (*Pericles*, Act I, scene 1, lines 164–165).

For Rogers, empathy followed unconditional positive regard, acceptance, or love, each and all of which were predicated on the therapist's congruence, genuineness, or authenticity, both in terms of awareness and communication. In an article that addresses hope in a context of a time of global despair, Weingarten (2010) develops the concept of 'reasonable hope': 'Unlike hope, which often sets up unrealistic expectations, reasonable hope, consistent with the meaning of the modifier, suggests something both sensible and moderate, directing our attention to what is within reach rather than what may be desired but unattainable' (p. 3). She describes the characteristics of reasonable hope including that it is relational, and a practice, both of which shift hope from a one- or a one-and-a-half person psychology to a two-person psychology. Clearly taking a constructivist approach to reasonable hope, which Weingarten also characterises as maintaining that the future is open, uncertain, and influenceable, and as accommodating doubt, contradictions, and despair, she discusses the 'co-creation' of hopefulness with clients, arguing that therapists who practice reasonable hope are more likely to engage in the co-creative process necessary to encourage their clients to do the same. Just as Weingarten suggests that doubt and despair are not antithetical to reasonable hope but can run parallel (citing Perlesz, 1999), or are in dialectic relation to it (citing Byrne & McCarthy, 2007), we argue that, alongside reasonable hope, we can and need to hold reasonable hopelessness. By being able to experience and accept both, we are likely to be able to be authentic, about all forms of hope and hopelessness. Thus, the fourth and theoretical challenge of this argument (see Table 8.1) is to shift our thinking about hope from being a noun to a verb (see Tudor, 2007) and, therefore, to talk about hop*ing* rather than hope; and, as Weingarten (2010) put it, from being a feeling to being a practice.

We refer to Weingarten as taking a constructivist position, as she refers to the co-construction of hope. Other implications of a constructivist view of therapy (which is a two-person psychology) include:

- That meaning constantly evolves through dialogue;
- That discourse creates systems (such as theories of personality), not the other way around; and
- That therapy is the co-creation, in dialogue, of new narratives, which, thereby provide new possibilities about the past, present, and future—on the basis that the past and the future is in the present (developed from Summers & Tudor, 2000).

In this mode of psychology both hope—or hoping—and hopelessness are in the relationship. A poignant and local example (in Vienna) is in the film *The Third Man* set in post-war Vienna, including the Prater (a famous amusement park in Vienna), written by Graeme Greene and directed by Carol Reed in 1949. The hopelessness experienced and expressed by Holly Martins (the anti-hero in the film), has been present in his relationship with Anna Schmidt (the heroine) from their first meeting to their last encounter. I (Keith) have seen the film many times and always get a lump in my throat when I watch the final scene when Anna walks past Holly (see Figure 8.2 and https://www.youtube.com/watch?v=h4whXHjXysw).

This is also a good example of alternative narratives in that, in the novel on which the film was based (Greene, 1950), Holly and Anna walk out of the cemetery 'side by side' (p. 157), thereby giving the reader (or, at least, this reader) the hope that they end up together! Nevertheless, in the film version, Holly and Anna's hopelessness reflects that of the post-war environment—and brings us to a final mode of psychology.

Two-person-plus psychology

Alongside the interest and development in ideas about the therapeutic relationship or therapeutic relating (see Summers & Tudor, 2000; Tudor, 2008c), there is increasing acknowledgment of the importance to psychotherapy outcomes of client factors as well as other extratherapeutic factors, i.e., factors outside therapy that are therapeutic (see Bohart & Tallman, 1999; Bozarth, 1998a; Duncan et al., 2004; Miller et al.,

Accepting hopelessness as a hopeful process 127

Figure 8.2 Still from *The Third Man*
Source: Reed (1949).

1995). These encompass the client's active participation in therapy and their proactive choice and realistic expectations of therapy as well as their levels of psychosocial functioning, secure styles of attachment, psychological mindedness, and social support. One example of empathy in this mode is Rogers' (1986) definition of empathy as 'in itself a healing agent' (p. 129); he continues, 'It is one of the most potent aspects of therapy, because it releases, it confirms, it brings even the most frightened client into the human race. If a person can be understood, he or she belongs' (p. 129). Elsewhere, Rogers (1975/1995d) succinctly describes one of the profound consequences of empathy: 'Empathy dissolves alienation' (p. 151). It is no accident that those therapists and others—such as community and youth workers as well as political activists who focus on the social/political world—often work and organise in groups and communities, and that those who analyse alienation (Wyckoff & Steiner, 1971) and psychopathology as forms of alienation (Tudor & Worrall, 2006), often work therapeutically in and with groups. Thus, I (Keith) have suggested an addition to Stark's (1999) taxonomy of a two-person-plus psychology (Tudor, 2011c), which represents the existence and impact of the world beyond the 'two persons' involved in a particular therapeutic relationship, i.e., a 'two-person-plus psychology'. With regard to hope—and hopelessness—two-person-plus psychology views both as part of our existential human condition, and thus that hope springs *external*.

This existential point—and its link with time—is beautifully and poetically summarised by Shakespeare (1605/2004) in *All's Well That Ends Well*: 'He hath abandoned his physicians, madam; under whose | practises he hath persecuted time with hope, and | finds no other advantage in the process but only the | losing of hope by time' (Act I., scene 1, lines 13–16). We refer to the existential view as we think that existentialists have a useful perspective about anxiety, including that, given the state of the world or the impact of the human world, we should probably be more rather than less anxious. Thus, rather than pathologising our anxieties and feelings of hopelessness, for example as 'ecological anxiety disorder', it may be useful to acknowledge or even develop greater anxiety about ecology and how we are compromising both the present and the future of our planet. In this context, we agree with the point Keys (2018) made in her keynote speech about the privilege of hopelessness, especially in relation to other struggles and the struggles of others which we think are—or should also be— our struggles (e.g., men being involved in anti-sexism work, white people in anti-racist work, etc.). However, we have each also been in situations as political activists in which hopelessness was not allowed and 'the struggle' was based on a psychology of false and relentless hope, which, we suggest, represents an insufficient psychological analysis of a political situation, response, and/or movement. In this sense, and precisely to avoid the kind of burnout Keys acknowledges, we think it's crucial to allow for hopelessness, somewhere and sometime, in order to build and maintain authentically hopeful or hoping relationships. Indeed, Žižek (2017) writes about 'the courage of hopelessness' which appears a useful antidote to the sense of hopelessness leading to passivity and inactivity. Earlier, we cited authors who advocated the importance of hope with regard to the client's treatment (i.e., Hoffman, 1992; Loewald, 1960; Timulak, 2007). Fromm (1968) takes this further when he writes about hope as 'a psychic commitment to life and growth' (p. 13); while Buechler (1995), contra Hoffman and others, states clearly that 'I don't believe it is, specifically, the analyst's hope that engenders hope in the patient, but the analyst's whole relationship to life' (p. 72).

Here we offer an example of what we see as a desirable shift from a one-person to a two-person psychology with regard to hopelessness, taken from one of our clinical practices.

> I worked for a number of years with a woman who referred to herself as chronically depressed. Initially she described this in a self-blaming way, and focused on the origins of her depression in her childhood, exacerbated by the lack of a long-term personal relationship in her 20s and 30s. While her first experience of therapy had healed some deeply-held issues that caused her pain, and also given her tools with which to manage other aspects of her depression, we would say that it had also trained her to think about it in terms of a one-person psychology as she still viewed herself as being depressed and being responsible for that, and, as a result, was feeling pretty hopeless about her future. When she came to me, she was in the process of leaving her relationship (of some 15 years), which she described as having been unsatisfactory from the beginning. Although she complained a lot about her husband, she was still essentially blaming herself for the failure of the marriage. Gradually, through the course of the therapy, she came to see the relationship itself as 'depressed' or, more accurately, that she and her husband had co-created what Rowland (2002), inspired by Warner's (1991, 1998) work on fragile

and dissociated process, referred to as 'depressed process', which, by definition, suggests that the process is between people and, therefore, represents more of a two-person psychology mode.

This same client had a strong interest in the environment and was very knowledgeable about and active with regard to a specific aspect. She had a good sense of herself and her contribution in this context and, although she experienced certain frustrations with others about particular attitudes and approaches to the environment and the direction of campaigns in which she was involved, she was generally enlivened by her work in this context. Much of the last part of the therapy was spent discussing and processing these experiences, which reflected the healing power of the social and especially the natural environment, and, thus, a two-person-plus psychology.

We mentioned earlier the environment as another element of 'the between' (and as providing hope), and we would say that our own acceptance of hopelessness has been and is both fostered and healed by the environment and, specifically, by our relationship with land and certain landscapes (see Chapter 10). In this sense, there is a very real way in which hope springs external, and that the antidote to the privilege of hopelessness is to find what is hopeful in and of the environment, world, and Earth. In concluding his overview of hope and hopelessness, Akhtar (2015) refers to the goodness that already exists in the world, citing 'altruism, courage, freedom, democracy, poetry, art, and love—that strengthens our hope and make our hopelessness bearable' (p. 18).

This brings us to the fifth and final (personal and societal) challenge of hope and hopelessness (Table 8.1), which is to finds ways of acknowledging the impact of the environment on the client and the therapy, and the client's relationship with their environment, which is, to a small extent, represented by some of our other work, especially Neville (1997, 1999, 2000, 2005, 2007, 2012, 2014), Tudor (2013b), and Key & Tudor (2023), as well as this present work.

Conclusion: The necessity of hopelessness—and acceptance

> To live is to suffer, to survive is to find meaning in the suffering.
> (Nietzsche, 1882/1974)

In ending this meditation on hopelessness, we quote a less well-known passage about hope from Romans 5:3, another book of the New Testament: 'And not only *so*, but we glory in tribulations also: knowing that tribulation worketh patience; And patience, experience; and experience, hope'. In other words, we need to face our suffering, alienation, and tribulations, including the objects and subjects of our hopelessness. Moreover, as we have argued throughout this chapter, all of this—from being able to distinguish between hopelessness and helplessness, through being able to maintain our activity rather than collapsing into passivity (privileged or otherwise), to being able to bear suffering, alienation, and tribulations—requires (alongside patience and experience) acceptance, positive regard, and love, also in all modes of therapeutic action.

9 Five kinds and four modes of empathy

In his discussion of the emergence of human consciousness, cultural philosopher, Gebser, suggests that the phenomenon of empathy is grounded in what he calls our 'archaic' consciousness; that is to say, the dim, pre-egoic consciousness experienced by our Stone Age ancestors. In Chapter 2 we discuss Gebser's (1949/1986) structures of consciousness; in this chapter, we focus on the implications of (t)his conceptualisation for empathic understanding (as Rogers tends to put it) or, more broadly, empathy. We begin with an overview of the stages of human consciousness, before considering Gebser's five stages of empathy—archaic, magical, mythical, mental-rational, and integral—as enacted in the therapeutic relationship. Finally, drawing on Stark's (1999) work on modes of therapeutic action and Keith's addition to this taxonomy a 'two-person plus psychology' (Tudor, 2011c) (discussed in Chapter 8), we consider how different modes of empathy further our thesis of belonging, becoming, and being with the planet.

Stages of human consciousness

Gebser traces the evolution of human consciousness through five stages or 'mutations' of increasing complexity, each clearly distinguishable from the preceding stage; that is, the archaic, the magic, the mythic, the rational, and the integral. Some millennia—and some 7,500 generations of human beings—later, our consciousness century may be dominated by one or another of these modes of consciousness: we may experience each of them, and we may experience shifting between them.

Our contemporary consciousness is multi-structured or, to change the metaphor slightly, multi-layered. We may thank Freud and Jung for pointing out that even when we are acting 'rationally', our magical and mythical consciousness is hard at work. The complexity of human behaviour comes out of the interplay of these several 'layers' or 'levels' of consciousness in whatever we do. Gebser (1949/1986) suggests that the acknowledgement and appreciation of these discrete structures is a step towards their integration with the rational structure in a more 'evolved' way of experiencing and, therefore, knowing the world. In this chapter, we focus on Gebser's model of the structures of consciousness with regard to the concept and practice of empathy, and, specifically, 'two-person' and 'two person plus' empathy.

DOI: 10.4324/9781003397731-12

Archaic empathy

Archaic consciousness is the most primitive state—both in the sense that it is earliest and in the sense that it is the least complex. For the first million or so years of human existence, human beings had no sense of themselves as separate from their environment. As far as we know, primitive humans were governed by instinct, and their consciousness was exceedingly dim. In this archaic consciousness, they had no sense of themselves as individuals, no sense of time and space, and lived in a state of ego-less unity with their environment. Their relationship to nature was dominated by impulse and instinct.

In archaic consciousness, the therapist and client don't inhabit separate worlds. Thus, empathy based in this kind of consciousness will be based on the experience of oneness with the other and with the universe which Hart (2010) links to Freud's (1915/1984b) primary process thinking and Luquet's (1981) primary mentalisation (see also Fonagy, 2001).

Human beings can, if we choose, change our ordinary state of consciousness to a less complex state through auto-suggestion or deep relaxation. Humans can also enact such change by entering a trance by hypnosis, or by chanting, music, dancing, or drumming. We can meditate. We can stop all mental activity for a time and let ourselves slip into a much simpler state of being. If we just sit, cease doing anything, remain in a state of passive attention, deal with intrusive thoughts and images by simply letting them go, we find we can enter a state of trance in which our sense of an individual reflecting ego, of the boundary between our internal and external worlds, becomes greatly diminished. We can enter a state of bliss, not ecstasy or transcendental experience perhaps, but silent, ego-less bliss, in which we and the universe are comfortably one. We can let go of ego, let go of the desire to be a distinct individual, and be content with experiencing the oneness of the greater organism of which we are a part. This is the simplest form of meditative trance, which is, literally, a regressive experience, i.e., a return to the archaic structure of consciousness through the shutting down of the other structures. The use of group trance in healing was and is common in pre-scientific cultures. (Of course, not all meditation is regressive; different forms of consciousness-changing meditation belong to the magical, mythical, and integral structures, and we can meditate within the mental structure without changing our mode of consciousness at all.)

We are inclined to think of meditation as a private and personal thing, even when people meditate together. Yet, historically and cross-culturally, meditation seems most commonly a group activity. In our experience, the kind of meditation we are talking about is most powerful in its impact when undertaken in a group. Each member of the group lets go of the boundary around the self and allows in the experience of the 'thisness' of the universe. The group members are in no way focused on each other, but share in the immediacy of what *is*. We think there are grounds for calling this phenomenon, and other group trance phenomena, collective archaic empathy.

Magical empathy

With the emergence of homo erectus (about 750,000 BCE) we find signs of human beings acting in a world of differentiated objects, exercising some control over them through the use of simple tools. There was, as then, no sense of personal identity or any ability to distinguish the part from the whole or internal experience from external. They seem to have experienced no sense of identity apart from the clan, and their world was a world of numinous power which could be dealt with only by magic. They had little language; they communicated through the direct experience of physical sensations or images. Their lives were totally enmeshed in the rhythms of nature. Gebser (1949/1986) calls this consciousness 'magical'. The magical structure, as Gebser determines, 'is spaceless and timeless and has an emotional and instinctual consciousness responsive to the demands of nature and the earth' (p. 76).

In magical consciousness, the therapist experiences the client's world somatically. Gebser suggests that, in this structure, consciousness is not so much in the individual human as in the world. Magical humanity tried to gain control over the transcendent power of nature through magic and sorcery, ritual, totem, and taboo, experiencing this magical world through a group-ego, sustained by the clan. It is in the magical structure that empathy, considered an experience of the primal sensing and feeling states of other members of the clan, is first a distinguishable phenomenon. Empathy is, for Gebser, a primitive phenomenon, utterly basic to the human condition.

Not all therapists experience these phenomena, but they are too common to be ignored. In mainstream writing about therapeutic interaction, the phenomena seem not to exist or are belittled as 'merely projection', evidence of therapists' lack of adequate ego-boundaries. In New Age writing, it is more generally viewed as evidence of a higher, or more evolved, consciousness. Alongside Gebser, we argue that the world of magical consciousness knows no ego-boundaries; that we have access to a mode of consciousness which deals with reality in just this way. In doing so, we want to avoid either romanticising or disparaging magical consciousness which, as Gebser asserts, can be either efficient or deficient.

From the viewpoint of our ordinary rational consciousness, we are inclined to view such phenomena as the transmission of a sensation or image from one self-contained person to another, in time and across space. We are also inclined to see a cause and effect relationship between the experience of the client and the reflection of it in the therapist. Gebser's (1949/1986) concept of a consciousness which experiences an ego-less, time-less, space-less, unitary world 'in which each and every thing intertwines and is interchangeable... [and] which operates without a causal nexus' (p. 48), challenges us to look at the phenomenon somewhat differently. If we drop our anthropocentric and ego-centric assumptions, we can imagine a reality in which both client and therapist are equal participants, in which the shared somatic or imaginative experience of client and therapist are not related as cause and consequence, or transmitted from one to the other, but are literally co-incidental.

Mythical empathy

After the last ice age (about 12,000 BCE) this primal consciousness was displaced by a new kind of consciousness, characterised by the development of imaginative thinking and the development of language. This shift, from magical to mythical consciousness, took human experience from an instinctual/emotional mode to an imaginative/verbal one. Humans ceased to experience themselves as being totally merged with nature. We see the beginnings of individual consciousness, the differentiation of self from other, the separation of internal and external awareness, the expression of human experience of the cosmos in image and story. Through the power of imaginative or 'mythical' thinking, humans were able to develop the sophisticated civilisations and complex societies of the ancient world; and, with them, the great narratives which expressed their experience of the universe.

In mythical consciousness, the therapist experiences the client's world imaginatively. Where the magical structure of consciousness is sensate, pre-rational, and pre-verbal, the mythical structure is imaginal, irrational, and verbal. It maintains the collective identity of the magical along with a fairly dim sense of individuality. Mythical empathy does not give us a direct experience of how you are and feel. Rather, it enables us to imagine how you are and feel; and it enables this because at the mythical level our separate stories are a common story. Mythical empathy involves the therapist entering into the client's story, recognising its universality as well as its uniqueness, being in the story with the client.

Mythical empathy arises out of a limited (relative to rational consciousness) sense of separate self. The magical structure does not distinguish self from not-self; the mythical structure knows self and not-self as a polarity, a complementarity; the mental structure knows self and not-self as a duality. In our mythical consciousness, we are both one and separate. The gap between us is crossed by imagination, not by conceptualisation.

Imaginal therapies, such as Jungian active imagination and Assagioli's psychosynthesis, depend on the ability to engage mythical consciousness. The therapist enters the imaginal world of the client and stays with the client's images, not interpreting, not rationalising, being an affirming presence in the imaginal world, helping the client to tell the story. Likewise, sand-tray therapy (often associated with a psychoanalytic orientation) and psychodrama (Moreno) depend on a willingness to cross the border into the client's personal story and an ability to recognise in this the universal story. In mythical consciousness, the boundary between self and other is permeable. Many therapists utilise the mythical structure when they cease reflecting and responding, and simply 'tune in' to the client and wait for a 'vision'.

Psychoanalysis labels this crossing of boundaries as either projection or identification, maintaining the assumption that the therapist and client are two separated, intact entities who are constrained to relationships to one another within an objectively real world. Classical Jungians discuss such phenomena as expressions of a collective or objective psyche. Post-Jungians, such as Hillman (1982), take seriously the notion of the *mundus imaginalis*, a level of reality located between the material, sensate world and the world of ideas or spirit. This is the world in which therapist and client find themselves enacting together the myth of the 'Wounded Healer'. It is the world of shared stories, visions, and dreams.

For most of us, most of the time the mythical world is experienced diluted by reflection, abstraction, and pre-conception. To stumble into our mythical consciousness can be a disturbing experience. For this reason, therapists who work with clients within this structure are likely to invite a crossing into the mythical world by enacting some sort of ritual. This is as true for the sand-tray practitioner setting up the tray and its icons; as it is for the psychodramatist guiding the protagonist in setting up the scene for enactment. In such therapies the return to ordinary consciousness is likewise ritualised.

The mythical world is far more unitary than the conceptualised world of mental-rational consciousness. It does not manifest the either/or of dualistic, rational thinking. Rather, its world is bipolar, both/and, taking the rational mind's oppositions (body/mind, conscious/unconscious, self/other, health/pathology, goodness/badness, subject/object, female/male, spirit/matter, one/many, even truth/falsehood) as complementary manifestations of a unitary reality. The mythical world is not a world of 'dead matter' like the world of rational, mechanistic science. It is ensouled, alive, replete with divinity (or divinities). The 'mythically empathic' therapist is able to move about in this numinous, fascinating, and sometimes frightening world with their client.

Mental-rational empathy

About 1,000 BCE, a fourth structure of consciousness, which Gebser (1949/1986) calls 'mental', began to emerge in Europe and Asia. Human beings became capable of rational and directed thought, began to identify being with thinking rather than feeling, to be aware of time, space, and quantity as we commonly understand them today. The emergence of discursive or abstract thought totally changed the relationship between human beings and their world. They became able to stand outside their world and reflect on it. They even became able to stand outside themselves, finding themselves not merely conscious, but conscious of their own consciousness. They became aware of time as more than duration and natural rhythm. They became fully aware of themselves as individuals, aware of cause and effect, able to act in a directed way on their world, no longer submerged in their environment and social group. They became able to build abstract political structures rather than tribal ones, to develop secular-scientific ways of perceiving and exploring the world.

With the collapse of the Roman Empire, Europe experienced a regression for some centuries to a magical-mythical consciousness. It was only in the 12th century that the Celtic and Germanic tribes made the same transition as had been made by the Greeks and Hebrews 2,000 years earlier, from mythical to mental consciousness. Gebser makes much of Petrarch's discovery of landscape as the discovery of 'objectified space', and of Da Vinci's discovery of the laws of perspective. The Renaissance celebrated the discovery of the person, and the fully fledged ego-centered human history. With the emergence of science, the human ego began more and more to assert itself against nature, faith, and the darkness of myth and magic. By the 17th century, reason reigned supreme in what the European elite perceived to be the most advanced civilisation of all time. The mental-rational structure enables the therapist to experience the client's world conceptually.

In his theory of structures of consciousness, Gebser (1949/1986) distinguishes between efficient and deficient structures. Magical, mythical, and mental consciousness can all have either efficient (positive) or deficient (negative) manifestations. From Gebser's perspective, the rational structure of consciousness which has dominated European culture for the past 400 years is not a higher form of consciousness which has emerged from the mental structure through an inevitable evolutionary progression, but a deficient form of mental consciousness, as it is cut off from its magical and mythical roots. It is an evolutionary dead end. It has seen the reduction of the universe from living organism to a collection of objects, the body from the temple of the soul to a piece of matter. It has seen the privileging of the intellect over other human capacities, the identification of intellect with the male and the relegation of the devalued physical-emotional (magical) and imaginative-intuitive (mythical) to the female. The fantasy of rational egoic control over the human machine and rational scientific control over the planetary one, have proved both futile and destructive.

In distinguishing the efficient mental structure of the great classical civilisations and the early renaissance from the deficient mental (rational) structure of the modern age, Gebser (1949/1986) notes, particularly, the discovery of objectified space, the development of the self-contained self, and the development of dualistic thinking. While the early mental structure is closely in touch with its magical and mythical roots, the rational structure is divorced from them. In the logic of a purely rational/materialistic/scientific consciousness, the notion of empathy is nonsense. In the hubris of positivistic psychology, even the existence of consciousness was denied. Rogers defied such absurdities, but in his early theorising about the nature of empathy was clearly concerned to develop a logical, systematic, and abstract way of explaining the phenomenon and its implications for therapy. He accepts the assumption that therapist and client exist in separate, rational worlds; assumes that one can look only from one direction at a time, and that, while the therapist knows the client's frame of reference, they don't experience any confusion of identity or become engulfed in the client's experiencing. From this perspective, the therapist's value to the client depends on the latter's determination to maintain his distinct separateness. Rogers (1958) expresses this idea with some emphasis:

> Am I strong enough in my own separateness that I will not be downcast by his depression, downcast by his fear nor engulfed by his dependency? Is my inner self hardy enough to realise that I am not destroyed by his anger, taken over by his need for dependence, nor enslaved by his love, but that I can exist separate from him with feelings and needs of my own? When I can freely feel this strength of being a separate person, then I can let myself go much more in understanding and accepting him.
>
> (p. 15)

Nevertheless, there is some ambiguity, for Rogers (1951) also sees the relationship as something which transcends these separate identities:

> In terms of the therapeutic situation, I think this feeling says to the client, I have a real hunger to know you, to experience your warmth, your expressivity—in whatever form it may take—to drink as deeply as I can from the experience of you in the closest, most naked relationship we can achieve. I do not want to change you to suit me; the real you and the real me are perfectly compatible ingredients of a potential relationship which transcends, but in no way violates, our separate identities.
>
> (p. 164)

Rogers' (1951) reflections on this observation sound like an apology for it not being an adequately 'scientific' statement:

> This whole idea seems important to me, not so much from a scientific standpoint, but simply because of its apparent importance in the process which my clients have been undergoing... Whether I'm kidding myself theoretically or not, this feeling of emotional adequacy in a therapeutic relationship seems very essential in creating a free and spontaneous relationship with clients.
>
> (p. 164)

We find the same uneasy, ambivalent relationship between practice and 'proper scientific thinking' in Kohut. Rogers (1986) points to the contradictory nature of Kohut's statements about empathy. He cites, with approval, Kohut's (1978) statement: that 'Empathy, the accepting, confirming and approving human echo evoked by the self, is a psychological nutrient without which human life as we know and cherish it, could not be sustained' (p. 715). He contrasts this with that of Goldberg (1980), a colleague of Kohut's: 'Empathy is employed only for data-gathering; there is no way it could serve us in our theory-building. In the clinical situation, the analyst employs empathy to collect information about current events in the patient's inner life' (p. 483). Kohut's practice may have convinced him of the power of empathy, but neither he nor his colleagues appear to be able to entertain the unscientific notion that empathy might, of itself, be healing. (For a more detailed comparison between Rogers and Kohut, see Kahn, 1985, and Tudor and Worrall, 2006.) This same ambivalence is reflected in Kohut's handling of an incident where, as analyst, he was at a loss for something to say to a despairing and suicidal woman client, so he gave her two fingers to hold. Immediately, he had to atone for this unwarranted warmth by making an interpretation: 'I immediately made a genetic interpretation to myself. It was the toothless gums of a young child, clamping down on an empty nipple' (cited in Rogers, 1986, p. 132).

In these extracts from their work, Rogers and Kohut seem to be struggling, consciously or not, between what Gebser regards as the efficient and deficient mental structures. It is the deficient structure which is represented by their notions of credible science. Rogers is staying in the efficient structure, while acknowledging the incorrectness of his position from the perspective of conventional science. Kohut is drawn by impulse towards the efficient expression, but rejects its apparent irrationality and chooses the more theoretically correct position, but deficient structure. Rational empathy aims to understand the inner world of the client, not to experience it. Having a ready-made interpretative system to assist in this understanding tends to turn understanding into diagnosis and reinforce the subject/object duality which is central to rational consciousness.

In *Client-Centered Therapy*, Rogers (1951) consciously and deliberately works within a mental-rational framework. Take his reflections on the proposition: 'The best vantage point for understanding behaviour is from the internal frame of reference of the individual himself' (Rogers, 1951, p. 494). He argues that human behaviour, no matter how bizarre it may appear to the observer, is always rational and purposive and 'in response to reality as it is perceived' (Rogers, 1951, p. 494). Rogers takes the perfectly rational view that while it would be desirable to 'empathically experience all the sensory and visceral sensations of the individual' (p. 494), this is impossible. Admitting that a great deal of the client's experience of the phenomenal world is not brought to the conscious level, he argues that on the one hand, it is unsatisfactory to try to understand the client's unconscious experiencing through an external interpretative framework; and, on the other hand, that to stay with the client's awareness gives us an incomplete picture. He acknowledges that the therapist's understanding of the client's phenomenal world will be, at least partly, derived by inferences from elements of that world which belong to the therapist and client's common experience. Throughout his discussion, the client's world is clearly the client's and the therapist's world is clearly the therapist's. Contents of one can pass to the other only by communication and (less accurately) by observation.

Rational empathy is essentially an act of intellection. The therapist strives to understand the world of the client. It has no necessary connection with feeling, and is certainly not to be mistaken for sympathy. There is no losing of boundaries. What is yours is yours and what is mine is mine, and there must be no confusion. Nevertheless, though 'cool', rational therapy might have been consistent with the theoretical constructs out of which Rogers was working at this stage, his experience of what worked drew him to suggest that this was not enough. The therapist must be touched by the experience of the client:

> I think clients are very much aware of the difference between the counsellor who listens and understands, and simply does not react, and the one who understands and in addition really cares about the meaning to the client of the feelings, reactions and experiences which he is recording.
>
> (Rogers, 1951, p. 164)

Integral empathy

Gebser's investigation of the evolution of human consciousness came from his sense, in the 1930s, that European consciousness was undergoing some sort of change: that something new was emerging in the 20th century. It seems to have started with his studies of Rainer Maria Rilke's use of language, finding there a transcendence of dualism, an aperspectivity, and a view of qualitative time, which he went on to find in other European writers, notably Paul Valéry and T. S. Eliot. As a refugee in Paris, in the late 1930s, Gebser sought in art, literature, music, science, architecture, and psychology, the evidence of a new sort of consciousness, against the background of a disintegrating mental-rational world and a regression to magical consciousness.

Three elements stand out in Gebser's analysis of what he called the integral structure of consciousness. The first is time-freedom. Archaic and magical humanity seem to have had no sense of time at all, living in a continuous present. For mythical humanity, time was rhythmical, constantly returning to its beginning. For mental-rational humanity, time became continuous and sequential, and eventually mechanically quantifiable. What identifies an integral sense of time, for Gebser (1949/1986), is the re-owning of pre-rational, magic, timelessness and irrational, mythical, temporicity alongside mental, measured time, which 'makes possible the leap into arational time-freedom' (p. 289).

Logically enough, Gebser suggests, that, just as archaic humanity could not feel what the experience of magical consciousness might be, and just as mythical humanity could not imagine what mental consciousness might be like (pre-mental humanity did not have 'ideas'), rational humanity cannot conceptualise the experience of integral consciousness. Gebser himself claims only to have observed the past and present trajectory of consciousness and, on this basis, to have guessed at its future direction. We want to suggest that client-centred and experiential psychotherapy is in this trajectory, at least as far as the understanding of empathy is concerned.

The integral structure of consciousness also has a new sense of space. Archaic and magical humanity lacked all spatial consciousness, because it lacked a defined sense of a self as observer. Mythical humanity emerged from this enmeshment in nature and became aware of an external world, but self-consciousness was still too weak to experience objective space. It was only in the beginnings of mental consciousness that human beings became able to locate events in objective space. Central to this experience was the discovery of perspective, which demands a point from which the world is viewed and an individual to view it. In the emergent, four-dimensional, integral consciousness, it becomes possible to view the world without locating the viewer in a particular position in space.

A third element in Gebser's analysis is the ego. Archaic and magical consciousness were ego-less. Mythical consciousness holds only a dim sense of self as distinct from the clan. Mental-rational consciousness allows the development of separate egoic identity. Integral consciousness is, in Gebser's language, 'ego-free'.

Gebser sees the deficiency in rational consciousness as deriving from its arrogant devaluation and suppression of the earlier structures. In the collapse of this structure in the 20th century, he saw both the danger of slipping back into a deficient magical-mythical structure and the promise of evolution to an integral structure. For the unwillingness of our rational-scientific civilisation to acknowledge the more primitive structures in no way makes them go away. We still think magically and mythically as well as rationally, whether we acknowledge it or not. The past structures are still present in us. We are inclined to equate consciousness with the sense of self we experience at the mental level. Yet, we constantly shift between this mental-rational consciousness and the more primitive structures which preceded it.

Both client-centred and experiential psychotherapy belong to the humanistic-existential cluster of therapies which, for all their many differences, have historically defined themselves in opposition to the rational-mechanistic propositions of behaviourism and psychoanalysis. Humanistic-existential therapies have been concerned to challenge the assumptions of high modernism: the dualistic assumption (particularly the mind/body dualism); the mechanistic/deterministic assumption (through a focus on volition and spontaneity); the masculist assumption (through a prizing of the feminine); the assumption of the absolute primacy of intellect (through a focus on experience and feeling); the materialist assumption (through a willingness to acknowledge non-material reality). However, within this cluster of therapies, and even within the smaller cluster of client-centred and experiential psychotherapies, there are different and contradictory voices. In this discussion, we consider two of them: person-centred empathy as described in the later writings of Rogers (1986a), and experiential empathy as described by Alvin Mahrer (1983).

Rogers' mature understanding of the nature of empathy is outlined in one of his later papers. Reiterating his ideas on the nature of the therapeutic relationship, he states:

> The third facilitative aspect of the relationship is empathic understanding. This means that the therapist senses accurately the feelings and personal meanings that the client is experiencing and communicates this acceptant understanding to the client. When functioning best, the therapist is so much inside the private world of the other that he or she can clarity not only the meanings of which the client is aware but even those just below the level of awareness. Listening, of this very special, active kind, is one of the most potent forces for change I know.
>
> (Rogers, 1986/1990, p. 198)

While this is not too far removed from Rogers' earlier explanations of what he means by empathy, we note that here he is imaginatively placing himself within the world of the client rather than constructing that world out of communication and observation. He is also less coy about the possibility of being in touch with something of the unconscious world of the client. There is less of a sense of therapist and client being in their separate, egoic space. These differences are taken considerably further later in the paper, when he goes beyond what has been confirmed by research and speaks from the edges of his personal experience

Psychologically, the emergence of the aperspectival, arational, integral world demands a disenchantment with narrow rational consciousness and a re-owning of the earlier structures. This allows the emergence of a new structure of consciousness for which we don't as yet have an adequate language. We find in Rogers' statement acknowledgement of a phenomenon with magical-mythical elements.

Magical-mythical healing operates through what are for us 'non-ordinary' states of consciousness, independent of linear space and time, not knowing the duality of mind/body and self/other, locates core identity not in the individual but in 'something larger', and does not know the laws of logic.

Those inside or outside the client-centred community who regard rational consciousness as the peak and culmination of evolutionary progress will see this statement of Rogers' as an indication that he 'lost it' in his old age. They will warn us that this honouring of magic and irrationality is regressive, an unfortunate intrusion of magical-mythical New Age consciousness into a perfectly adequate rational-humanistic system of thought. Indeed, Wilber (1983) warns us of the dangers of the 'pre/trans fallacy', that is, the tendency of some of us to mistake regressive phenomena for progressive ones, to mistake the pre-egoic for the trans-egoic, the pre-rational for the trans-rational, the pre-personal for the trans-personal, the magical for the mystical. However, he also points to the tendency of others of us to make the opposite mistake. For Wilber, as for Gebser, trans- or post- states are distinguished from pre- states in that they retain the foundation of ego, rationality, and control which they transcend.

In the above passage, Rogers is talking about an experience which he cannot justify rationally. We might be inclined to label it irrational. However, Gebser (1949/1986) takes pains to distinguish the irrational from the arational:

> It is of fundamental importance that we clearly distinguish between 'irrational' and 'arational', for this distinction lies at the very heart of our deliberations... There is a fundamental distinction between the attempt to go beyond the merely measurable, knowing and respecting it while striving to be free from it, and rejecting and disregarding the measurable by regressing to the immoderate and unfathomable chaos of the ambivalent and even fragmented polyvalence of psychic and natural interrelation.
>
> (p. 147)

Rogers' (1986/1990) reflections are hardly those of someone who has abandoned rationality and slid into immoderate and unmeasurable chaos! Neither has he abandoned his sense of self, but he is able to hold the paradox of experiencing self-sense and transpersonal sense simultaneously. In reflecting on his experience, he shows an awareness of a paradox, or at least an irony, in finding that a focus on individual experiencing should lead to an experience of oneness. He quotes, with approval, a participant in one of his workshops:

> I found it to be a profound spiritual experience. I felt the oneness of spirit in the community. We breathed together, we felt together, even spoke for one another. I felt the power of the 'life force' that infuses each of us—whatever that is. I felt its presence without the usual barricades of 'me-ness' or 'you-ness'—it was like a meditative experience when I feel myself as a centre of consciousness. And yet with that extraordinary sense of oneness, the separateness of each person present has never been more clearly preserved.
>
> (Rogers, 1986/1990, pp. 137–138)

Later, in the same paper, Rogers (1986/1990) comments on a particular example of an 'intuitive response' in a therapeutic interaction:

> I have come to value highly these intuitive responses. They occur infrequently... but they are almost always helpful in advancing therapy. In these moments I am in a slightly altered state of consciousness, indwelling in the client's world, completely in tune with that world. My nonconscious intellect takes over. I know much more than my conscious mind is aware of. I do not form my responses consciously, they simply arise in me, from my nonconscious sensing of the world of the other.
>
> (p. 148)

Again, we could argue that an altered state of consciousness, identification with the client, and a sense of nonconscious knowing, point to magical-mythical structure of consciousness. These are not highly evolved capacities, restricted to the genius, the saint, or the shaman, but fairly basic ones which we seem to share with animals. There is certainly no basis for romantically privileging these capacities. However, if we follow Gebser in arguing that the capacity to simultaneously experience these capacities and maintain a reflective awareness of them signals something new in the evolution of human consciousness, we may wish to view the whole phenomenon somewhat differently.

Finally, we make the same point regarding experiential psychotherapy as described by Mahrer (1983) who, in his critique of the limitations of client-centred therapy, sets out three assumptions on which he believes the approach is based:

a   Therapist and patient are assumed to be two fundamentally separate and intact entities.
b   Their relationship is predominated by the patient's frame of reference. The patient has this frame of reference, and the therapist acknowledges and uses the patient's frame of reference.
c   Both therapist and patient are assumed to exist within an encompassing world of objective reality upon which the patient's frame of reference is but one perspective. (p. 143)

In Gebser's language, Mahrer (1983) sees client-centred therapy operating within a fairly advanced mental-rational structure. In contrast, he locates his own experiential therapy within the emerging integral structure. In the reality in which Mahrer works,

> the personhood or identity of the therapist can assimilate into or fuse with the personhood or identity of the patient... the locus of the therapist can occur internally within the patient... [The therapist is] able to share both the internal and external domains of the patient... When the patient attends to a meaningful focal centre, the therapist can likewise share the same attentional

centre. [In the course of therapy] the locus of relationships radically shifts from that of external, separated therapist and external, separated patient... to either the relationship of patient (and therapist) with the meaningful attentional centre, or to the relationship between patient and deeper personality process (and therapist)... [and] patient and therapist exist in multiple phenomenal worlds constructed by the patient, the therapist, and both conjointly.

(p. 145)

In such a context, empathy is entirely revisioned. Instead of maintaining the separation of identities, as the mental-rational expression of client-centred therapy was determined to do, experiential empathy depends on the dissolving of the boundaries between therapist and client: 'Ordinarily, about 80 to 90 per cent of an experiential session is spent with the therapist sharing the patient's attentional centre. During all this time, the therapist is internal to the patient, aligned and fused with the patient' (Mahrer, 1983, p. 197).

A precondition to such a unity of experiencing is the minimisation of therapist/patient roles, which Mahrer sees as problematic and severely inhibiting successful therapy. The experiential therapist's aim is to experience the world of the patient, concretely, not to be content with the 'as if' approach of the client-centred therapist. Accordingly, the experiential therapist's aim is to enter the patient's world from their common personhood, not from within a role relationship. They don't sit facing the patient but beside them; they don't seek to reflect what the patient is thinking and feeling, but to express what they are thinking and feeling in common; they don't observe the patient as the other, for both have their eyes closed; they don't seek to relate to or even communicate with the patient as self to other; rather, seek to experience exactly the same world. They don't seek to enter this world by a conceptual or imaginative leap but by sharing the same physical sensations.

Experiential empathy begins with the client becoming aware of the sensations in their body and describing these to the therapist. The therapist adopts these sensations as their own:

> Something is happening in your body right now. It may be in your throat or chest or head or legs or somewhere. I want to have the same thing in my body. I want to have the same feelings, the same sensations that are going on in your body right now. Describe where the feelings are and what they are like, so that I can have them too, no matter where they are or what they are like. Then we can move ahead.

(Mahrer, 1983, p. 235)

Moving ahead involves the therapist attending, not to the patient, but to whatever the patient is attending. The therapist does not guess what the patient is experiencing, but expresses whatever sensations and images they are experiencing themselves. Therapist and patient don't interact with each other; rather, they interact as one person with the shifting focus of attention. As the therapist experiences more and more intense sensations, and increasingly precise and vivid images, there is no censoring or selection on the basis of 'This is mine; that is theirs'.

Mahrer's reflections on this practice bear comparison with Rogers' reflections on the practice of empathy. Like Rogers, Mahrer finds the practice healing in itself. Like Rogers, he notices a shift in and out of an altered state of consciousness. Like Rogers, he claims to be aware of a deeper potential, a deeper transpersonal reality. Like Rogers, Mahrer is constantly confirmed in his conviction that beyond the frightening darkness of the client's deeper potential is a positive energy.

Obviously, in evaluating such a practice, we are at risk of falling into Wilber's (1983) pre/trans fallacy, one way or the other. Such a practice clearly involves magical and mythical processes. We argue, however, that such practice integrates them with mental processes, transcending the constructs of the 'merely rational' world rather than resiling from (or abandoning) them. The experiential therapist is simultaneously inside and outside the experience, just as the protagonist in psychodrama may be simultaneously a three-year-old child in hospital and an adult observing his own performance, or the person in hypnotic trance may be observing his own trance behaviour. The experience of operating in two or more states of consciousness simultaneously is common enough. Perhaps in our re-owning of the earlier strata of our consciousness, this is the best most of us can manage. Fully integrated consciousness may be still emergent!

Four modes of empathy as therapeutic action

In her book *Modes of Therapeutic Action*, Stark (1999) offers a taxonomy of approaches to the field of psychology (across all forces and traditions), which she refers to as 'modes':

- One-person psychology.
  In this mode or model of psychology (Stark uses both terms), the goal of treatment is a strengthening of the client's ego through insight, facilitated predominantly by the therapist's interpretations. Most commonly associated with classical psychoanalysis, there are forms of reflective listening and ways of focusing the client that foster such insight and strengthening. In this mode of therapeutic action, the purpose of treatment/therapy is on the 'enhancement of knowledge'; the unit of study is 'the patient and the patient's internal dynamics' (Stark, 1999, p. xvi); and the role of the therapist is that of 'an objective observer of the patient' (p. xvi). An example of empathy in this mode is Rogers' (1974/1995f) reflection that 'I and my colleagues realized that this empathic listening provided one of the least clouded windows into the workings of the human psyche, in all its complex mystery' (p. 50). Here, Rogers, somewhat unusually, views empathy as a means to an end, in this case, insight into the workings of the human psyche.

- One-and-a-half-person psychology.
  In this mode, the goal of treatment is the provision of experience. Stark explains the difference between these two modes as a representing a shift in

interest from nature (and drives) to nurture (the quality of maternal care), informed, notably by object relations and self psychology. This goal is facilitated predominantly by the provision of a corrective experience (Alexander & French, 1946) through a reparative or developmentally needed relationship (see Barr, 1987; Clarkson, 1990, 1995). Although Stark (1999) views the corrective experience being conveyed 'by way of the real [therapeutic] relationship' (p. xvii), I (Keith) suggest that 'this is more of an "I–It" relationship than an "I–Thou" or "Thou–I" relationship' (Tudor, 2011c, p. 51), precisely because it is the therapist designing and doing or offering the correction or repair *to* the client. In this mode, the purpose of treatment is filling in the structural deficit; the unit of study is the client's parents' failure, whether the absence of good (i.e., not 'good enough' parenting), or the presence of bad (Fairbairn, 1952); and the role of the therapist is to be 'a new good (and, therefore, compensatory) object' (Stark, 1999, p. xviii). In this mode, empathy involves a continuous process of checking with the client to see if understanding is complete and accurate. It is carried out in a manner that is personal, natural, and free flowing: it is *not* a mechanical kind of reflection or mirroring. (Raskin & Rogers, 1989, p. 189)

We suggest this is an example of one-and-a-half person empathy as the continuous process of checking may well be reparative for the client.

- Two-person psychology.
  In this mode, therapy—and what is healing—is 'interactive engagement with an authentic other' (Stark, 1999, p. xix); in other words, the therapeutic relationship itself. The client is viewed as an active and proactive agent who has an impact on the therapist and the relationship, and, for their part, the therapist working in this mode is required to draw on and use more of themselves *in* the relationship, precisely as the authentic other. Whilst the idea that therapy *is* the therapeutic relationship has its antecedents in psychoanalysis, humanistic psychologists and therapists, notably Taft (1933/1973) who first coined the term 'relationship therapy', elaborated this over some 50 years before the 'relational turn' in psychoanalysis, which is generally considered to date from the publication of Greenberg and Mitchell's (1983) work *Object Relations in Psychoanalytic Theory*. In this mode of psychology, the purpose of treatment is the development of a therapeutic relationship, however brief, which acts as a mirror of the client's other relationships and, thereby, a reflection of their relationships, past and present, outside therapy. Thus, the unit of study is the relationship, including what are commonly referred to as ruptures and repairs between the therapist and client. An example of empathy in this mode is Rogers' (1952/1967b) definition that 'Empathic understanding—[is] understanding with a person, not about him' (p. 332).

Some years later, in reviewing this taxonomy, and influenced by some of the literature on ecopsychology and ecotherapy, as well as my views of the power of influence and change beyond the therapist and the clinic, I (Keith) offered an addition to these three modes, namely that of a 'two-person plus psychology':

- Two-person-plus psychology (Tudor, 2011c)
  In this mode, what is healing is engagement in and with the environment (which is why we see this as relevant to our current interest), based on the view that, as human beings, we are part of and not separate from the environment. This mode acknowledges more explicitly (than two-person psychology) that the client is a person-in-context and that that context may be an important part of the therapy and, thus, therapy in this mode may well involve others (partner, family, group), and/or take place outdoors. The purpose of therapy is to repair or resolve the client's alienation, whatever form that takes (see Tudor, 1997/2017a). The unit of study is the interface of the client with (in) their environment and thus the 'environment' of the therapeutic relationship, while the role of the therapist is to draw on themselves also as a person-in-context in order to help the client. An example of empathy in this mode is (as noted in Chapter 8), Rogers' (1986b) later view that empathy is:

  > in itself a healing agent. It is one of the most potent aspects of therapy, because it releases, it confirms, it brings even the most frightened client into the human race. If a person can be understood, he or she belongs.
  > (p. 129)

We think that this mode of psychology is more consistent (then the other modes) with Gebser's ideas about structure and consciousness, and well as the layers of empathy. We also think that it provides a framework for challenging anthropocentric and ego-centric assumptions in therapy (in theory and in practice); de-centring the individual; and developing ideas about and concepts in 'we psychology', including the social brain (Siegel, 1999) and the collective brain (Muthukrishna & Henrich, 2016), and, most importantly, in developing more empathy for our/the environment and planet.

10 Experiencing and perceiving

Keith Tudor and Alisoun Neville

In this chapter we address and develop the brief reference Bernie and Keith made in Chapter 4 (in the context of the discussion about Rogers' therapeutic conditions) to '*the experiencing Earth*' (p. 76)

The sixth, basic, and assumed condition

In his two major formulations of the necessary and sufficient condition for therapy, which Rogers refers to as therapeutic personality change and therapeutic process, respectively, he describes this condition as follows:

> That the client *perceives*, at least to a minimal degree, conditions 4 and 5, the *unconditional positive regard* of the therapist for him, and the *empathic* understanding of the therapist.
>
> (Rogers, 1959, p. 213)

> The final condition as stated is that the client perceives, to a minimal degree, the acceptance and empathy which the therapist experiences for him.
>
> (Rogers, 1957, p. 99)

Notwithstanding the slight difference between these statements, it is clear that Rogers set great store by the client's perception of the therapist's experience of them, and, therefore, that this might be viewed as the litmus test of the efficacy of therapy both within and beyond the client-centred framework, and, more broadly, any facilitative relationship (Rogers, 1957). Around the same time, Rogers (1958/1967c) refers to this 'basic' and 'assumed' condition as one in which 'the client experiences himself as being fully *received*' (p. 130). In the context of our present focus and concern, it is interesting that Rogers introduces this statement by commenting that: 'If we were studying the process of growth in plants, we would assume certain constant conditions of temperature, moisture, and sunlight, in forming our conceptualization of the process. Likewise in conceptualizing the process of personality change in psychotherapy' (p. 130). Here, as elsewhere in his writing, Rogers draws on agricultural and environmental analogies and metaphors; and, by focusing on the 'conditions' of therapy, is, in effect, positioning them as

DOI: 10.4324/9781003397731-13

environmental conditions. Taking an organismic perspective (as we do), we are interested in the maintenance, enhancement, and reproduction of the experiencing organism (Rogers, 1963), and, in order to do that with regard to the environment, we have to think and feel beyond the anthropocene.

Although Barrett-Lennard (1962) found that success in psychotherapy was positively related to the client's perception of the therapist's conditions/attitudes (contact, congruence, acceptance, and empathy), this sixth condition is largely ignored within person-centred literature. Exceptions include Van der Veen (1970), Watson (1984), Toukmanian (2002), Tudor (2001, 2011a, 2013c), and Tudor and Worrall (2006).

Watson (1984) reviews the importance and empirical status of this condition:

> from a phenomenological perspective, only the client has direct access to his or her own perceptions in the process of self-reflection; unless the client gives a self-report, other persons must infer the client's perceptions indirectly from other overt behavior. From this standpoint, adequate assessment of the therapist-provided conditions requires that the client be the source of the ratings.
>
> (p. 21)

Applied to the living world as though it is a client, it is clear that, with regard to our human-provided 'conditions', treatment of and relationship with our living world, 'the environment' and the planet (see Chapter 6), we're not doing so well.

Toukmanian (2002) describes 'perception' as the core element in person-centred and experiential psychotherapies and as 'a key construct that permeates all aspects of Rogers' theory of therapy and personality change' (p. 115). She argues that perception, even though not explicitly dealt with in Rogers' work, looms large in his emphasis on 'the primacy of subjective knowing, his existential view of the person, his conception of the nature of the therapeutic relationship, and his definitions of many of the theory's foundational constructs' (p. 115).

I (Keith) have written several publications critiquing the notion of the (three) so-called 'core conditions' (i.e., the therapist's congruence, unconditional positive regard, and empathy), and two specific articles that reclaim the three 'lost conditions' (of psychological contact, client incongruence, and client perception) (Tudor, 2000, 2011a). I have also published with colleagues in which we have applied the six conditions to a number of activities, namely, therapy (Ioane & Tudor, 2017; Komiya & Tudor, 2016; Singh & Tudor, 1997); learning, organisation, and environment (Embleton Tudor et al., 2004; Tudor & Lewin, 2006); supervision (Tudor & Worrall, 2004b; see also Gibson, 2004); and online therapy (Rodgers et al., 2021).

Knowing and advancing this aspect of Rogers' theory, during the week (in 2019) we spent writing this book at Bernie's home on Mt. Toolebewong, Victoria, Australia, which included a daily walk in the woods, I (Keith) suggested to Bernie that, in considering this sixth condition, we might write about belonging, becoming, and being from the point of view of our respective mountains. In doing so, we are inspired by heuristic research enquiry as developed by Moustakas (1990) and Sela-Smith (2002), which we consider compatible with the PCA and this current project.

> When someone feels an internal draw and hears the call from the deepest recesses of the self, it is almost impossible not to notice. This may be something that is being consciously or unconsciously experienced as incomplete and that needs to be completed. It may be something that is discordant that needs to be brought to harmony or something that is unclear that needs to be clarified. It may be something that is misunderstood that needs understanding or something that is dissociated that needs to be integrated. Perhaps it is something that has not been known before that seeks to be known.
>
> (Sela-Smith, 2002, p. 64)

In this spirit, we (Alisoun and Keith) introduce and write about the two mountains.

Toolebewong, Victoria, Australia

I miss my father deeply. I must recall him to write to this passage, to do honour to his relationship, and mine/ours, with a parcel of land on Mount Toolebewong, a home shared with lyrebirds, bracken, snakes, wombats, and two 'barely habitable' buildings, in which I spent my most formative years.

But this is Australia. At the time of writing, we—my family—don't know the true name of the mountain. Inheriting the notion that 'Toolebewong' translates as 'misty mountain' I have always marvelled at the fog settling across the road and into the fern gullies, sensing into the presence of the fog itself and the many mysteries it conceals. I am told, more recently, it translates in Woiwurrung language as 'Where the raven sat on the tree' and know that these are questions I could ask the Wurundjeri.

It was hard work living there as a child. It was hard to understand why, in the late 1970s, my friends enjoyed the warmth of carpet and electricity while my parents installed themselves and my infant brother in front of tractors to prevent the power reaching our home. The State Electricity Commission were the enemy in those years, for Mum, Dad, and our neighbours, most of whom lived in the co-operative (an intentional community) up the road. This collective shared the concern that 'development' would follow the tractors, and would make the mountain harder to protect. The state did not agree, or at least chose not to care. We watched with horror as the power lines were laid, the ragwort took hold in the bush, the imported deer pushed out the goannas, and half acre blocks appeared up the road. There were dogs and more cars, and sections of bush rapidly cleared to make more of the view.

Dad's sense of responsibility to the living earth guided his life decisions, his reciprocal relationships and obligations to place. It was tangible for him, literal even, as he battled with leaking pipes and empty water tanks year after year after year.

Dad spoke to me of rising oceans and mountains of plastic, many years before these ideas had the (persistently inadequate) traction they have now.

Experiencing and perceiving 149

Figure 10.1 Mt Toolebewong at dusk
Source: Photo—Alisoun Neville.

Figure 10.2 Mt Toolebewong—The Shed
Source: Painting—Alisoun Neville.

I read this at his funeral, an extract from T. S. Eliot's (1922/1963) *The Wasteland*:

> If there were water
> And no rock
> If there were rock
> And also water
> And water
> A spring
> A pool among the rock
> If there were the sound of water only
> Not the cicada
> And dry grass singing
> But sound of water over a rock
> Where the hermit-thrush sings in the pine trees
> Drip drop drip drop drop drop drop
> But there is no water.
>
> (lines 346–358)

Looking back, through the window

I have struggled, in different ways to Dad perhaps, with what this means in a still-colonised country, in which the notions of reciprocity and obligations take on specific meanings. With reference to the discussion of Rogers above, I am drawn to the implications for settler relationships with Indigenous/First Nations peoples, in which, writing from a settler location in the nation-state called Australia, the point of view of the mountain cannot meaningfully be considered without reference to the point of view of the peoples from whom those lands were taken.

Acknowledging first the inherently situated and local nature of these questions, I draw on writings by Indigenous peoples more broadly, in recognition of the contributions of Indigenous intellectuals and activists to theories and frameworks of decolonisation (Tuck & Yang, 2012).

Tallbear (2019) reminds us that 'the settler state cannot be decolonized' (p. 33):

> The issue is not only that material dispossession of land and 'resources' builds the settler state but also that 'dispossession' undercuts co-constitutive relations between beings. Property literally undercuts Indigenous kinship and attempts to replace it. It objectifies the land and water and other-than-human beings as potentially owned resources. One can see the settler property regime undercutting kinship between Indigenous people... [and] Indigenous relations with place overturned by the settler-state imposition of private property.
>
> (p. 32)

Recentring a commitment to being in relation, Tallbear proposes 'an explicitly spatial narrative of caretaking relations' and calls on us to practice small acts of visionary resistance and deep narrative and ontological revision that forgo the relentlessly violent love for the nation-state in favor of loving and caring for our relatives, both human and other than human, whose lives depend on these lands.

(p. 36)

She is echoed in her call by Moreton-Robinson (2019), to erase the epistemology which nourishes the settler's being.

Tallbear's (2019) vision feels accessible, comforting even, until she reminds me it cannot be integrated with the settler state, the colonial dreaming 'that is ever co-constituted with deadly hierarchies of life' (p. 25). Tuck and Yang (2012) point out that the disruption of Indigenous relationships to land represents a profound violence that is reasserted each day of occupation. To own and/or otherwise occupy the lands that are stolen in this context, as my parents did, and as we children now inherit, will not be remediated by simple declarations that we are aligned in our love for 'Mother Earth and all her children' or other moves to innocence (Moreton-Robinson, 2019, p. 72; Tuck & Yang, 2012).

A similar tension may underpin what Yunkaporta (2019) sees as an oversimplification in contemporary discourses on Indigenous knowledges and sustainability. He notices there is a significant focus on examples of sustainable practices by Indigenous peoples pre-colonisation, but very little/inadequate attention to contemporary implications. The Indigenous peoples participating in these conversations, Yunkaporta believes, may be offering formulaic self-narratives and cultural artefacts, 'a window for outsiders to see into a carefully curated version of their past' (p. 19). Crucially, Yunkaporta adds, this view is one-way: 'We're not sharing what we see when we look back through that window' (p. 19).

The language I have is inadequate

In reflecting further on the proposition put to me by Keith, that we might consider Rogers' sixth condition from the perspective of the mountain, I am confronted also by this: I feel a call, an internal draw from the land with which I have lived in closest relation, but I don't speak its language. I don't know what it is I am listening to, or how to take heed of the feedback I am offered. In his extraordinary memoir *Displaced: A Rural Life*, Kinsella (2020) writes of a landscape in the Western Australian Wheatbelt that he calls Jam Tree Gully, where he lives and with which he is intimately familiar. Kinsella says a group of York gums remind him of 'a depth of ontology of presence that resists our descriptions, even our immersions' (p. 63) and acknowledges that:

The language I have is inadequate and I cannot and would not access the language that can talk of it—not only do I not have the right, but I could never decode it. I will never really comprehend its complexities and intensities but through poetry I go as close as I can to doing so, I hope. You can't substitute understanding, but you can at least respect it.

(pp. 62–63)

Kinsella locates himself as a settler for whom the 'terra nullius legal deletion of Aboriginal rights of presence, possession, and *language of land* has many ongoing manifestations' (p. 27), including, most crucially:

> This *is* Ballardong Noongar land. It is stolen land and it needs to be returned. And then a discussion has to take place on how coexistence might work. I feel a deep belonging, but also an unbelonging because of this injustice.
>
> (p. 20)

Kinsella (2020) writes in detail of the land on which he lives, but troubles the language and assumptions of possession: 'land is never to be owned, and will accept you or reject you in ways you're not even aware of. I feel a connection though I know I unbelong.... Respect, acknowledgment, and letting the land have the say, not the exploiters' (p. 10). Kinsella suggests that an ethical presence in this country has to address the driving question: 'How can we coexist justly and fairly?', a discussion which 'has to begin with Aboriginal people as to how the land might be respected' (p. 20).

My own ideas and anxieties about formal ownership/possession of Wurundjeri lands tend to loosen their grip when my hands touch the earth in Dad's vegetable garden, my knuckles bitten while pulling weeds from the dirt, my legs buckling to harvest the far too prolific potatoes, my arms scratched and strong to keep the boysenberries in check. I feel in touch with Dad's approach while I am doing this work. He didn't appear to overthink it. He spent his years trying to convince the garden fences that he was smarter than the wombat and convincing everybody else to accept his buckets of raspberries and Jerusalem artichokes. He wasn't much one for rest or creature comfort. He enjoyed working hard, sharing the bounty widely, and saw taking care of the land as the path to its respect.

Yunkaporta (2019) warns (or promises) that

> future survival of all life on the planet will be dependent on human beings being able to perceive and be custodians of the patterns of creation again, which in turn requires a completely different way of living in relation to the land.
>
> (p. 252)

Later, he teaches that 'being in profound relation to place changes everything about you—your voice, your smell, your walk, your morality' (p. 255). I am a child again, and there is so much to learn.

My mother was more focussed on the environmental weeds, which spread fast outside the fences of this garden. The ragwort which grew, and regrew, and grew again. The silence amongst the tea trees, the loss of mountain ash. Like her, my siblings and I sit daunted by the labour required for the leaking roof, the broken toilet, the relentless need for a firebreak, wood for the fire, and other mounting tasks. There is a lot of work involved and other ways to pay our dues.

My parents didn't necessarily underthink the questions I pose here. As a child I remember Dad's involvement in local politics: his role through council in the handback of lands once occupied by Coranderrk reserve; and following my mother to support a Gunditjmara-led protest against a new Alcoa plant, across the state in Portland. Tallbear's focus is firmly here, not in the past, and asks the question echoed above by Kinsella (2020): 'How do we relate well in this place without that inherently eliminatory dreaming?' (p. 26).

Kinsella's (2020) vision is a shared/collective endeavour, which he relates most directly to his family, as 'aloneness cannot heal land and community—but together we can' (pp. 16–17). He describes the land as in a process of healing, in an interim moment of repair. Tallbear (2019) emphasises material connectedness among many generations, encompassing

> those whose bodies may now/still exist within organismically defined understandings of life… [as well as] entities that do not meet that definition, and other bodies whose materiality has been transferred back to the earth and out into that web of relation, or whose bodies are not yet formed of already existing matter.
>
> (pp. 25–26)

I notice these words again when I read Dad's opening words in this book, about his hopes for his children and his grandchildren, and how the process of writing reminds him he is alive. I recall our discussions about the cosmos as he lay ill, when we shared wild speculations on the presence or absence of spirits in my emerging novel.

To be in good relation

I trust it is clear in his writing that Dad's ethic of care, of love, extended well beyond family and land/earth. He celebrates Rogers for his contributions to philosophy through, among other things, the nature of the good life, what it means to be human, the ethics of helping, the nature of human relationships. When asked about his ethics of giving by one of many Persians he befriended in his final years—a great number of whom were seeking asylum and whom he emotionally, practically, and/or financially assisted—he said he was bought up to believe that if someone needs help, you help them. As simple as that. Putting this into action helped him manage his rage at the pure inhumanity of successive Immigration policies/Ministers/Prime Ministers in Australia. Kinsella reminds me that relationships are complex because they are, but that right is right and wrong is wrong. I wish Dad was alive to read Kinsella's book. He would have found so much joy in the reading, not least because Kinsella too believed in an open door, and had been hit by lightning a few more times than Dad. They were both men chased by, but seemingly unafraid of, the chaos of nature's storms.

A core premise of the therapeutic role rests on what may be made possible through the client's experience of a good/secure relationship. I talk often with other therapists, and with the people who come to see me, about creating and holding relational safety, including processes of rupture and repair, and attending to dissonance in the spaces between and within our bodies.

To be in good relations as Tallbear asks of us, requires a broader lens, and is incompatible with the settler state. For Dad and Keith, the current planetary emergency is 'forcing us to abandon the ways of imagining the world which have led us to that emergency' (p. 24 [Chapter 1]), and demand directly of their readers that we 'overcome our paralysis and act' (p. 15 [Chapter 1]).

My response to these questions is visceral, not always finding safety, as my very embodiment carries the structures of the nation/settler state within which these relationships occur. My ideas of—and commitments to actions in—good relations continue to evolve, stretched by the work and memories of my father, by my/our relationships to Mt Toolebewong and other forms and locations of love, and by a currency of conversations with Wurundjeri and other Indigenous peoples. Imagining Dad's life and relationships once more from the potential perspective of the mountain, I find much to embrace in his works of love and repair. Kinsella (2020) puts this simply, and helps me look ahead: 'We don't have to be stuck with the damage—it can be undone' (p. 147).

In the early months of the coronavirus pandemic and lockdowns, I moved in next to Dad, in a house close to his on the 'property' on Mt Toolebewong. We, his children, wanted to protect him from the virus and, despite his stubborn and persistent stoicism, we worried about him being there by himself. It soon became freezing, as April turned to May, the window blinds were not installed and the solar system shut down when I turned on the second heater. He taught me again how to split wood for the pot belly, pump water between the tanks, and how to be still in the bush. When the great symbol of the virus, the bat, swept in from the roof and under my bedroom door, he walked up twice through mud and rain to help me sleep in peace. We both swore about the Wi-Fi, at different times but at the same feverish pitch.

When Dad's knees allowed him, and my feet allowed me, we walked slowly between the trees. We sat one time to rest and he pointed out a line of ground ferns that followed the track of the underground stream. It spoke to him, and through him to me, of the pulsing heart of the universe.

I thank my Dad for this pulsing heart within him. A heart so huge, and a heart he shared with so many, and yet we were all left wanting more. There is no such thing as enough of a heart like that. And I thank him for teaching me to notice this heart within me, to know that I am inseparable from, and have obligations to, that stream, and to the traditional owners of those waters and the lands that surround them.

I end by sharing a poem I wrote while I was there:

> I asked if he would sit
> But he stood strong
> Making fire for me
> Was more important

Figure 10.3 Toolebewong Trees
Source: Painting—Alisoun Neville.

> Than the screams in his legs, his back, his mind
> He bent in the middle
> Stooped and ready
> Pushing wood towards metal
> Seeking splits
> And small splints
> Fitting for fire.

Helvellyn, Cumbria, England

> Ko Helvellyn te maunga | Helvellyn is the mountain.

There are a number of ways of referring to and describing this mountain, and although I (Keith) describe it is 'my mountain', I do so in the spirit of association (my), not possession (mine). In this contribution, I attempt to give voice to different perspectives or voices about and of Helvellyn, and thus is written about it (third person), addressing it (second person), imagining I am it (first person), and about me and it (first person plural). In reversing the usual order in the conjugation of verbs ('I am', 'you are', 's/he is', 'we are', etc.), I am working from the outside in, and from the impersonal to the personal—and ending with the plural. In the context of Alisoun's poignant, political, and poetic piece, I acknowledge that writing about Helvellyn as my—or the—mountain is or appears to be a lot easier for me as being from and writing about England, than it is for her to write about Mt. Toolebewong as a settler in the land known as Australia or would be for me to write about the Waitakere, the range of hills in West Auckland (where I live) as a settler in Aotearoa New Zealand. I write 'appears to be' following an exchange of emails with Alisoun who challenged my original statement as being 'too easy and simplistic a position, as it elides both the British role in colonisation and the ongoing actions and impacts of a British nation-state built on the extraction of resources from external lands and peoples' (A. Neville, personal communication, May 2022). I appreciate the challenge and, as I think and reflect, recognise that, of course, my ability to access and have a relationship to Helvellyn is predicated upon certain privileges, i.e., financial security (which includes having walking boots—and now being more aware of their origins and manufacturer), leisure time (including holidays), etc., all of which is enabled by wealth created not least by historical colonisation and current colonialism—and makes my relationship with it more complex, and perhaps especially so as I write from a distance.

Helvellyn (– it)

> Helvellyn… is a mountain in the English Lake District, the highest point of the Helvellyn range, a north-south line of mountains to the north of Ambleside, between the lakes of Thirlmere and Ullswater. Helvellyn is the third-highest point both in England and in the Lake District, and access to Helvellyn is easier than to the two higher peaks of Scafell Pike and ScaFell. The scenery includes

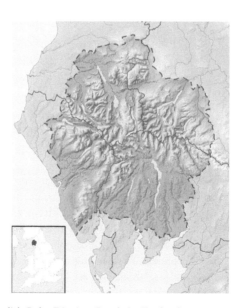

Figure 10.4 The English Lake District, Cumbria, England
Source: Reproduced under the Creative Commons Attribution-Share Alike 3.0 Unported license.

three deep glacial coves and two sharp-topped ridges on the eastern side (Striding Edge and Swirral Edge).

(Wikipedia, 2022)

Writing more personally about Helvellyn in his pictorial guide to this Lakeland fell, Wainwright (1955) notes that:

> Legend and poetry, a lovely name and a lofty altitude combine to encompass Helvellyn in an aura of romance... There is some quality about Helvellyn which endears it in the memory of most people who have stood on its breezy top; although it can be a grim place indeed on a wild night, it is, as a rule, a very friendly giant. If it did not inspire affection, would its devotees return to it so often?
>
> (p. 2)

Still others have offered poetic descriptions of 'old Helvellyn' (William Wordsworth) and 'mighty Helvellyn' (Sir Walter Scott), and topographical descriptions such as 'lofty Helvellyn' (Adam Walker). In an early fragment of prose, Wordsworth (1787) sees 'the Spirit of these Mountains... [as] throned on Helvellyn' (quoted in Owen & Smyser, 2013, p. 24).

Helvellyn stands at 3,118 feet or 950 metres high, and its coordinates (in terms of the global positioning system) are: 54°31'38"N 3°00'58"W. This positioning has more meaning from me since I have been living in Aotearoa New Zealand where, at 36°56'59.99"S 174°36'59.99"E, I am about as far away from Helvellyn as I can be—its antipodal point lies some way south-east of the South Island of New Zealand, only 1,722 miles from where I live!

Notwithstanding these facts, it is a mountain with which I have strong personal associations. My parents (who were from Liverpool and Wallasey) loved fell-walking and took my two older brothers and I to the Lake District most years. At age six, I climbed—or, rather (I suspect), was more carried up—Catbells from Manesty near Keswick and a couple of years later I climbed Helvellyn, the first of many such walks up this mountain from all ascents and, aided by Ordinance Survey maps and Wainwright's (1955) guide, in all weathers. When my father died in 1990, I and other members of my family walked up to Red Tarn where we scattered his ashes. I have had the great pleasure of introducing, my son, Saul, aged seven, to Helvellyn, ascending by Striding Edge (above and left), up which he positively scampered! Later, in 2011, my mother's ashes were also scattered at the side of Red Tarn.

In 2009, I immigrated with my family to Aotearoa New Zealand. As part of my engagement with living in a bicultural nation, specifically with tangata whenua (people of the land), I was introduced to the concept and practice of pepeha, which is a set form of words in te reo (the Māori language) that provides an introduction to the person speaking. It includes them (and/or others) acknowledging the mountain, and the river and/or sea to which they relate—as well as the waka (originally a seagoing canoe), tribal affiliations, and connections to both ancestors and living relatives. When I was learning about how to formulate this, I knew at once that my mountain was Helvellyn: ko Helvellyn te maunga | Helvellyn is the mountain.

Figure 10.5 Striding Edge towards High Spying How
Source: Photo by Gary Rogers, 2005, reproduced under Creative 2.0 CC BY-SA 2.0.

As I now say this quite regularly, I have developed more of a relationship with this mountain. It is the third highest mountain in England, the country of my birth; as the youngest of three children in my family of origin, I am the third highest in my family. As a humanistic therapist, I have trained in, practice, and promote 'third force' psychology. These are significant 'thirds' in my life.

Helvellyn (–you)

In *The Spell of the Sensuous*, quoting a poem about a rock, written by someone from the Omaha people in North America, Abram (1997) makes the point that 'Here words do not speak *about* the world; rather they speak *to* the world, and to the expressive presences that, with us, inhabit the world' (p. 71). In a similar spirit, a number of poets, not least some of the Lakeland poets, have written in a way that addresses the mountain directly, mostly notably Bryan Walter Proctor (1877) in his eponymous homage:

> Helvellyn! Blue Helvellyn! Hill of hills!
> Giant amongst the giants! Lift thy head
> Broad in the sunlight! No loose vapour dims
> Thy barren grandeur; but with front severe,

> Calm, proud, and unabashed, thou look'st upon
> The heights around, – the lake and meadows green
> …
> Behind thee cometh quick the evening pale.
>
> (p. 307)

Proctor talks to Helvellyn as embodied, with limbs ('thy huge limbs that lie | Sleeping far'), a head ('thy head', 'thy summit'), a heart ('thy heart [within which] a secret spirit may now abide'), and veins ('thy veins'). He personifies in Helvellyn other elements thus: 'thy music' (the winds), and 'thy echoes' (the 'rolling thunder'); and, finally, ascribes certain attributes to the mountain: 'thou… fairly ascending', and 'thy lonely state'. This, at least in Proctor's words, is a mountain truly personified.

This association with Helvellyn as 'you' has been enhanced by my basic understanding but continuing study of te reo Māori. In Māori, grammatically, mountains (along with rivers, sea, waka, and certain categories and groups of people) take the more formal 'o' category, as distinct from the more informal 'a' category (Thornton, 1998), thus: 'tō maunga' (your [singular] mountain, which is formal and correct), as distinct from 'tau maunga' (your [singular] mountain, which would be informal and incorrect). What this does—at least for this Pākehā (non-Māori) mind—is to change my relationship with you, Helvellyn, as a respected elder. This is further nuanced by the fact that, of course, your (associative) mountain is not '*your*' (possessive) mountain, a point Alisoun makes (above). Thus, if I ask someone 'Ko wai tō maunga?' ('What's the name of your mountain?'), they would generally answer, 'Ko ____ te maunga', i.e., '*The* mountain is ____' (and not '*My* mountain is ____'.)

Finally, in and from this perspective, I am aware that I have written about I and me to you, Helvellyn, but not about what you, Helvellyn, say to me and us. The closest I get to this is when I am sitting, wedged into the rocks by the side of Red Tarn, cradled by you, being still, and listening, simply listening. In this sense I am perhaps close to Wordsworth's invocation of the Spirit of these mountains which instructs us in 'the lore of Nature' (Wordsworth, 1787, as quoted in Woof, 2015, p. 75).

Helvellyn (–me/I)

Helvellyn

I am pale yellow moorland,
I am blue.
I remember exploding—or was it me?
And, in the dim and distant past, hosting alpine plants and ringlets.
And gave water—which was taken.
I am bleak, I am Winter, I am rain—I am you.
I am popular, and, in that popularity, abused.

I am mined, and undermined.
I have and show my scars, and still spit the stones.
I am ridiculed—and yet...
I am welcoming and kind.
I hurt and kill. (It's impersonal)
I render—and surrender,
I am pale yellow moorland,
I am blue.
I am.

(Tudor, 2022a)

Helvellyn (–us)

The idea that I am one with this/my/the mountain is encapsulated in the Māori whakataukī or saying, 'Ko au te awa, ko te awa ko au | I am the river, and the river is me'. There is a real sense in which I feel and am at one with Helvellyn and feel at home and with it. Yet, it is not an easy relationship. Whilst I have mostly good memories of my childhood, walking on this and other mountains, I have also struggled with it/you. The last two times I have walked to the top of Helvellyn (in 2011 and 2014), I have been all too aware of my lack of fitness, age, and mortality. In 2014 I spent a long time there and thought a lot about mortality—which was both a challenge and a gift. At the same time, when I have made it to Red Tarn, where my parents' ashes are scattered, I have a real sense of coming home, returning to source, and renewing.

Figure 10.6 Helvellyn—Striding Edge, Red Tarn, Red Tarn Beck, Swirral Edge, and Castye Cam
Source: Photo by Simon Ledingham, 2006, reproduced under Creative Commons Attribution Share-alike license 2.0 CC BY-SA 2.0.

Experiencing and perceiving 161

Thinking and feeling about my relationship with Helvellyn, not least in the context of this book, I return to Rogers—and Bernie—and think about the conditions of temperature, moisture, and sunlight. How has this changed the mountain and, therefore, us? Rereading Chapter 6, I am reminded that Helvellyn is still evolving—at 450 million years old, it is a relative youngster. Somewhere between 28,000 and 14,700 years ago, Helvellyn would have looked like a nunatak, that is, a rocky island protruding above an ice field. It is strange—at least to me—to think of Helvellyn, which appears so permanent, as evolving and changing but, as I do, I can get in touch with relating to it/you as a living world. I am reminded of the impact of climate change. For Cumbria, climate change brings a 20 per cent increase in Winter rainfall (Holdgate, 2019/2022) which, in turn, brings risk of flooding. In February 1997, heavy rainfall caused a landslide on the western flanks of Helvellyn which deposited 40 tonnes of debris on a local trunk road (Wilson, 2003). As streams widen their channels—on Helvellyn, Nethermostcove Beck, Red Tarn Beck, Glenridding Beck, Helvellyn Gill, and Whelpside Beck—there is a greater need for flood defences, which leads to more building on the mountain. I am reminded of the species on Helvellyn: the Herdwick sheep, ravens, peregrine falcons, buzzards, ring ouzels, skylarks, wheatears, and the rare mountain ringlet butterfly; and, in the coves east of

Figure 10.7 Helvellyn—The Eastern side, looking down onto Red Tarn from Striding Edge
Source: Photo from Wikimedia Commons, 2012, reproduced under Creative Commons Attribution Share-alike license CC BY-SA 4.0.

Helvellyn's summit, remnant populations of arctic-alpine plants, which have been there since the last Ice Age: including the downy willow, mountain avens, the Alpine mouse-ear, and Alpine meadowgrass. I don't know much about these but as I look at their images, I find them familiar. I am reminded of the impact of the increase in human population over time, and of the impact on the human traffic on the mountain—and of the pollution that a number of them leave. I am always upset about the amount of litter left by humans on this—and other—mountains. I am reminded of forest loss. Between 2001 and 2021, Cumbria lost 14.3k ha of tree cover: a 17 per cent loss (Global Forest Watch, 2022). As a response, Holdgate (2019/2022) states: 'Double the woodlands and restore the bogs and we would offset the emissions of nearly half the resident population of Cumbria.'

As I remind and inform myself of these facts and figures, I re-mind: I turn my mind to Helvellyn; I feel more connected; I mind. I realise that unless I can really think of—and feel—myself as (more) a part of it/you, I miss the sense and essence of being not just part of, but of *being* this living world, which is the project of this book. Like Alisoun, I feel my language is inadequate. The language of wholes, of 'we'ness, of homonomy or belonging is harder than the language of individuals and parts—which is why I am drawn to the concept and language of the organism; in both understanding and being the maintenance, enhancement, and reproduction of the experiencing organism; and how this applies to and *is* us, i.e., our living world.

Part 3
Freedom—with responsibility

This last part of the book comprises two chapters which, building on the intellectual foundations of the book, offer visions of freedom—for therapy and for therapists.

Freedom is a core value of and concept in PCP, which is most clearly expressed in Rogers' perspectives on education and encapsulated in the title of his book on the subject *Freedom to Learn* (Rogers, 1969, 1983; Rogers & Freiberg, 1994; see also Embleton Tudor et al., 2004)

Rogers was one of the few founding fathers—or mothers—of an approach to psychology or therapy to have written anything on education (and/or training), which is another reason why we should take his work in this field seriously. As Rogers (1959/1967f) claims:

> If we value independence, if we are disturbed by the growing conformity of knowledge, of values, of attitudes, which our present system induces, then we may wish to set up conditions of learning which make for uniqueness, for self-direction, and for self-initiated learning.
>
> (p. 292)

We hope that Chapters 11 and 12 offer some stimulus, if not conditions, for reflection, uniqueness, self-direction, and critique that promotes freedom to practice and to think about practice.

DOI: 10.4324/9781003397731-14

11 Setting therapy free

In *The Science Delusion: Freeing the Spirit of Enquiry*, Rupert Sheldrake (2012) argues that modern science is being held back by centuries-old assumptions that have hardened into dogmas. He nominates ten such dogmas that most scientists take for granted, and sets out to refute them.

1 That everything is essentially mechanical.
2 That all matter is unconscious.
3 That the total matter and energy is always the same.
4 That the laws of nature are fixed.
5 That nature is purposeless, and evolution has no goal or direction.
6 That all biological inheritance is material.
7 That minds are in heads and are nothing but the activities of brains.
8 That memories are stored as material traces in brains and are wiped out at death.
9 That unexplained phenomena like telepathy are illusory.
10 That mechanistic medicine is the only kind that really works.

These dogmas or beliefs (Sheldrake uses both terms interchangeably), he argues, are powerful not because scientists think about them critically but because they don't. The *facts* of science are real enough, but the belief system which governs conventional scientific thinking is an act of faith, grounded in a 19th century Western ideology that tradition and 'science' were the only trustworthy bases of knowledge and for action. There is plenty to point at in 20th-century science to discredit the notion of a mechanical, steady state universe but, as Sheldrake is at pains to point out, mainstream Western scientists have preferred to hang on to the 19th-century materialist worldview than to look closely at the assumptions on which their belief system is based.

Sheldrake, a biologist, is closely associated with what is sometimes called 'the new science'. Indeed, his book *A New Science of Life* published in 1981 introduces us to that expression and its particular significance. Around the same time, physicists David Bohm and Fritjof Capra were writing about 'new physics' and 'new paradigm science'. Rogers places himself in their company when he writes in *A Way of Being* (1980/1995i) of the influence on his ideas of a line of radical thinkers from holistic philosopher Jan Smuts to complexity theorist Ilya Prigogene. A central figure in this

DOI: 10.4324/9781003397731-15

company is Alfred North Whitehead, whose philosophy of organism (nowadays more generally known as process philosophy) provided a critical theoretical stimulus to Bohm, Sheldrake, and others, such as Prigogine and Conrad Waddington who contribute to a post-19th-century understanding of life, the universe, and everything.

Our purpose here is not to repeat Sheldrake's arguments challenging the dogmas of conventional science; rather, to use his list of dogmas as a starting point for a discussion of Rogers' challenge to mainstream psychological science and his radical reconceptualisation of therapy. Rogers engages both with setting science free from its dogmas and setting therapy free from the trap it had fallen into—of allowing its theory and practice to become embedded in the dogmas of a scientific worldview which could no longer be taken to represent the whole truth about reality. For Sheldrake, a major element in the scientific delusion is the notion that all matter is unconscious, that nature is purposeless, and that evolution has no direction. Rogers gradually realised that his theory and practice were incompatible with such dogmas.

'This book is, I believe, about life'[1]

The image of the clockwork universe operating under fixed laws has been basic to the Western scientific endeavour since Newton. It affects our very image of what science is. When Sheldrake challenges this image he is writing within a tradition which is sometimes labelled the 'radical enlightenment' (Gare, 2006; Israel, 2009; Jacob, 1981/2006), an alternative tradition in European science which turned to Spinoza, rather than Newton and Descartes, for inspiration. The central hypothesis in this way of thinking about the world may be expressed as 'nature is alive, and we are part of her'.

During the 18th and 19th centuries, the machine theory of life was challenged continually by an alternative school of biology and philosophy called vitalism. Vitalists promoted the concept that organisms were more than machines; they were actually *alive*, that there was some force that shaped the forms of organisms and gave them purposive behaviour. Key figures who maintained the image of an organic universe in the 20th century include Henri Bergson, Alfred North Whitehead, Carl Jung, Arne Naess, and, we would argue, Carl Rogers. Process philosophy, the PCA, and ecophilosophy—and, for that matter, Jungian analysis—are all grounded in the radical idea that aliveness is a fundamental attribute of the universe.

Biologist and ecophilosopher Charles Birch (1993) remarks that it is physics, the science that gave rise to materialism, signals the demise of materialism. Birch warns us 'not to be too sure that the dominant image of the world given to us by the science of the past, which is called the modern worldview, is a picture of the real world' (p. 52). Nevertheless, mechanistic, reductionist thinking still represents orthodox science.

Vitalism remains the ultimate heresy. All biology can, it is alleged, be explained in terms of physics and chemistry. The universe is essentially composed of dead matter. (Although, some of the material entities within it have an extra component called 'life', which can easily be lost.) The vitalist philosophers, however, argued that life is at the very centre of being. The more radical of them, Whitehead argued that the universe is not only alive, but that every electron, atom, and molecule has something akin to experience. The universe can better be imagined as a living, experiencing organism than as a machine.

Sheldrake (1990) points out that when we allow ourselves to think of the universe as alive, it changes the way we think about everything, including the way we do science:

> As soon as we allow ourselves to think of the world as alive, we recognize that a part of us knew this all along. It is like emerging from winter into a new spring. We can begin to reconnect our mental life with our own direct, intuitive experiences of nature… And we can begin to develop a richer understanding of human nature, shaped by tradition and collective memory, linked to the earth and the heavens, related to all forms of life; and consciously open to the creative power expressed in all evolution.
>
> (p. 188)

Whether they are aware of it or not, person-centred therapists act on an implicit understanding that the world is alive. The foundations of the PCA—the actualising tendency and the formative tendency—make no sense at all in a universe composed of dead matter. Unfortunately, the assumptions of conventional materialist and reductionist science are hard to shake off. We readily enough accept the evidence that we are alive, that there is more to us than physics and chemistry, and we even pay animals and plants the compliment of acknowledging their aliveness. However, we are less inclined to accept the conclusion of Whitehead and Sheldrake that life is a quality of matter, not an add-on inserted at a particular moment by either a transcendent deity or a random chemical reaction.

If we take seriously the idea that the universe is alive we will no longer be trapped in the conventional therapeutic paradigm, where we imagine the therapeutic interaction to be an exchange between two distinct and separate individuals. We will see in the interaction of therapist and client the possibility of being 'open to the creative power expressed in all evolution'. We will have greater respect for traditional non-Western therapies which operate within an understanding that we are elements in an organic, animate universe in which we are intrinsically connected with all life, human and nonhuman. The phenomenon we call 'growing' or 'growth' in ourselves and our clients will become not something we do, or even something that happens to us as individuals, but a creative energy in which our lives are embedded. In our 'richer understanding of human nature' we will acknowledge that the healing that our clients experience is 'linked to the earth and the heavens'.

From the beginning, Rogers embraces science as the key to understanding human nature and the process of therapy. However, he strongly resists the notion that the essence of science is to be found in the adoption of the dominant mechanistic paradigm. In the preface to *Client-Centered Therapy* Rogers (1951) makes it clear that he doesn't accept the dogma of a mechanical universe:

> [This book] is about the client and me as we regard with wonder the potent and orderly forces which are evident in this whole experience, forces which seem deeply rooted in the universe as a whole. The book is, I believe, about life, as life vividly reveals itself in the therapeutic process—with its blind power and its tremendous capacity for destruction, but with its overbalancing thrust towards growth, if the opportunity for growth is provided.
>
> (p. xi)

Rogers' conceptualises therapy, even at this early stage, within an image of a universe which is organic, alive, and directional.

Rogers wrote his 1959 paper 'The theory of therapy, personality and interpersonal relationships, as developed in the client centred framework' within the cause and effect model conventional in mainstream science, through a discussion of conditions, process, and outcomes. However, even here, we find him pointing out that this is for reasons of convenience in understanding and that there is no clear distinction between process and outcome. In addition, he is clearly aware that the language of *the actualising tendency, organismic valuing process*, and *self-experience* makes no sense within the mechanistic framework. He was not alone. Other proponents of what is generally labelled the humanistic-existential paradigm in the field of psychology and the related field of psychotherapy likewise rejected the objectivist-mechanistic assumptions underlying mainstream psychological science. Rogers himself acknowledges the influence of Goldstein, Rank, and Angyal on his own thinking; and his contemporaries—Gordon Allport, Frederick Perls, Abraham Maslow, Karen Horney, Roberto Assagioli, and others—had no hesitation in talking about 'growth' and 'becoming'. Such phenomena are incompatible with the notion of a mechanical person within a clockwork universe.

In recent person-centred literature we find increasing attention being paid to the centrality of organismic thinking in Rogers' work. Elsewhere, Keith, arguing that Rogers' basic orientation is that of being an 'organismic theorist', makes the point that: 'Organismic psychology, which is in my view the lost tradition of 20th-century psychology, represents the attempt to put the mind and body back together and treat the human organism as a unified, organised whole' (Tudor, 2010, p. 58).

Tudor and Worrall (2006) place Rogers' organismic psychology firmly within the framework of Whitehead's process philosophy, arguing rightly that we are dealing not simply with a theory of individual psychology but with a cosmology. In his early writings, Rogers was somewhat tentative in his acknowledgement of the philosophical foundations of his theory. However, by the time he wrote in *A Way of Being* (originally published in 1980), of the two foundations of the PCA, i. e., the actualising and formative tendencies (Rogers, 1963/1995e), he had lost any discomfort or sense of ambivalence about rejecting the mechanistic paradigm as a framework for his ideas. The universe he is writing about in *A Way of Being* is not a huge machine, as Newton and mainstream science would have us believe, rather it is alive, a universe in which 'there is in every organism, at whatever level, an underlying flow of movement towards constructive fulfilment of its inherent possibilities' (Rogers, 1963/1995e, p. 117).

Ellingham (1997, 2001) points out a 'critical flaw' in person-centred theory, which is manifested in the dissonance between organicist and mechanistic concepts. He argues that person-centred theory as generally presented is a mix of concepts deriving from two disparate paradigms, two fundamentally different guiding visions of the world. Within person-centred theory we find a clash between the Cartesian-Newtonian paradigm, and an alternative view of reality: 'a paradigm variously labelled holistic, organismic, process, and from which has arisen field theory, general systems theory and ecopsychology' (Ellingham, 2001, p. 96).

We may argue whether Rogers' early writings are marred by this 'critical flaw', but there is no question of where he stood when he came to collate and write *A Way of Being*. When he wrote of the foundation blocks of the PCA, one of which, the actualising tendency, is 'a characteristic of all organic life', and the other, 'a formative tendency in the universe as a whole' (Rogers, 1963/1995e, p. 114), he was clearly not limiting himself to a reconceptualisation of therapy; rather, contributing to a reconceptualisation of the nature of the universe.

Rogers' conviction that there is an inherent tendency in all life to expand and develop itself was shared with many of his contemporaries who identified with a humanistic-existential approach to therapy. Where he differs from most of them is his increasingly explicit formulation of the idea that when we observe our clients 'striving, in the only ways they perceive as available to them, to move toward growth, toward becoming' (p. 119), we should take 'a broader view' and understand their 'becoming' to be embedded in a cosmic becoming.

In explaining what he means by the formative tendency Rogers writes:

> We are tapping in to a tendency which pervades all organic life—a tendency to become all the complexity of which the organism is capable. And on an even larger scale, I believe we are tuning into a potent creative tendency which has formed our universe, from the smallest snowflake to the largest galaxy.
>
> (p. 134)

It is an idea which can be traced to the mediaeval philosophy of Giordano Bruno and the enlightenment philosophy of Baruch Spinoza. We find it reiterated in Sheldrake and other scientists in a variety of disciplines. Most pertinently, it is enunciated by Rogers' contemporary, the Norwegian philosopher and deep ecologist Arne Naess whose ideas have had a profound influence on the development of ecopsychology. He spells out the implications of the organic paradigm for our behaviour, advocating a widening and widening of the notion of 'self':

> Human nature is such that with sufficient allsided maturity we cannot avoid 'identifying' our self with all living beings, beautiful or ugly, big or small, sentient or not... We may be said to be in, of and for Nature from our very beginning.
>
> (Naess, 1995, p. 13)

It is after enunciating his theory of the formative tendency and placing the person-centred way of being firmly within the new scientific paradigm, that Rogers (1980/1995j) describes the 'persons of tomorrow' in a way which resonates with the deep ecologists: 'They feel a closeness to, and a caring for, elemental nature. They are ecologically minded, and they get their pleasure from an alliance with the forces of nature' (p. 351).

'A fruitful new approach'

Rogers was radical in his conviction that human beings are 'choosing' rather than 'caused', free rather than determined. Though, in psychology in the 1940s and 1950s, this kind of thinking was regarded as unscientific, Rogers took life and choice seriously. In this he was at the forefront of a shift in scientific thinking. While he was doing 'proper science' and establishing the credibility of client-centred therapy, his deep assumptions about life were incompatible with the mechanistic fantasy of modernist science. When Rogers (1951) asserts that 'in the psychological realm any simple S-R explanation of behaviour seems almost impossible' (p. 487), he was doing so against the background of an orthodox North American psychology which uncritically accepted the mechanistic paradigm.

John Watson thought he was bringing old-fashioned notions of psychology to an end when, in 1913, he wrote 'Psychology as the behaviorist views it'. In 1929, as Rogers was beginning his career as a therapist, Watson was declaring categorically that 'the most complicated of our adult habits are explicable in terms of chains of simple conditioned responses' (Watson, 1913, p. 3). Mainstream North American psychology tended to agree.

In 1929 behaviourism was the exciting new 'scientific' approach to psychology, fighting against the resistance of old-fashioned, introspective, and instinctual psychology. By the time Rogers wrote *Client-Centered Therapy* (in 1951) the publication of Clark Hull's *Principles of Behaviour* (1943) and B. F. Skinner's *Walden II* (1948), in which Skinner described a utopian society founded upon behaviourist principles, had moved behaviourist psychology to centre stage. It had become the orthodox doctrine, especially among the younger generation of psychologists. Meanwhile, Rogers was publicly accepting and promoting the heretical idea that consciousness, subjectivity, and spontaneity were real aspects of human experience, not the illusions that behaviourists such as Watson and Skinner asserted them to be. Even so, reflecting on his work, Rogers (1990) acknowledges that, early in his career, he had been 'quite deterministic in [his] views' (p. 204). Referring to an early study, regarding which he found himself reluctant to accept the findings, he says:

> I still must have thought that the major factors in the child's behaviour were external factors. It was the outside forces that determine what the person was going to do. I simply felt that there must be some flaw in the study.
>
> (p. 207)

In a 1946 paper, Rogers acknowledges that to some extent he shares with other psychologists a reluctance to admit the concept of human spontaneity into his scientific thinking. Nevertheless, he points out that the evidence of purposeful behaviour cannot adequately be explained in terms of the determinism which is the predominant philosophical background of most psychological work. In 1947, in his address as retiring president of the American Psychological Association, he challenged the prevailing orthodoxy by putting the radical proposition that an individual's behaviour is not determined by external conditions, arguing that, 'We discover within the person, under certain conditions, a capacity for the restructuring and the reorganization of self, and consequently the reorganization of behaviour, which has profound social implications' (Rogers, 1947, p. 368).

He went on to claim that acknowledging the ability of a person to discover new meaning in present and past experiences and to consciously alter behaviour in the light of this new meaning has profound significance for our thinking. We must, he argues, revise the philosophical basis of our work and acknowledge the presence in the organism of a spontaneous force which has the capacity of integration and redirection.

'A part of something larger'

Newton and Descartes were able to combine their belief in a clockwork universe with their Christian faith, by surmising that the creator wound the clock up (so to speak) in the beginning and left it to run down. As Enlightenment philosophy morphed into scientific materialism, the notion of a creator became surplus to requirements and was dropped from the paradigm. However, the clock continued to tick—and to wind down. In the dominant mechanistic image of conventional science, the universe is subject to entropy, leaking energy, wearing out, running down, and so on. Darwin (1859/2009) challenges that conclusion, suggesting that nature is becoming more complex, producing 'higher' forms of life from 'lower' ones; and, for 100 years or more, scientists were content to live with this contradiction. However, this contradiction could not be tolerated forever. When Rogers (1954/1967k) proposes that the 'actualizing tendency' is grounded in 'the directional trend which is evident in all organic and human life—the urge to expand, extend, develop, mature' (p. 351) he was making an observation which was beginning to be taken seriously in the physical sciences. In 1966, Albert Szent-Gyoergyi (1937 Nobel Prize winner in Physiology/Medicine), argued that there is a drive in living matter to perfect itself. He proposed that evolution is not to be imagined as an essentially blind and mechanical process, the product of chance genetic mutations and natural selection; rather, the consequence of a dynamic inherent in all living beings through which forms tend to reach higher and higher forms of organisation, order, and harmony. This is the context within which Rogers (1963/1995e) argues the significance of the formative tendency, observing that every form that we see or know has emerged from a simpler, less complex form, and that 'the universe is always building and creating as well as disintegrating' and 'this process is evident in the human being, too' (p. 126).

Sheldrake (2012) points out that conventional science still clings to the delusion that the 'the laws of nature are fixed' and that 'the total amount of matter and energy is always the same' in spite of abundant evidence pointing to a 'radically evolutionary view of nature' which 'implies an ongoing creativity, establishing new habits and irregularities as nature evolves and that human creativity is part of a vast creative process that has been unfolding through the whole of evolution' (p. 107).

Both Whitehead and Bergson, to whom Sheldrake is largely indebted, put creativity at the centre of the evolutionary process. Whitehead sees human development as a creative response to the lure of something beyond us. He suggests that there is a central organising force that actively seeks to realise the qualities of intensity, harmony, beauty, complexity, enjoyment, and peace.

In refuting the assumption that nature is purposeless, Sheldrake (2012) finds evidence both in his own discipline of biology, and in mathematics, chemistry, quantum mechanics, and complexity theory, which uses the metaphor of gravity to represent the attraction of every molecule, every sensate being, indeed the whole cosmos, towards the future. As Sheldrake puts it: 'Expansive energy, pushing from the past, gives the universe an arrow of time, while through gravitation everything is pulled towards a future unity, at least a virtual unity, and maybe an actual unity as well' (p. 150).

At the end of his discussion of an emergent universe, Sheldrake asks the question: 'What difference does it make?' He points out that, like animals and plants, we have intrinsic powers to maintain, grow, and heal ourselves. Our lives are embedded in larger systems: our societies and cultures, the solar system, the galaxy and, ultimately, the entire evolutionary universe. This resonates with Rogers' understanding that our own and our client's becoming is an element in the becoming of the universe, generated not simply by our own biology but by the cosmic process in which we are enmeshed.

In *On Becoming a Person*, Rogers (1961/1967c) makes it clear that he imagines each new moment as a moment of creation in which we may allow ourselves to be drawn towards the goal of beauty and complexity and become more than what we have been. In *A Way of Being* Rogers (1980/1995i) reiterates this when he suggests that every moment of becoming—whether at the atomic level, the cellular level, the individual human level, or the level of the entire cosmic organism—is an expression of this same dynamic source, and is attracted towards the fulfilment of its greatest possibilities. Furthermore, this creative moment that we experience is not just our private moment. It does not exist apart from the creative moment that the whole universe is experiencing.

In tune with evolutionary flow

One of the key proponents of the argument that the reductionist, mechanistic image of the universe is no longer compatible with the evidence is complexity theorist Stuart Kauffman who, like Sheldrake, suggests that it is time to abandon an understanding of the universe which has ceased to serve us well. Kauffman (2008) contends that we are coming to a new scientific worldview 'that reaches to emergence and to vast unpredictability and unending, ever new diversity and creativity that appear to be beyond natural law itself' (p. 30). He argues that creativity, meaning, value, and purpose are essential qualities of the universe and can be investigated scientifically. In the meantime, 'The universe in its persistent becoming is richer than all our dreamings' (Kauffman, 2000, p. 139).

Rogers would have no argument with that. Furthermore, he was prepared to undertake the challenge of pursuing the implications of this concept for a theory of personality and therapy, and concretising this concept in therapeutic practice. We (two) argue that we (all) need to take Rogers' concept of the formative tendency seriously, and to understand ourselves organically, as cells of a greater organism, so that our actualising, maintenance, and growth is not something we do as individuals, rather, are processes through which we participate creatively in the universe's *becoming*. We also need to take Rogers seriously when he asks us to think of self as process, not as content—and hence the importance of the prior concept of the organism. To think of self as process means we cannot think of ourselves apart from the world. There is one process, and our becoming is part of it:

> This process of the good life is not I am convinced, a life for the fainthearted. It involves the stretching and growing of becoming more and more of one's potentialities. It involves the courage to be. It means launching oneself fully into the stream of life. Yet the deeply exciting thing about human beings is that when the individual is inwardly free, he chooses as the good life this process of becoming.
>
> (Rogers, 1957/1967h, p. 196)

The idea of 'launching oneself fully into the stream of life' is radically at odds with the deterministic psychology which was the intellectual background of Rogers' project of developing an alternative approach to therapy. It is in line with the thinking of contemporary ecopsychologists such as Andy Fisher (2002), who argues that 'one of the main consequences of adjusting to environments that are at odds with our nature is that we come to live according to certain meanings— beliefs, concepts, rules, moral injunctions—that replace our own organismically felt meanings' (p. 76). When we and our clients, as Rogers (1957/1967c) puts it, 'choose as the good life this process of becoming' (p. 127), it is a becoming which is prompted by our organismically felt meanings and is in no way at odds with nature: 'With greater self-awareness, a more informed choice is possible; a choice more free from introjects, a *conscious* choice that is even more in tune with the evolutionary flow' (Rogers, 1963/1995e, p. 127).

'Almost mystical subjectivity'

Rogers' experience as a therapist did not sit well within the orthodox materialist and determinist paradigm of psychological science. Neither was it compatible with the competing paradigm of psychoanalysis, which was deterministic in its own way. In a paper originally published in 1955, Rogers (1955/1967d) reports that:

> As I have acquired experience as a therapist, carrying on the exciting, rewarding experience of psychotherapy, and as I have worked as a scientific investigator to ferret out some of the truth about therapy, I have become increasingly conscious of the gap between these two roles... and as I have become a better investigator, more 'hard-headed' and more scientific (as I believe I have) I have felt an increasing discomfort at the distance between the rigorous objectivity of myself as scientist and the almost mystical subjectivity of myself as therapist.
>
> (p. 200)

Rogers' solution to the antagonism which he reports between the scientific mindset of orthodox psychological science, which denied the relevance, indeed the very reality of consciousness, and the actuality of experience, was to call for a changed view of science, a view which abandoned the assumption that human behaviour could be only understood through objective observation. He insists, rightly, that scientific endeavour has always had its origin in personal subjective experience:

> Science, as well as therapy, as well as all other aspects of living, is rooted in and based upon the immediate, subjective experience of a person. It springs from the inner, total, organismic experiencing which is only partially and imperfectly communicable. It is one phase of subjective living.
>
> (p. 222)

In Rogers' mind, a subjectivist approach to the exploration of reality and the concept of organismic experiencing are intimately connected. He is using the same logic as cosmologist Alfred North Whitehead (1929/1978), palaeontologist Teilhard de Chardin (1959), biologists Conrad Waddington (1962) and Charles Birch (1993), philosopher Christian de Quincey (2002), and systems theorist Ervin Laszlo (2004), all of whom argue that, if experiencing and subjectivity exist anywhere in the universe, then there must be something akin to experiencing and subjectivity 'all the way through'. Like William James, Whitehead argues that the world has both an interior and exterior aspect. While Rogers puts forward this panexperientialist argument explicitly, it is implicit in his thinking that our organismic experiencing is part of something larger. Organismic experiencing involves subjectivity, and is not confined to human beings. Rogers (1973/1995g) acknowledges Martin Buber as one of 'my favourite thinkers' (p. 41) and refers to his work frequently in both *On Becoming a Person*, and *A Way of Being*. For Rogers (1955/1967d), Buber's phrase, the 'I–Thou relationship', means 'a timeless living in the experience which is *between* the client and me... It is the height of personal subjectivity' (p. 202). Subjectivity is not locked up in the individual ego, but shared with the 'thou' in a common experience. In view of Rogers' professed admiration for the thinking of Buber and the Chinese vitalist philosopher Lao-tse, we should, perhaps, conclude that Rogers follows them in extending the 'I–thou relationship' to the nonhuman world. Certainly, he is not confining his understanding of relationship to our connection(s) with(in) the human world when he cites Buber (and Lao-tse) approvingly:

> To interfere with the life of things is to harm both them and oneself... He who imposes himself has the small, manifest might; he who does not impose himself has the great, secret might... The perfected man... does not interfere in the life of beings, he does not impose himself on them, but 'he helps all beings to their freedom (Lao-tse).' Through his unity, he leads them too, to unity, he liberates their nature and their destiny, he releases Tao in them.
> (Buber, 1937, quoted in Rogers, 1973/1995g, pp. 41–42)

In the context of a psychological science (in the 1940s and 1950s) which was obsessed with objectivity and determinism, Rogers' focus on individual subjectivity was radical. Rogers himself was well aware of the radical implications of his position. As Thorne and Mearns (2000) note: 'Rogers knew only too well that he was not only presenting a clinical hypothesis but throwing down a gauntlet with profound existential implications for the living of a human life' (p. 100).

'Space is not a barrier and time has disappeared'

In his paper, 'Persons or science: A philosophical perspective', Rogers (1955/1967d) points out that belief in the findings of scientific research can only occur when there is a subjective readiness to believe. He notes that psychologists are ready to accept research findings which are compatible with their belief systems, even though the evidence is poor. Yet they reject findings which are incompatible with their assumptions, no matter how strong the evidence. The example he offers for the latter is their rejection of the scientific evidence for the phenomenon of extrasensory perception.

Rogers took such phenomena seriously. He expanded on the concept in *A Way of Being*. We should not fall into the trap of thinking that it was just a weird idea that took hold of him in his 80s, and fail to see that it is an integral part of the worldview which framed his thinking. The phenomena of extrasensory perception, telepathy, clairvoyance, intuition, and premonition make no sense within the reductionist mechanistic worldview, but are totally compatible with Whitehead's process philosophy and other models of reality which have emerged, like Whitehead's, from 20th century physics. In such models, the universe consists not of 'things' but of connections between events. Furthermore, in such a vision of reality, each momentary event or 'occasion of experience' (Whitehead's term) involves the whole universe: everything is connected. Einstein famously declared in a letter to a colleague that he was reluctant to accept the notion of 'spooky actions at a distance' (quoted in Born, 1971), but the evidence was against him. Research in quantum physics has adequately demonstrated that Whitehead (1925/1997) was correct in castigating what he called 'the fallacy of simple location'. The notion that the universe consists of distinct objects located in specific places serves us well in practical terms, but has little relation to reality as physics has revealed.

Research in interpersonal neuroscience is currently casting light on how the phenomena of mirror neurons and neural resonance show us to be enmeshed in each other's experience. Furthermore, psi research has become increasingly sophisticated and less constrained by the traditional limitations of laboratory research. Dean Radin (2006, 2009) and Russell Targ (2004) have summed up the evidence; Targ (2004) concludes that: 'After a century of increasingly sophisticated investigations and the more than a thousand controlled studies with combined odds against chance of 10^{104} to 1, there is now strong evidence that some psi phenomena exist' (p. 275).

Sheldrake argues strongly that the dogma that unexplained phenomena such as telepathy are illusory seriously retards the progress of science. Rogers (1973/1995h) expresses the hope that in the coming generations of psychologists there will be some who will dare to investigate the possibility that there is a reality which is not open to our senses,

> a reality in which present, past, and the future intermingled, in which space is not a barrier, and time has disappeared; a reality which can be perceived and known only when we are passively receptive, rather than actively bent on knowing. This is one of the most exciting challenges posed to psychology.
>
> (p. 256)

In another paper (on humanistic education), Rogers (1977/1995a) asserts that 'We need… to learn more about our intuitive abilities, our capacity for sensing with our whole organism' (p. 313). Elsewhere, Bernie (Neville, 2012) argues that when Rogers stresses the significance of the area of 'the intuitive, the psychic, the vast inner space that looms before us… the area that currently seems illogical and irrational' as 'next great frontier of learning' (p. 312), he does so within such a vision of the cosmos. He imagines intuition to be of the same nature as psi phenomena, and to be most manifest when our whole organism is 'in tune with the pulse beat of the world' (p. 313).

Rogers was adequately convinced that parapsychological science had demonstrated the existence of such phenomena as telepathy, precognition, and remote viewing. He observes that 'there is an increased respect for and use of intuition as a powerful tool' (Rogers, 1980/1995j, p. 344), and, in revising his earlier thinking about empathy (Rogers, 1978/1995d) includes a sense of direct, intuitive knowing.

Rogers hypothesises that empathic understanding is a necessary and sufficient condition for the particular kind of transformation that can take place through the interaction between therapist and client. Whitehead's process philosophy goes further, proposing that there is actually no space between us, and that we are not encapsulated in our individuality exchanging messages with each other; rather, we are all aspects of each other. When Rogers (1955/1967d) writes of 'complete unity, singleness, fullness of experiencing in the relationship… [and] a timeless living in the experience which is *between* the client and me' (p. 202), he has abandoned not only the mechanistic paradigm but the humanistic-experiential paradigm of the 1960s which prioritised the distinctive 'self' of the individual and provided the assumptive framework within in which the diverse therapies of the period emerged. He is closer to Christian de Quincey's (2005) radical definition of intersubjectivity as the 'mutual co-arising-and-engagement of interdependent subjects… that *creates* their respective experience' (p. 281). Intersubjectivity, de Quincey argues, is a process of co-creativity, where *relationship* is ontologically primary. It does not depend on individual subjects communicating with each other through language, interpreting each other's meaning and reaching agreement. Conventionally, we have imagined relationship as an artefact of the communication between two persons. In a process cosmology such as that developed by Alfred North Whitehead and expanded by de Quincey, the notion that therapist and client are fundamentally isolated individuals communicating through words and gestures across the space between them is an illusion—and a delusion:

> All individuated subjects co-emerge, or co-arise, as a result of a holistic 'field' of relationships. The being of any one subject is thoroughly dependent on the being of all other subjects with which it is in relationship.
> (de Quincey, 2005, p. 281)

We are relational beings. We do not exist except in our connectedness. For the ecopsychologist that connectedness extends to all human and nonhuman being. We are totally intertwined with the world. In the philosophy of Merleau-Ponty (1968), there is no boundary between self and other: we are an intrinsic part of a complex, living system, no longer able to separate ourselves as individual subjects, from the rest of the earth, human and nonhuman, as object. We are part of what he calls 'the flesh of the world', which is not mere insensate matter but a living being which both senses and is sensed.

> One can say that we perceive the things themselves, that we are the world that thinks itself—or that the world is at the heart of our flesh. In any case, once a body-world relationship is recognized, there is a ramification of my body and a ramification of the world and a correspondence between its inside and my outside and between my inside and its outside.
> (Merleau-Ponty, 1968, p. 136)

This is not new or news to indigenous people and wisdom traditions, but it is for much of the Western—and Northern—intellectual tradition and its discipline of psychology and its therapies.

'A potent, creative tendency'

Ellingham (2011) argues cogently that Rogers made a 'fateful wrong move' in retitling the relationship therapy he had inherited from Otto Rank as 'non-directive therapy' and, later, as 'client-centred therapy'. Notwithstanding our appreciation for, and agreement with, Ellingham's point, we recognise that a number of developments in person-centred theory that emphasise the power of relationship, and especially the 'we' of the therapist–dyad, i.e., Barrett-Lennard (2005), Schmid (2005), Tudor and Worrall (2006), and Tudor (2021, 2022) is solidly grounded in Rogers' relational perspective. It turns our attention away from thinking of the therapist's contact, congruence, unconditional positive regard, and empathic understanding as 'things' we must 'provide', techniques we must practice, skills we must exercise, or even attitudes we must possess—all elements in an atomistic/mechanistic vision of therapy.

Rogers acknowledged the influence of Buber in his focus on the 'we' in the therapist–client interaction. Moreover, he went further than Buber in acknowledging that the 'we' that we experience embraces our current client, all human beings, and all sensate creation; indeed, the whole universe.

For 30 years Arne Naess, the founding genius of the deep ecology movement, attacked our anthropocentric image of the planet and argued that human individual 'self-realisation' is simply one manifestation of the 'self-realisation' of the universe. Naess first distinguished 'deep' ecology from 'shallow' ecology in the 1970s and the distinction is now the basis for the division between ecopsychology and environmental psychology. Environmental psychology has been shaped by the dualistic, mechanistic, objectivist worldview of modern science which shapes most psychological thinking. Ecopsychologists, however, adopt a very different position, which owes much more to Spinoza than it does to Descartes and Newton. They reject the human-in-environment image completely. Humans do not live *in* an environment; we are as much part of the total relational field as anything else. As Naess (1973) contends: 'The total-field model dissolves not only the human-in-environment concept, but every compact thing-in-milieu concept—except when talking at a superficial or preliminary level of communication' (p. 101).

When Rogers (1963/1995e) writes of both client and therapist being a part of something larger and of 'tapping into a tendency which permeates all organic life.... A potent creative tendency which has formed our universe' (p. 134), he was locating his thinking in the same frame. In doing so, he was pointing to the limitations of the humanistic–existential paradigm which had provided the intellectual scaffolding for the development of client-centred therapy. He wanted to set therapy free from the focus on the individual, and the image of it as an interaction between two encapsulated egos. It had become clear to him that to identify self-actualisation with ego indicates a vast underestimation of who we truly are. Naess (1995) is even more explicit: 'Human nature is such that with sufficient all sided maturity we cannot avoid "identifying" our self with all living beings, beautiful or ugly, big or small, sentient or not' (p. 13).

In his final book, Rogers makes it clear that the way of being he was expounding does not only apply to our relations with other human beings. Like Buber, Gandhi, and 'ancient oriental sages' he believed that a respectful, compassionate, non-oppressive stance must extend beyond humankind to the whole of creation. The 'person of tomorrow' (Rogers, 1980/1995j) he suggests, will 'feel a closeness to, and a caring for, elemental nature'. People will be 'ecologically minded' and get their pleasure from an 'alliance with the forces of nature, rather than in the conquest of nature' (p. 351).

Rogers was convinced that humankind was experiencing a paradigm shift, citing with approval the statement of Nobel prizewinning chemist Ilya Prigogine that 'we are at the dawn of a new period, with all the excitement, the hopes and also the risks which are inherent in a new start' (p. 348). He made his own contribution to this paradigm shift. He had a major influence in setting therapy free first from the reductionist-mechanistic fantasies of the behaviourists and second from the individualistic psychology of the humanists. In doing so, we think he should be acknowledged as a major voice in the abandonment of the fantasy of the clockwork universe, joining Whitehead, Sheldrake, Laszlo, and the rest in recognising that we live:

> in a world that consists only of vibrating energy, a world with no solid base, a world of process and change, a world in which the mind, in its larger sense, is both aware of, and creates, the new reality.
>
> (Rogers, 1980/1995j, p. 352)

Note

1 The headings in this chapter are taken from Rogers' writings, thus: 'This book is, I believe, about life' (Rogers, 1951, p. xi); 'A fruitful new approach' (Rogers, 1947, p. 368); 'A part of something larger' (Rogers, 1965/1995e, p. 129); 'In tune with evolutionary flow' (Rogers, 1965/1995e, p. 127); 'Almost mystical subjectivity' (Rogers, 1955/1967d, p. 200); 'Space is not a barrier and time has disappeared' (Rogers, 1973/1995h, p. 256); and 'A potent, creative tendency' (Rogers, 1963/1995e, p. 134).

12 Setting therapists free

In Chapter 11 we discuss how psychotherapy is compromised by its alliance with modern science and, in turn, its 'scientific' assumptions. Using Sheldrake's arguments challenging the dogmas of conventional (modern) science as a framework, we elaborate the challenge that Rogers' ideas pose to mainstream psychological science. In this chapter, we take a similar, critical perspective as we elaborate challenges to the practitioners of that 'science', i.e., the therapists themselves.

Old and new challenges

We revisit and review a paper Rogers delivered as an invited address to the annual meeting of the American Psychological Association (APA) held in Honolulu, Hawaii, on 2 September 1972, and published the following year.

The original article, which appeared in the *American Psychologist*, was reprinted with minor editorial changes under the title 'Some new challenges to the helping professions' as a chapter in Rogers' book *A Way of Being*, and again in Kirschenbaum and Henderson's (1989) *The Carl Rogers Reader* (which reproduced the 1980 chapter). In his brief introduction to this chapter ('Some new challenges…'), Rogers (1973/1995h) reflects that the original paper was a passionate one: 'an outpouring of pent-up criticism' (p. 235); that, whilst, it was originally addressed to psychologists, it applied equally to members of other helping professions and to educators; and, that, whilst some of the language was intemperate and extreme, he did not apologise for it, as 'the issues raised are still valid and controversial' (p. 235)—and, indeed, as far as we're concerned, they still are.

In both the speech and the published article, Rogers (1973/1995h) addresses five questions, each of which, he argues, represents 'a possible move toward the enhancement, the deepening, the enrichment of our profession. Each one, in a word, represents for psychology a step toward self-actualization' (p. 387). In his original article, Rogers acknowledges that these challenges 'had little or no logical sequence' (p. 379). Here, reflecting the philosophical nature of the book, we address Rogers' questions in a slightly different order: one that addresses issues of ontology (Rogers' questions about being whole, and the nature of reality); of epistemology and methodology (about human science); of methodology and method (about professionalisation); and of method (about being designers). In

DOI: 10.4324/9781003397731-16

doing so, we make certain connections between Rogers' challenges to and concern about clinical psychology, psychology and, more broadly, the helping professions, and current concerns about holism; reality or realities; the nature of science; therapeutic interventions; and the professionalisation of therapy. We argue that meeting these challenges keeps therapists open to learning, adapting, and changing—even dancing!—and, in any case, free.

> The only man who is educated is the one who has learned how to learn; the man who has learned how to adapt and change.
> (Rogers, 1969, p. 104)

Can we permit ourselves to be *whole* people?

In his original address and article, Rogers discusses the problem of an educational system in which intellect is all: in which, we might say, thinking is privileged over feeling, the psyche over the soma, and, generally, parts of people rather than people as a whole. Rogers argues forcefully that this system produces dichotomised, dehumanised human beings. In terms of Rogers' critique of the education system, we are reminded of the work of the radical educationalist John Gatto, who identifies eight characteristics of children who are the product of state schooling: being indifferent and hostile to the adult world; having a lack of curiosity and an inability to concentrate; a poor sense of the future, and no sense of the past; a numbness of moral facility; and an unease with intimacy or candour; and being materialistic, and dependent, passive and timid in the face of new challenges. At an extreme, these are the characteristics of a psychopath and, indeed, Gatto (2002) refers to such schooling as the 'psychopathic school' (for further discussion see Embleton Tudor et al., 2004).

Being 'a whole person' is not generally supported by our social context and institutions, educational and others, especially in contexts and societies in or influenced by the Western intellectual tradition, principally due to the legacy of Cartesian dualism. Although, taking a longer view of history, it is important to acknowledge that this dualistic split between mind and body has dominated Western thinking for only the past 400 years (see chapters in Part I of this book). Neither is being whole, holy (spiritual), and, indeed, healthy, all of which share a common etymological root (see Tudor, 1996, 2008b), particularly supported by the dominant language and paradigms of psychology and therapy which generally think about and view people as 'parts' (for a critique of which see Tudor & Worrall, 2006), and as having separate cognitions and behaviours. For the answer as to whether we can permit ourselves to be whole—men, women, or however we identify—we need to look to the concept, psychology, and language of holism.

Holism, from the Greek word ὅλος (holos), meaning all, whole, entire, total, was in modern times, a term coined by Smuts (1926/1987), which he defines as 'The tendency in nature to form wholes that are greater than the sum of the parts through creative evolution' (p. 88). It is a concept that has been developed especially by organismic psychologists and theorists, notably Goldstein (1934/1995);

it is central to gestalt psychology and informs gestalt therapy, as well as much alternative medicine, whose practitioners tend to take an holistic approach to healing. The emphasis on the wholeness of the organism is also found in more recent work in neuroscience (see Damasio, 1994/1996). Holism is, if you like, the conceptual and theoretical base for thinking about human beings—and, indeed, beyond human beings—as whole, rather than as parts or atoms, and is thus the opposite of reductionism. For some years we have been interested in the language of wholes and in developing this language when talking and working with clients, supervisees, and trainees, e.g., 'So, you're totally compassionate towards your partner *and, at the same time*, you're feeling angry in every fibre of your being'. The language, and its implications, is very different from the atomistic and compartmentalised view of people represented by: 'So, there's a part of you that's compassionate…, and there's another part of you that's feeling angry.'

The challenge of being a whole person—whether that is being able to think and feel at the same time, to be objective and subjective, personal and professional, personal and political, or even humanistic and psychodynamic (see Gomez, 2004; Tudor, 2013b), in short to be 'both… and' rather than 'either… or'—is to be able to be and do so in a world, especially the Western and Northern world, in which many are often not permitted and/or discouraged to be or to experience ourselves as whole.

One manifestation of this in the professional sphere is the tendency of professional organisations to split and divide (see Caplow, 1966; Shaw & Tudor, 2022). For example, in the field of psychotherapy in Aotearoa New Zealand, there have been various iterations of the title and, therefore, scope of the main psychotherapy association since its inception some 75 years ago:

1   1947 New Zealand Association of Psychotherapy
2   1974 The New Zealand Association of Psychotherapists, Counsellors and Behaviour Therapists (Incorporated)
3   1981 The New Zealand Association of Psychotherapists and Counsellors (Incorporated)
4   1987 The New Zealand Association of Psychotherapists (Inc)

Whilst there were good reasons advanced at the time for each change (see Manchester & Manchester, 1996), there is a sense in which some of these separations and distinctions represent what Freud (1930/1985) refers to as 'the narcissism of minor differences' (p. 305), which only fuels splits and antagonisms, for instance between psychotherapists and counsellors, rather than contributing to the mental health of the population such associations and its members seek to serve.

Is this the only reality?

Drawing on distinctions which he himself acknowledges dated back to the work of William James, Rogers talks about different types of consciousness, including drug-induced states of expanded consciousness, extra-sensory perception, mystical experiences, paranormal phenomena, psychic discoveries, clairvoyance, pre- and simultaneous cognition, telepathic communication, and the 'separate reality' Carlos Castaneda explored in his meetings with the Yaqui Indian, Don Juan (see Castaneda, 1968, 1971).

Rogers' challenge about diverse consciousness and multiple realities is exciting partly because it acknowledges different experiences and partly because it offers a more horizontal and, we think, egalitarian vision of consciousness (see Chapter 2). We contrast this with more topographical systems of the mind, as proposed by Freud (the conscious, the preconscious, and the unconscious) and, for that matter, the archaeological view of the psyche implied by the term 'depth psychology' and, in PCP by 'relational depth' (Mearns, 1996; Mearns & Cooper, 2005), for a critique of which, see Tudor and Worrall (2006), and Tudor (2014/2017b).

In the bicultural context of Aotearoa New Zealand in which Western forms and frames of knowledge are both challenged by post-colonial studies, decolonisation, and indigeneity, and expanded by indigenous wisdom traditions and their ontologies, epistemologies, and methodologies, Rogers' (1973/1995h) last comment on this particular question is particularly interesting. He suggests that:

> there may be a few who will dare to investigate the possibility that there is a lawful reality which is not open to our five senses; a reality in which present, past, and future are intermingled, in which space is not a barrier and time has disappeared; a reality which can be perceived and known only when we are passively receptive, rather than actively bent on knowing.
>
> (p. 386)

Another and contemporary application is to online teletherapy, which Rodgers et al. (2021) discuss with regard to Rogers' (1957, 1959) conditions of the therapeutic relationship.

The significance of this is that *what* we understand and experience as 'reality', the essence of things, or the subject of our interest or concern, influences and frames *how* we understand and investigate these phenomena—which brings us to epistemology, or theories of knowledge.

Dare we develop a *human* science?

Rogers challenges psychologists to develop a *psychological* science rather than a pseudoscience, one which reflects and represents a personal, subjective knowledge or science rather than an objective, Newtonian science; one which is open to human experience; a science of 'man' (Rogers, 1968) which encompasses: inner cognitive processes; the exploration of inner meanings, including dreams, and the phenomenological world as well as external behaviour. Rogers also makes a plea that the study of such science should promote curiosity and creativity.

Thus, in terms of *how we know what* we know about different consciousness (as above and Chapter 2), we are more persuaded by the view that, to take a phrase from Carper's (1978) work in nursing, there are different 'ways of knowing', i.e.,

- Empirical—which comprises factual knowledge that can be empirically verified. The bias of much of Western research is often disguised by the elision of 'empirically supported treatment' and research that is based on empiricism with 'evidence-based' practice and research. Empirical knowledge is one form of knowledge and one way of knowing, but not necessarily the best or most appropriate for the study of complex organisms such as human beings; and there are many forms of evidence (see Tudor, 2018c, and below).
- Personal—which derives from personal self-understanding through reflective practice and the kind of empathy whereby you put yourself in another's shoes. This way of knowledge, and its collective variant (see below), is valued in indigenous traditions and some Western traditions of knowledge and research such as heuristics and ethnography.
- Ethical—that is knowledge and attitudes, which derive from ethical frameworks and, ultimately, moral philosophy. In research terms, this concerns axiology, from the Greek word αξία (axia), meaning worth or value. Following Levinas (1983), who viewed ethics as 'first philosophy', we would argue that this is the first way of knowing.
- Aesthetic—which, from the Greek αισθάνομαι (aisthanomai) meaning 'I perceive, feel, sense', refers to knowing in and from relating to the here-and-now. In this context, it supports personal knowing and research.

To Carper's taxonomy, we would add:

- Collective—which reflects ways of knowing in community and through generations. We should also note that, in discussing 'science', Rogers was emphasising 'human' in reference to a science that could be more humanised and, in this sense, humanistic, as distinct from dehumanised and/or inhuman. He was not emphasising human over the nonhuman world, though, in order to acknowledge this, we might also add to Carper's taxonomy, ecological ways of knowing.

In 1973 Rogers evaluated this challenge as unmet; 50 years on, we think that, in this respect, our epistemological world, as well as our professional world (see below), has changed—for the worse.

Neither psychotherapy nor counselling are sub-branches of medicine; yet, despite offering a different science and, specifically, an epistemology of human beings based on a knowledge of the mind and body through relationship, and personal, ethical, aesthetic, and collective ways of knowing, therapy appears to have lost confidence in itself. It seeks to follow psychology and medicine in its approach to and language of 'diagnosis' (dynamic formulation), 'treatment', and 'cure'. One example is the Classical school or approach within transactional analysis (TA), which was founded by Dr Eric Berne, himself a medical doctor and psychiatrist (and who dedicated his major work on TA to his father, who was also a doctor, in Latin). Berne (1972/1975b) wrote about stages of cure as: social control, symptomatic relief, transference cure, and script cure. Compare this language with that from the radical psychiatry tradition of TA which, influenced by Karl Marx and Wilhelm Reich, defined alienation as: 'Alienation = Oppression + Mystification + Isolation', and argued that 'Liberation = Awareness + Contact + Action' (Wyckoff & Steiner, 1971). These formulae informed their psycho-political, radical therapeutic practice, and current understandings of alienation (see Tudor, 1997a; Tudor & Worrall, 2006).

Perhaps the most significant example of the way in which the epistemology—or epistemologies—of therapy is being threatened is by the dominance of 'evidence-based practice' in which 'evidence' is based only on an empirical way of knowing and, in the case of the Layard agenda whereby happiness is achieved by means of brief cognitive behavioural therapy, an economic way of knowing—or, at least, organising services (Layard, 2005) (for responses to which, see Dalal, 2018; Loewenthal & Proctor, 2018; Tudor, 2008/2018b).

Research in counselling and psychotherapy is dominated by medical and economic models and the 'drug metaphor', which seeks and implies that there is a specific 'treatment' for specific 'conditions'. Compare this to what Rogers said in an interview recorded in the last year of his life and published posthumously: 'It's so unfortunate that we've so long followed a medical model and not a growth model. A growth model is much more appropriate to most people, to most situations' (in Rogers & Russell, 2002, p. 259).

It is, in our view, unfortunate that most government guidelines for therapy practice and research follow and promote the medical model and not a growth model, and are thus, by definition, irrelevant to and biased against therapeutic approaches based on growth models. Furthermore, such government guidelines and bodies generally present their criteria as neutral, discount qualitative research methods and other 'practice-based evidence' (Morgan & Juriansz, 2002), and, therefore, other therapeutic approaches, let alone other wisdom traditions with their own epistemologies (and ontologies, methodologies, and methods). I have been somewhat surprised, for example, that in universities in Aotearoa

New Zealand, kaupapa Māori research methodology, i.e., research based on Māori wisdom, protocol, and cultural principles (G. Smith, 1997; L. Smith, 1999), is not taught as a matter of course in research papers, although, in more recent years, there has been a lively debate—in Aotearoa New Zealand and other countries—about decolonising and indigenising curricula.

Finally (on this), it is more than unfortunate that some psychotherapy education/training programmes spend even any time teaching the widely discredited *Diagnostic and Statistical Manual of Mental Disorders* (DSM) (for example, Karter & Kamens, 2019), which offers psychiatric—and some might say, an insurance-based—approach to 'mental disorders', rather than *psychotherapeutic* understandings of distress, dis-ease, and alienation.

Giving away our knowledge (science), our ways of knowing, and our languages compromises the integrity of independent therapy and renders it and its practitioners less authoritative. This is why we favour therapy education courses based in universities to position themselves as sciences rather than arts.

Dare we do away with professionalism?

This challenge was, in Rogers' (1973/1995h) words, 'the radical possibility of sweeping away our procedures for professionalization' (p. 243). 'I know what heresy that is', he wrote, continuing

> what terror it strikes in the heart of the person who has struggled to become a 'professional.' But I have seen the moves toward certification, licensure, attempts to exclude charlatans, from a vantage point of many years, and it is my considered judgment that they fail in their aims.
>
> (p. 243)

Fifty years ago, Rogers advanced a number of concerns:

1 That professionalisation tends to freeze the profession in a past image.
2 That certification is not equivalent to competence, and that licensure or, here, registration does not guarantee competence or good practice. Rogers put this quite baldly: 'There are as many *certified* charlatans and exploiters of people as there are uncertified' (p. 244).
3 That professionalism builds up a rigid bureaucracy.

The debate and decision about professional registration in the United Kingdom (in the mid-2000s) cut across 'theoretical lines', in that there were (and probably still are) many humanistic practitioners in favour of the state registration of psychotherapists as well as the statutory regulation of psychotherapy. In Aotearoa New Zealand, the profession, in the form of the New Zealand Association of Psychotherapists, sought and obtained registration and, thus, we inhabit a 'post-regulation' landscape in which a relatively small but significant and active minority choose not to register and still practise psychotherapy but do not call themselves psychotherapists (see Tudor, 2011b, 2017/2020). For a number of years, the New Zealand Association of Counsellors has debated whether to follow psychologists and psychotherapists in becoming 'agents of the state'.

The arguments against statutory regulation have been well made in a number of publications. Here, specifically with regard to Rogers' challenges and concerns, we make a number of brief points.

1 That there are a number of models of regulation—from the least restrictive (self-regulation, negative licensing, and co-regulation), through more restrictive (reservation of title, and/or certain core practices), to the most restrictive (reservation of title and practice) (see Macleod & McSherry, 2007). Professions need to apprise themselves of these in order to decide which model is most suitable for the profession, the context it inhabits, and the clients it serves in our changing world.
2 That, as there is no evidence that the state registration of psychotherapists or counsellors protects the public, most legislation under which professions are

regulated, such as, in Aotearoa New Zealand, the *Health Practitioners Competence Assurance Act 2003* (which, significantly, was closely based on the *Medical Practitioners' Act 1995*), is not the appropriate legislation under which to seek recognition. This is important if professions are to consider how they protect the public, and ensure competence, and not to devolve or upload that responsibility to the state. This is a particularly poignant observation to make in Aotearoa New Zealand, as it was only 60 years ago that the *Tohunga Suppression Act 1907*, under which Māori healers and political activists were outlawed, was repealed (in 1962) (see Woodard, 2014).

3   That, as the activities of the 'responsible authority', the Psychotherapists Board of Aotearoa New Zealand, have demonstrated, state registration has led to an increasing and an increasingly rigid, persecutory, and avaricious bureaucracy (Tudor, 2017/2020b). Since it was established in 2007, the Board has consistently sought to extend its powers from simply organising the registration of psychotherapists to approving supervisors who, it has explicitly stated, it regards as 'agents of the Board'; to seeking to register and thereby to restrict overseas 'visiting Educators' (see Tudor, 2012), a proposal which was mediated by the profession; and, currently, to accredit education/training programmes and courses—a process that, to date, has taken some 12 years! In doing so, the Board (which comprises six unelected practitioners and two lay people) is clearly heading towards the most restrictive model of regulation, i.e., reservation of title and whole-scale practice restriction, and stands as a caution to psychotherapists in other countries to be careful what they wish for (Tudor, 2013a).

4   That, in addition, to the number of publications which address the arguments for and against statutory regulation of therapy, there is now an established literature that is highly critical of other moves towards increasing professionalisation; of 'defensive therapy'; of 'short-termism' in therapy; and of the increasing managerial and audit culture in therapy and other helping professions (see below).

Some argue that professionalisation, and even state registration, brings with it certain recognition and status. Certainly, over the past 50 years, psychology has self-actualised, but, arguably, it is at the expense of aligning itself alongside, even inside, the medical profession and the medical model. It is, however, a *self*-actualisation, i.e., actualising a particular self-concept of what it means to be a 'professional', rather than organismic actualising which tends and trends to both homonomy (belonging) and autonomy (self-determination), or social actualisation (Keyes, 1998). In an increasingly regulatory and bureaucratic world, we need to reclaim the internal locus of control and self- and co-regulation with regard to our selves, our peers, and our profession(s), rather than simply seeking external confirmation of our identity and status (see Embleton Tudor, 2017/2020).

Do we dare to be designers?

This challenge was 'to develop an approach which is focused on constructing the new, not repairing the old' (Rogers, 1973/1995h, p. 240). In elaborating, we refer to an approach to TA which Keith and a colleague and friend, Graeme Summers, developed over 20 years (Summers & Tudor, 2000; Tudor & Summers, 2014). Drawing on field theory and social constructivism, 'co-creative TA' emphasises the present-centred nature of the therapeutic relationship—or therapeutic relating—and the co-creative nature of transactions, life scripts (which they rename 'co-creative identity'), ego states ('co-creative personality'), and games (co-creative confirmations). They frame this approach within a positive health perspective on and in TA, as distinct from what they view as an undue emphasis on psychopathology, and argue that co-creative TA provides a narrative or story about TA itself that offers new and contemporary meanings to old transactional truths. They talk about this kind of therapy as offering clients new relational possibilities, what Stern (1998) refers to as a 'ways-of-being-with', which, of course, echoes, Rogers' idea of the PCA being a way of being. Interestingly, in the light of Rogers' challenge about being designers, in their original article, Graeme and Keith argue that, as helping professionals, we need to see ourselves as transactional designers as much as transactional analysts (Summers & Tudor, 2021). As de Bono (1992) put it: 'With analysis we are interested in what is. With design we become interested in what could be' (p. 63). This fits well with the question Rogers (1973/1995h) goes on to elaborate about the wider view of psychologists and, more broadly, other helping professionals: 'whether [we] can develop a future-oriented, preventive approach, or whether it will forever be identified with a past-oriented remedial function' (p. 240). Addressing this question himself, Rogers argues:

> That we need to be radical in the true sense of the word and get to the root of things, which may involve leaving our secure offices and getting out into the community; and include taking our practice outdoors and working with people in the/ir environment.
>
> That we need to be at the heart of designing environments. How many of us are involved in designing our working environments?
>
> That we need to be involved in building flexible institutions which account for and prioritise human relationships, and continuing relationships with the community—and, we would add, our environment.
>
> That we need to be significant in relationships between minority groups, and to bring about improved communication in 'interface situations', as Rogers puts it: 'between these often bitter and alienated groups and the culture that has often mistreated them'.
>
> (p. 243)

Looking back further

At the beginning of his article, Rogers (1973/1995h) writes that he was tempted to reminisce about certain developments in the profession, which he identified as:

> the struggle to prove that psychologists could actually and legally carry on psychotherapy, involving various professional struggles with psychiatry; the attempt to open up therapy to detailed scrutiny and empirical research; the effort to build a theoretical formulation that would release clinical work from

the dying orthodoxy of psychoanalytic dogma and promote diversified and creative thinking; the efforts to broaden the scope and the vision of clinical and other psychologists; and perhaps finally the effort to help psychologists become true change agents, not simply remedial appliers of psychic Band-Aids.

(p. 236)

Whilst Rogers chooses not to yield to the temptation of reminiscing about these efforts, we do want to revisit what Rogers obviously considered to be major achievements that the psychology profession had made to date (then over some 50 years), as I think that, in a number of ways, psychology as a discipline and as a profession has taken some retrogressive steps, which have both impacted on and echo in other helping professions.

- Regarding *the right to practice*. Whilst this now may not be a problem for the majority of psychologists, the fact that, in many countries, psychologists have allied themselves with the medical profession and, specifically, with other health professionals who have sought and gained state registration, means that it has become harder for other related professionals, such as therapists, to practice without also being state registered. Indeed, what we refer to as 'the domino argument', i.e., 'psychologists are registered, so we should be registered, too', is now being used in arguments for statutory regulation. The professional struggles for legitimacy that psychologists had with psychiatrists have been replaced by struggles that other professionals with less power or standing are having with the state and with agents of the state—and, in some cases, with psychologists (see Dillon, 2017/2020).
- Regarding *detailed scrutiny*. Rogers does not elaborate on what he means by this, but we—and others—would argue that there is now too much scrutiny of therapy, with the result that it is becoming too defensive (Clarkson, 1995); too 'straight' (Samuels & Williams, 2001); too managed and audited (King & Moutsou, 2010); and too safe and domesticated (Totton, 2011).
- Regarding *research*. Whilst therapy has opened up to 'empirical research' (as Rogers put it), this, too, has not come without problems, most of which derive, again, from psychology being overly influenced by medicine and the medical paradigm regarding research. There are some signs of good news, in that the so-called 'gold standard' of research is beginning to be challenged from within the medical establishment by people such as Rawlins (2008), and by the American Psychological Association (APA), whose definition of 'evidence-based psychological practice' has stated that it comprises: 'the integration of the best available research *with clinical expertise in the context of patient characteristics, culture and preferences* [emphasis added]' (APA, 2006, p. 273). This reflects the view that practitioners can and should be informed both by researchers and academics and by clients, and holds the possibility if not the promise that we can move away from the obsession with a restricted 'evidence-based practice' to a more open, inclusive, and diverse 'practice-based evidence' (see Morgan & Juriansz, 2002).

- Regarding *theoretical formulation(s) which promote/s diversified and creative thinking*. In his original article Rogers (1973/1995h) writes forcibly about 'the dying orthodoxy of psychoanalytic dogma' (p. 236) and, whilst this, in its dogmatic form, has largely died, and, clearly, there are many different theoretical formulations of psychology and therapy, psychoanalytic and psychodynamic thinking is still hegemonic; and, across theoretical orientations, 'diversified and creative thinking' (p. 236) is a minority, even a peripheral, activity. Despite the fact that it is commonly accepted that the therapeutic relationship is central to therapeutic effectiveness and that such relationship is informed by factors common to and across therapeutic approaches and modalities, most education and training is still organised in terms of therapeutic orientation and modality. For psychologists, this means that, by and large, cognitive behavioural therapy is privileged over forms of therapy within humanistic psychology.
- Regarding *a broader scope and vision for clinical and other psychologists*. We would say that the scope and vision of clinical psychologists have, with rare exceptions, narrowed: community psychology, popular and influential in the 1970s and 1980s, has all but disappeared, and few people talk about 'critical psychology', a tradition which is still supported by the e-journal *The Journal of Critical Psychology, Counselling and Psychotherapy* (https://www.egalitarianpublishing.com/jcpcp.html).
- Regarding *psychologists as change agents*. Whilst there still are some community psychologists and some radical psychologists, these appear to be a dying breed, which leaves organisational psychologists as the predominant change agents.

Picking up the challenge

Rogers (1973/1995h) ends his article by asking psychologists (the APA in 1972) and, in a sense and more broadly, other helping professionals and professions: 'Do we dare?' (p. 387). In Māori culture, as part of the pōwhiri (welcome) process, one of the hosts may lay down a wero or challenge, usually in the form of a leaf. Wero literally means 'to cast a spear', and, if laid down, is done so by an elder with some authority. It is up to the manuhiri or visitors whether or not to pick up the challenge. In 1972, with some 45 years' experience in clinical psychology, Rogers was certainly an elder with some authority. Interestingly, with the exception of one short letter from Lee Steiner (1974), there is no evidence, at least within the pages of the *American Psychologist*, that Rogers' challenge was ever picked up by the APA. Although Rogers has been rated as one of the most influential psychologists of all time (Haggbloom et al., 2002), it appears that, with regard to his challenge, he was not taken seriously. Not surprisingly, we do take him—and his challenge—seriously and consider his article as ahead of its time.

Reading it again, now over 50 years on, it has lost none of its validity, controversy—or emotionality—and still sounds quite radical. Rogers certainly 'dared' to attack some of the 'sacred cows' (then and now) of the professional world. It is also remarkably prescient in that, part Nostradamus and part Cassandra, it anticipated many of the key struggles in the helping professions today. Perhaps the greatest challenge for us, and the next generation or two, is to continue to address these challenges so that colleagues in another 40 years are not saying similar things about the challenges that they will be facing—and, by way of ending, we pick up Rogers' challenge and respond: 'Yes, we dare.'

A manifesto for daring

1   We can and must dare to continue to develop a human science in which we are confident in our contribution as helpers in whatever profession, and not least if we identify as humanistic practitioners, and that this contribution is equally if not more valid for our clients than one based on a medical model.
2   We can and must dare to be designers, and, with our clients, to 'co-create' possibilities, solutions, and more possibilities.
3   We can and must dare to do away with the professionalism and professionalisation of therapy, and to reclaim these activities for the vocational, political, spiritual, and subversive practice they are—or, at least, and especially in post-regulatory societies, to allow for a pluralism in professions in which diverse and divergent views about these activities can be argued, without fear, favour, discrimination, or oppression.
4   We can and must dare to be and to reclaim ourselves as whole people, and not to compartmentalise our or other people's psyches; and to develop the language of wholes as distinct from parts.
5   We can and must dare to acknowledge and honour the reality of different realities, and to hold psychologies and psychotherapies that have and acknowledge spirit.
6   We can and must dare to dare; to paraphrase T.S. Eliot (1915), to dare disturb the universe. We suggest that this includes being reflective; being critical—for those in education, this may be framed as being 'a critic and conscience of society' (as enshrined in the New Zealand *Education Amendment Act 1990*); being able to discriminate (see Dalal, 2011/2019); being radical, i.e., getting back to our roots, being 'bolshie', i.e., in the minority, being disobedient (see Steiner, 1981); and being intolerant when faced with oppression and injustice.

Epilogue

Given that Bernie died during the project that was/is this book, I (Keith) decided to write and co-ordinate a final chapter which stands as an epilogue to the book and to Bernie's work and life.

13 Setting Bernie free

A eulogy

Keith Tudor

This is a chapter I didn't want to write.

I began writing this chapter while Bernie Neville, co-author of this book, was alive and, by the time I will have finished and revised this, and you, the reader, are reading it, Bernie will be dead—or, at least, no longer with us in the form in which we have known him. When, in late January 2021, I heard the news of his diagnosis and prognosis, notwithstanding my own grief, I knew that I wanted to complete this book project or, at least, to complete as much of it as possible while he was still alive. Herein lay my first loss, in that I recognised that the process of completing the book would now be different—as it has been.

Bernie and I wrote about our relationship in the Introduction to this book and, indeed, the whole book represents the culmination of our intellectual and personal relationship over some 15 years. Therein lies a second loss, as I know that Bernie had more to say and to offer, that he and I had much more to discuss and debate, and that I—we all—had more to 'download' and learn from and with him.

In one of the hypograms in Chapter 2, we (Bernie and I) quote Keller's (1986) words on substance: 'I am not a separate and enduring substance but an event in which the universe composes itself' (p. 186). That being the case, I can only say that the universe composed itself well and wisely in the substance we knew as Bernie for the 82 years of his life.

One of the things I appreciated about Bernie is that he lived his life in a way that embodied the theory he espoused: as a process. I know other colleagues and friends appreciated this about him, and so invited some who were close to him and his ideas to offer their thoughts about him.

Bernie Neville—The substance that was, and is

The person

> Bernie was a person. This sounds simple and simple-minded. It is. But being a person is not easy. Especially today. Being a person means being genuine, humane, empathically connected to others. It means not succumbing to forces that pull one from those stances of attitude and practice, whether in

DOI: 10.4324/9781003397731-18

counselling and psychotherapy, education, philosophy, or politics, all areas where Bernie's personhood shined through.

(Jeff Cornelius-White)

My memories of Bernard William 'Bernie' Neville center on my first impression of his kind character, gentle manners and nice smile. Afterwards, I experienced his capacity for interesting conversations combined with a self-effacing, humble attitude. I will always treasure our friendship; our personal contacts, although not frequent, were always significant.

(Alberto Segrera)

Bernie walked his talk. Three scenarios come to mind immediately. Bernie was famously hospitable, and staying in his home in Melbourne, I realised that, at 81, with quiet compassion and humility he was still choosing to use the inferior outside bathroom facilities so that the women refugees with whom he shared his home could continue to feel safe and comfortable having sole use of the indoor bathroom. Visiting our home, he observed a series of interactions between our daughter, with her puppy, and her father (Keith), and he became a sweet and tough advocate for the young ones (sweet for our daughter and tough with Keith), bringing to bear his customary sense of humour, his scholarship, and his lively intelligence. It became a long, whiskey-fuelled, robust discussion in which there were no obvious winners, but good humour and much food for thought. I remember, also with great affection, the time he took us to his home in Yarra and shared joyful memories of his family growing up, and I observed his deep connection to and respect for the land there. Whether as teacher and academic, internationalist, or steward of the land, from his writing about life and the world to the smallest interpersonal interactions, Bernie was consistent in trying to understand meaning and motive, and in taking action. Like so many, I was enriched by our encounters.

(Louise Embleton Tudor)

At the launch of the Australian edition of *The Life of Things* (Neville, 2012) Bernie's former colleague from LaTrobe University, David Tacey commented that Bernie lived and breathed everything that had been written into *The Life of Things*.

Bernie's personhood meant to me something ordinary yet amazing, commonplace yet rare, idiosyncratic yet universal. I don't feel like I can find the words to convey what I'm trying to say, but what I can say is that Bernie had something special that enriched me and likely many others with whom he came into contact, and, by extensionality, those with additional degrees of separation.

(Ross Crisp)

The last time I saw Bernie, he gave me an extra-large black T-shirt with multicoloured writing on it. He told me I should wear it. I didn't understand what it said or why I should wear it. I immediately put it on top of the collared shirt I was wearing. It hung low in its oversized fit. I felt awkward because of the weight and size, more than the sudden change in garb. Eventually, I asked questions or he explained, and I googled for information on the topic. I don't recall that part. The point of this story is not what did the shirt say or why he wanted me to wear it. The point is that I knew I should wear it because Bernie had asked me. I knew that I was being a given a gift beyond cotton fabric, a gift connecting humanity through Bernie's undeniable, inexplicable, indisputable personhood. When I felt the heaviness of the fabric and considered my internal state, I realised I was swimming not only in the size of the shirt, but in my smallness to fill out the meaning of the shirt as a gift, as a connection, and as less of a literal and figurative person than Bernie.

(Jeff Cornelius-White)

The common man and an 'Aussie bloke'

During a morning-tea break at the PCE conference in Vienna in 2018, Bernie told me that he preferred to speak in the manner of the 'common man'. He did so for audiences that listened attentively to his ideas concerning the evolution of Carl Rogers' theory and practice, the Gods of classical mythologies, and the seers of multiple realities, among them Alfred North Whitehead (his favourite philosopher), Jean Gebser, Carl Jung, and Arne Naess.

(Ross Crisp)

Very quickly after Bernie and I had first met (in 2006), Bernie kindly invited me to visit him in Australia. Fortunately, I was able to do so the following year during which I ran a workshop in Melbourne sponsored by the Victorian Association of Humanistic and Transpersonal Psychology. I'll never forget the way Bernie introduced me by saying simply 'This is Keith Tudor. He's a good bloke'! It was the shortest but one of the warmest introductions I have ever experienced. Moreover, he followed this up at the end of the day's workshop when he closed by saying, 'Thanks, Keith, that was ripper'! (I didn't know what 'ripper' meant, but understood that it was positive.) As I got to know Bernie, I found him to be equally at ease in an intense and academic discussion about ideas and a playful and sometimes equally intense conversation about sport—usually the relative merits of the Australian Wallabies and the New Zealand All Blacks; and equally at home, at home, at a conference, in a workshop, in a street café, and a late night bar. I loved the intellect, the heart, the man, and the 'bloke'. Sometimes, after a long day, which might have involved a workshop or some writing, a meal, and sometimes a film (which always seemed to be intense Australian, and which I'm sure is a genre), he would often say 'Fancy a drink?' and we'd walk, slowly, to one of the local bars in Thornbury (where he lived in Melbourne), have a night cap, and shoot the breeze. They were precious times.

(Keith Tudor)

Figure 13.1 Bernie Neville—on Mt Toolbewong
Source: Photo—Keith Tudor, 2019).

The in-between

> Bernie belongs to an era in which person-centered therapists and their clients focus upon the 'in-between', and the 'we' of interaction in which they participate in each other's process of becoming. In encounter groups, I observed his gift for self-disclosure that conveyed his humanity and genuineness, and which was at the same time apposite to the often controversial topics being discussed by other participants.
>
> (Ross Crisp)

The educator

> We were both more interested in education than in psychotherapy and shared the sense that it was missing the real gold and settling for fools' gold to focus only on the transactional level dynamics of the human dramas that unfolded in person-centered gatherings. We both believed that humanity needed an educational process that would reconnect us with the deeper mythic flows of being. Bernie taught me how to see in the small moments of encounter the mythic songs and to hear in the voices of participants traces of gods who had been part of human psychological reality for millennia.
>
> (Maureen O'Hara)

> Bernie, the academic, is a restless educator in his marrowbone and is on the dancing edge of theoretic understanding; linking ideas that peel open the mind and experience of student and academic alike. His enthusiasm when exploring new theorists and new ideas is electric and stimulates the personal researcher in

each of us. The non-exhaustive list of Carl Rogers, Eugene Gendlin, Jean Gebser, G. Feuerstein, R. Kegan. K. Egan, and, of course, Alfred North Whitehead reveal the multi-perspectival life of this beloved strolling educator.

(Patricia McCann)

One man, many tribes

> Our dear Bernie was an assiduous participant in international forums, world conferences, and other PCA meetings, notwithstanding the very long displacements this demanded from his native Australia. His benevolent appearance was combined with his ample experience as a person-centered educator and a passion for humanising organisations and exploring and developing the philosophical foundations for social and transcendental implications.
>
> (Alberto Segrera)

Drawing on Warner's (2000) metaphor of the PCA as being 'one nation, many tribes', I see Bernie Neville as not belonging to a single tribe or village but as the local balladeer, who occasionally wanders from tribe to tribe, village to village, sending a welcoming smile before him, arriving to sit comfortably at the fireside, establish relationships and networks, and sharing his stories from other communities. The villagers always welcome him with a ready smile, focus on him as he attempts to learn their language as a sign of respect, and share food with him. He, in turn, hears stories of their current and profound issues, listens deeply to what is underneath their words, and responds to their spoken and unspoken need.

Bernie the balladeer also travels beyond the nation and tribes of PCE and brings back the folded, colourful cloth of other nations (of process philosophy and Jungian psychology) which promise so much. He unfolds the cloth at our feet so we can see the brilliance of multiple perspectives in the stories and gifts he brings. He then leaves the wisdom behind until he comes again.

> Next time, the village hears that he is coming and stand to greet him, but he arrives from an unexpected direction: he has walked a different path, and explored different notions but nevertheless arrives again at the village to be greeted like a favourite brother. He is not clothed in the same apparel, does not offer the same songs or stories. He makes people feel comfortable but is nonetheless thought-provoking. Yet he is still the favourite brother who shares wisdom.
>
> (Patricia McCann)

Breadth and depth

> The launch of his book *The Life of Things*, held at the Phoenix Institute in Melbourne, was a festive occasion—with much repartee—that honoured Bernie's vision for a person-centered ecopsychology. For myself, his book remains especially memorable for its clarity in conveying the breadth and depth—and the paradoxes and contradictions—of Rogers' ideas that are applicable to all social situations.
>
> (Ross Crisp)

One of the first workshops I heard Bernie talk at was about the ancient Gods. To be honest, I didn't get it at all. It all seemed a bit esoteric and far removed from the more pragmatic person-centred theory and literature I was used to. But as I listened more, and tuned into what Bernie was trying to communicate, I realised there was a depth to his thinking that I had initially missed, and that I needed to 'catch up' with him in order to understand where he was coming from. I realised I had underestimated this tall, lanky Australian with a dry sense of humour. He didn't fit my image of a serious philosophical thinker with profound insight into the world. But, as I came to know him more, both in person and through his writing, I came to appreciate just how much we will miss him. Gods bless you Bernie, for all that you have passed on to us, and for so much more left hinted at, but still unsaid.

(Brian Rodgers)

Trickster and brother

The news of Bernie's impending death arrived as a gut punch. That trickster memory kept Bernie preserved in my mind's eye as the larger than life young Aussie that I first encountered almost 50 years ago so it is hard to take in this mortal reality. We met when I took my maiden flight with Carl Rogers, Natalie Rogers, Jared Kass, John K Wood, and Maria Bowen as facilitator at the first PCA workshop in California. From the very beginning I was enchanted by his intellectual curiosity and integrity and the way he, like me, saw the radical philosophical depth of Rogerian thought… My own thinking about the paradigmatic radicalism of Rogers' ideas was greatly strengthened by conversations with Bernie over the years. At the other side of the world, Bernie remained in my heart as the brother I only saw occasionally but was always part of my psychic universe. His work and his bold yet delicate way of being have lit up the world. As he said at the end of his last book about the mythic dynamics in a time of the global COVID-19 pandemic, 'Whether we summon them or not, the gods are present'. May they be with him and us at this time of loss and gratitude.

(Maureen O'Hara)

The last time I spoke to him (12 February 2021), Bernie was at home. He looked frail but was still alert, and was sitting up and enjoying a whiskey. We spoke for a few minutes, some of them about the book, and then he needed to go. I said, 'It'd be great to see you and talk again, but, if this is the last time we speak, kei te pai | all good'. He smiled. Then, in acknowledgement of that shared story (noted above), I said, 'That was ripper'! Without a moment's hesitation, Bernie responded, 'That was *bloody* ripper'!

(Keith Tudor)

Setting ourselves free

All this is true—and, of course, it is also about setting us free to let Bernie go: to recognise that he has gone, *and* that he remains. Whether we conceptualise this as 'His spirit remains', 'His spirit lives on', or whatever, I know that some essence of Bernie is in me, and will remain as long as I live, and so on.

At funerals, people often read poems, and sing song or hymns. Some of these suffer from being overused and, thereby, losing some of their potency. One such is the poem by Henry Scott-Holland 'Death is nothing at all' (which was, in fact, part of a sermon, entitled, 'Death: The king of terrors' that he preached in 1910 during the period King Edward VII was lying in state). When I first heard the poem, I liked it. Later, I came to think that it was comforting partly as it discounted the reality of death, loss, distance—and, indeed, 'reality'. However, in the weeks between January 2021 (hearing the news about Bernie) and (completing this manuscript), I kept coming back to this poem. Reflecting on it and on this book, it seems to me to represent much of what we are saying in the book—about the nature of life, 'things', substance, relationship, continuity, and, therefore, time and space.

So, with sadness, fondness, laughter, and a sense of continuity and anticipation, we (Bernie and I) end this particular particle and connection between us, and between us and you the reader and the world, with this poem.

> Death is nothing at all.
> It does not count.
> I have only slipped away into the next room.
> Nothing has happened.
>
> Everything remains exactly as it was.
> I am I, and you are you,
> and the old life that we lived so fondly together is untouched, unchanged.
> Whatever we were to each other, that we are still.
>
> Call me by the old familiar name.
> Speak of me in the easy way which you always used.
> Put no difference into your tone.
> Wear no forced air of solemnity or sorrow.
>
> Laugh as we always laughed at the little jokes that we enjoyed together.
> Play, smile, think of me, pray for me.
> Let my name be ever the household word that it always was.
> Let it be spoken without an effort, without the ghost of a shadow upon it.
>
> Life means all that it ever meant.
> It is the same as it ever was.
> There is absolute and unbroken continuity.
> What is this death but a negligible accident?

Why should I be out of mind because I am out of sight?
I am but waiting for you, for an interval,
somewhere very near,
just round the corner.

All is well.
Nothing is hurt; nothing is lost.
One brief moment and all will be as it was before.
How we shall laugh at the trouble of parting when we meet again!
(Scott-Holland, 1910)

Thanks, Bernie—that was bloody ripper!

References

Abram, D. (1997). *The spell of the sensuous*. Random House.
Aczel, A. (2003). *Entanglement*. Plume.
Akhtar, S. (2015). Hope and hopelessness: An introductory overview. In S. Akhtar & M. K. O'Neil (Eds.), *Hopelessness: Developmental, cultural, and clinical realms* (pp. 3–19). Karnac.
Alexander, F. (1946). The principle of the corrective emotional experience. In F. Alexander & T. French (Eds.), *Psychoanalytic therapy: Principles and application* (pp. 66–70). Ronald.
Alexander, F., & French, T. (Eds.). (1946). *Psychoanalytic therapy: Principles and application*. Ronald.
Alford, C. F. (1994). *Group psychology and political theory*. Yale University Press.
Amatuzzi, M. M. (1984). The jungle, the way and the goal. In A. S. Segrera (Ed.), *Proceedings of the first international forum on the person-centred approach*. Universidad Iberamericana.
American Psychological Association Presidential Task Force on Evidence-based Practice. (2006). Evidence-based practice in psychology. *American Psychologist*, 61(4), 271–285. https://doi/10.1037/0003-066X.61.4.271.
Angyal, A. (1941). *Foundations for a science of personality*. Commonwealth Fund.
Asay, T. P., & Lambert, M. J. (1999). The empirical case for the common factors in therapy: Qualitative findings. In M. A. Hubble, B. L. Duncan, & S. D. Miller (Eds.), *The heart and soul of change: What works in therapy* (pp. 33–36). American Psychological Association.
Atwood, G., & Stolorow, R. (1996). *A meeting of minds: Mutuality in psychoanalysis*. Analytic Press.
Baldwin, L. V., & Dekar, P. R. (2013). *In an inescapable network of mutuality: Martin Luther King, Jr. and the globalization of an ethical ideal*. Cascade Books.
Barr, J. (1987). The therapeutic relationship model: Perspectives on the core of the healing process. *Transactional Analysis Journal*, 17, 134–140. https://doi.org/10.1177/036215378701700402.
Barrett-Lennard, G. T. (1962). Dimensions of therapist response as casual factors in therapeutic change. *Psychological Monographs*, 76(43), 1–36. https://doi.org/10.1037/h0093918.
Barrett-Lennard, G. T. (1997). The recovery of empathy—toward others and self. In A. C. Bohart & L. S. Greenberg (Eds.), *Empathy reconsidered: New directions in psychotherapy* (pp. 103–121). American Psychological Association.
Barrett-Lennard, G. (2005). *Relationship at the centre: Healing in a troubled world*. Whurr.
Barrett-Lennard, G. T. (2009). From personality to relationship: Path of thought and practice. *Person-Centered & Experiential Psychotherapies*, 8(2), 79–93. https://doi.org/10.1080/14779757.2009.9688482.

References

Barrett-Lennard, G. (2013). *The relationship paradigm: Human being beyond individualism*. Palgrave Macmillan.

Bazzano, M. (2012). Immanent vitality: Reflections on the actualizing tendency. *Person-Centered & Experiential Psychotherapies*, 11(2), 137–151. https://doi.org/10.1080/14779757.2012.672930.

Berne, E. (1962). The classifications of positions. *Transactional Analysis Bulletin*, 1(3), 23.

Berne, E. (1975a). *Transactional analysis in psychotherapy*. Souvenir Press. (Original work published 1961)

Berne, E. (1975b). *What do you say after you say hello? The psychology of human destiny*. Penguin. (Original work published 1972)

Bion, W. R. (1967). Notes on memory and desire. *Psychoanalytic Forum*, 2, 272–273.

Birch, C. (1993). *Regaining compassion for humanity and nature*. Chalice Press.

Birch, C. (2008). *Science and soul*. UNSW Press.

Birch, C., & Cobb, J. (1981). *The liberation of life*. Cambridge University Press.

Blair, L. (2011). Ecopsychology and the person-centred approach: Exploring the relationship. *Counselling Psychology Review*, 26(1), 47–56.

Bohart, A. C. & Tallman, K. (1999). *How clients make therapy work*. American Psychological Association.

Bohm, D. (1980). *Wholeness and the implicate order*. Routledge and Kegan Paul.

Bohm, D. (1996). *On dialogue*. Routledge.

Born, M. (1971). *The Born-Einstein letters*. MacMillan.

Bowen, M. V.-B. (1984). Spirituality and person-centred approach: Interconnectedness in the universe and in psychotherapy. In A. S. Segrera (Ed.), *Proceedings of the first international forum on the person-centred approach*. Universidad Iberamericana.

Bozarth, J. D. (1998). *Person-centred therapy: A revolutionary paradigm*. PCCS Books.

Bregman, R. (2020). *Humankind: A hopeful history* (E. Moore & E. Manton, Trans.). Bloomsbury.

Breit, S., Kupferberg, A., Rogler, G., & Hasler, G. (2018). Vagus nerve as modulator of the brain-gut axis in psychiatric and inflammatory disorders. *Frontiers in Psychiatry*, 9, 44. https://doi.org/10.3389/fpsyt.2018.00044.

Brown, M. (1990). *The healing touch: An introduction to organismic psychotherapy*. Liferhythm.

Buber, M. (1937). *I and Thou*. T&T Clark. (Original work published 1923)

Buechler, S. (1995). Hope as inspiration in psychoanalysis. *Psychoanalytic Dialogues*, 5, 63–74. https://doi.org/10.1080/10481889509539050.

Bühler, C. (1972). *Introduction to humanistic psychology*. Wadsworth Publishing.

Byrne, N., & McCarthy, I. (2007). The dialectical structure of hope and despair: A fifth province approach. In C. Flaskas, I. McCarthy, & J. Sheehan (Eds.), *Hope and despair in narrative and family therapy: Adversity, forgiveness and reconciliation* (pp. 36–48). Routledge.

Cameron, R. (2000). Subtle energy awareness: Bridging the psyche and soma. *Person-Centred Practice*, 10(2), 66–74.

Cameron, R. (2002a). In the space between. In G. Wyatt (Ed.), *Contact and perception* (pp. 259–273). PCCS Books.

Cameron, R. (2002b). Subtle body work. In T. Staunton (Ed.), *Advances in body psychotherapy* (pp. 148–171). Brunner-Routledge.

Cameron, R. (2004). Shaking the spirit. In K. Tudor & M. Worrall (Eds.), *Freedom to practise: Person-centred approaches to supervision* (pp. 171–188). PCCS Books.

Cameron, R. (2015). *The unseen dance: Subtle interactions and their implications for the therapeutic relationship* [Doctoral thesis, University of Edinburgh]. Edinburgh Research Archive. https://era.ed.ac.uk/handle/1842/11811.

Caplow, T. (1966). The sequence of professionalization. In H. M. Vollmer & D. L. Mills (Eds.), *Professionalization* (pp. 20–21). Prentice Hall.
Capra, F. (1983). *The turning point*. Harper Collins.
Carkhuff, R. R. (1969a). *Helping and human relations Vol I: Selection and training*. Holt, Rinehart & Winston.
Carkhuff, R. R. (1969b). *Helping and human relations Vol II: Practice and research*. Holt, Rinehart & Winston.
Carper, B. (1978). Fundamental ways of knowing in nursing. *Advances in Nursing Science*, 1(1), 13–23.
Casteneda, C. (1968). *The teachings of Don Juan: A Yaqui way of knowing*. Ballantine Books.
Casteneda, C. (1971). *A separate reality: Further conversations with Don Juan*. Simon & Schuster.
Ceballos, G., Ehrlich, P. R., Barnosky, A. D., García, A., Pringle, R. M., & Palmer, T. M. (2015). Accelerated modern human-induced species losses: Entering the sixth mass extinction. *Science Advances*, 1(5), e1400253. https://doi.org/10.1126/sciadv.1400253.
Chalquist, C. (2007). *Terrapsychology: Reengaging of the soul of place*. Spring Journal Books.
Charles, R. (2004). *Intuition in psychotherapy and counselling*. Whurr.
Clark, P. U., Dyke, A. S., Shakun, J. D., Carlson, A. E., Clark, J., Wohlfarth, B., Mitrovica, J. X., Hostetler, S. W., & McCabe, A. M. (2009). The last glacial maximum. *Science*, 325(5941), 710–714. https://doi.org/10.1126/science.1172873.
Clarkson, P. (1990). A multiplicity of psychotherapeutic relationships. *British Journal of Psychotherapy*, 7(2), 148–163. https://doi.org/10.1111/j.1752-0118.1990.tb01329.x.
Clarkson, P. (1995). *The therapeutic relationship*. Whurr.
Coats, L. L., Cole, K. L., & Mead, J. I. (2008). 50,000 years of vegetation and climate history on the Colorado Plateau, Utah and Arizona, USA. *Quaternary Research*, 70(2), 322–338. https://doi.org/10.1016/j.yqres.2008.04.006.
Connell, R. (2008). *Southern theory: The global dynamics of knowledge in social science*. Allen & Unwin.
Cook, F. H. (1989). The jewel net of Indra. In J. B. Callicott & R. T. Ames (Eds.), *Nature in Asian traditions of thought: Essays in environmental philosophy* (pp. 213–229). State University of New York Press.
Cooper, M. (2001). Embodied empathy. In S. Haugh & T. Merry (Eds.), *Empathy* (pp. 218–229). PCCS Books.
Cornelius-White, J. H. D. (2007). The actualizing and formative tendencies: Prioritizing the motivational constructs of the person-centered approach. *Person-Centered & Experiential Psychotherapies*, 6(2), 129–140. https://doi.org/10.1080/14779757.2007.9688436.
Crucifix, M. (2012). Oscillators and relaxation phenomena in Pleistocene climate theory. Philosophical transactions. *Series A, Mathematical, Physical, and Engineering Sciences*, 370(1962), 1140–1165. https://doi.org/10.1098/rsta.2011.0315.
Csikszentmihalyi, M. (1990). *Flow: The psychology of optimal experience*. Harper and Row.
Dalal, F. (2018). *CBT: The cognitive behavioral tsunami*. Routledge.
Dalal, F. (2019). *Thought paralysis: The virtues of discrimination*. Karnac Books. (Original work published 2011)
Damasio, L. (1996). *Descartes' error: Emotion, reason and the human brain*. Vintage. (Original work published 1994)
Darwin, C. (2009). *On the origin of the species*. John Murray. (Original work published 1859)
David Suzuki Foundation. (1992). *Declaration of interdependence*. www.davidsuzuki.org/About_us/Declaration_of_Interdependence.asp.
de Bono, E. (1992). *Serious creativity*. HarperCollins.

References

Dell, W. (2005). *Notes for a new mind*. Universal Publishers.

de Quincey, C. (2002). *Radical nature: Rediscovering the soul of matter*. Invisible Cities Press.

de Quincey, C. (2005). *Radical knowing: Understanding consciousness through relationship*. Park Street Press.

Dillon, G. (2020). The road to registration: The New Zealand Association for Psychotherapy and its long search for identity and recognition through legislation. In K. Tudor (Ed.), *Pluralism in psychotherapy: Critical reflections from a post-regulation landscape*. Tuwhera Open Access Books. https://ojs.aut.ac.nz/tuwhera-open-monographs/catalog/book/1 (Original work published 2017)

Donald, M. (1991). *Origins of the modern mind*. Harvard University Press.

Donald, M. (2001). *A mind so rare*. Norton.

Duncan, B. I., Miller, S. D., & Sparks, J. A. (2004). *The heroic client: A revolutionary way to improve effectiveness through client-directed, outcome-informed therapy*. Jossey-Bass.

Egan, G. (1980). *The skilled helper*. Cengage Learning.

Egan, K. (1997). *The educated mind*. University of Chicago Press.

Eliot, T. S. (1915). The love song of J. Alfred Prufrock. *Poetry: A Magazine of Verse*, June, 130–135.

Eliot, T. S. (1963). The wasteland. In *Collected poems (1909–1962)* (pp. 61–86). Faber & Faber. (Original work published 1922)

Ellingham, I. (1997). On the quest for a person-centred paradigm. *Counselling*, 8(1), 52–55.

Ellingham, I. (2001). Carl Rogers' 'congruence' as an organismic not a Freudian concept. In G. Wyatt (Ed.), *Congruence* (pp. 96–115). PCCS Books.

Ellingham, I. (2011). Carl Rogers' fateful wrong move in the development of Rogerian relational therapy: Retitling 'relationship therapy' 'non-directive therapy'. *Person-Centred and Experiential Psychotherapies*, 10(3), 181–197. https://doi.org/10.1080/14779757.2011.599515.

Embleton Tudor, L. (2020). The neuroscience and politics of regulation. In K. Tudor (Ed.), *Pluralism in psychotherapy: Critical reflections from a post-regulation landscape*. Tuwhera Open Access Books. https://ojs.aut.ac.nz/tuwhera-open-monographs/catalog/book/1 (Original work published 2017)

Embleton Tudor, L., Keemar, K., Tudor, K., Valentine, J., & Worrall, M. (2004). *The person-centred approach: A contemporary introduction*. Palgrave.

Embleton Tudor, L., & Tudor, K. (1996). Is the client always right? A person-centred perspective. *Cahoots*, 55, 33–43.

Embleton Tudor, L., & Tudor, K. (Ed.). (2002). Psyche and soma [Special issue]. *Person-Centred Practice*, 10(2), 61–65.

Fairbairn, W. R. D. (1952). *Psychological studies of the personality*. Routledge & Kegan Paul.

Feldenkrais, M. (1981). *The elusive obvious*. Meta Publications.

Fernald, P. S. (2000). Carl Rogers: Body-centered counselor. *Journal of Counselling & Development*, 78(2), 172–179. https://doi.org/10.1002/j.1556-6676.2000.tb02575.x.

Finke, J. (2018). Beyond and on the side of orthodox client-centeredness—On balancing the conceptual framework of PCT. *Person-Centered & Experiential Psychotherapies*, 17(1), 19–36. https://doi.org/10.1080/14779757.2017.1398677.

Fisher, A. (2002). *Radical ecopsychology: Psychology in the service of life*. State University of New York Press.

Fisher, A. (2013). *Radical ecopsychology: Psychology in the service of life* (2nd ed.). State University of New York Press.

Fonagy, P. (2001). *Attachment theory and psychoanalysis*. Other Press.

Fonagy, P., Gergely, G., Jurist, E., & Target, M. (2002). *Affect regulation, mentalization and the development of the self.* Other Press.
Fordham, M. (1957). *New developments in analytical psychology.* Routledge and Kegan Paul.
Fossey, D. (1983). *Gorillas in the mist.* Houghton Mifflin.
Fox, W. (1990). *Toward a transpersonal ecology: Developing new foundations for environmentalism.* Shambhala.
Frankl, V. (1969). *The will to meaning.* New American Library.
Freud, S. (1984a). The ego and the id. In J. Strachey (Trans. & Ed.) & A. Dickson (Ed.), *The pelican Freud library Vol.11: On metapsychology* (pp. 339–407). Penguin. (Original work published 1923)
Freud, S. (1984b). The unconscious. In J. Strachey (Trans. & Ed.) & A. Dickson (Ed.), *The pelican Freud library Vol.11: On metapsychology* (pp. 159–222). Penguin. (Original work published 1915)
Freud, S. (1985). Civilization and its discontents. In J. Strachey (Trans. & Ed.) & A. Dickson (Ed.), *The pelican Freud library vol.12: Civilization, society and religion* (pp. 243–240). Penguin. (Original work published 1930)
Fromm, E. (1968). *The revolution of hope.* Harper & Row.
Gare, A. (2006). *Reviving the rational and enlightenment: Process philosophy and the struggle for democracy.* Paper presented at the 6th International Whitehead Conference, 3–6 July, Salzburg, Austria.
Gare, A. (2007/2008). The arts and the radical Enlightenment. *The Structurist*, 47, 20–27.
Gare, A. (2014). Deep ecology, the radical Enlightenment and ecological civilization. *The Trumpeter*, 30(2), 184–205.
Gare, A. (2017). *The philosophical foundations of ecological civilization: A manifesto for the future.* Routledge Environmental Humanities.
Gatto, J. T. (2002). *Dumbing us down: The hidden curriculum of compulsory schooling.* New Society Publishers.
Gebser, J. (1986). *The ever-present origin* (N. Barstad & A. Mickunas, Trans.). Ohio University Press. (Original work published 1949)
Gendlin, E. (1981). *Focusing.* Bantam.
Gendlin, E., & Lemke, J. (1983). A critique of relativity and localization. *Mathematical Modelling*, 4, 61–72.
Gentry, A. H. (1988). Changes in plant community diversity and floristic composition on environmental and geographical gradients. *Annals of the Missouri Botanical Garden*, 75, 1–34.
Gibson, D. (2004). On being received: A supervisee's view of being supervised. In K. Tudor & M. Worrall (Eds.), *Freedom to practise: Person-centred approaches to supervision* (pp. 31–42). PCCS Books.
Gillman, L. N., Wright, S. D., Cusens, J., McBride, P. D., Malhi, Y., Whittaker, R. J. (2015). Latitude, productivity and species richness. *Global Ecology and Biogeography*, 24(1), 107–117. https://doi.org/10.1111/geb.12245.
Global Forest Watch. (2022). *Forest loss.* https://www.globalforestwatch.org/.
Goldberg, A. (Ed.). (1980). *Advances in self-psychology.* International Universities Press.
Goldstein, K. (1995). *The organism.* Zone Books. (Original work published 1934)
Gomez, L. (2004). Humanistic or psychodynamic: What is the difference and do we have to make a choice? *Self & Society*, 31(6), 5–19. https://doi.org/10.1080/03060497.2004.11086244.
Greenberg, J. R., & Mitchell, S. (1983). *Object relations in psychoanalytic theory.* Harvard University Press.
Greene, G. (1950). *The third man.* Penguin.

Greening, T., Rogers, C., May, R., & Friedman, M. (1986). Good and evil. In R. May, C. Rogers, A. Maslow, and other humanistic psychologists (Eds.), *Politics and innocence: A humanistic debate* (pp. 10–42). Saybrook Publishers.

Greenway, R. (1995). The wildness effect and ecopsychology. In T. Roszak, M. E. Gomes, & A. D. Kanner (Eds.), *Ecopsychology: Restoring the Earth, healing the mind* (pp. 122–135). Sierra Club Books.

Guardini, R. (1955). Die begegnung: Ein beitrag zur struktur des daseins [The encounter: A contribution to the structure of existence]. *Hochland*, 47(3), 224–234.

Haenga-Collins, M., Solomon, M., Woodard, W., Rodgers, B., & Tudor, K. (2019). Bicultural encounter. *Person-Centered & Experiential Psychotherapies*, 18(3), 255–273. https://doi.org/10.1080/14779757.2019.1650806.

Haggbloom, S. J., Warnick, R., Warnick, J. E., Jones, V. K., Yarbrough, G. L., Russell, T. M., Borecky, C. M., McGahhey, R., Powell, J. L., Beavers, J., & Monte, E. (2002). The 100 most eminent psychologists of the 20th century. *Review of General Psychology*, 6, 139–152. https://doi.org/10.1037/1089-2680.6.2.139.

Hakl, H. T. (2014). *Eranos: An alternative intellectual history of the twentieth century*. Routledge.

Hall, C., & Lindzey, G. (1957). *Theories of personality*. Wiley.

Hall, C., & Lindzey, G. (1970). *Theories of personality* (2nd ed.). Wiley.

Hall, C., & Lindzey, G. (1978). *Theories of personality* (3rd ed.). Wiley.

Hall, F., & Neville, B. (2011). The effects of an Australian heritage: Counselling in a land down under. In C. Lago (Ed.), *The handbook of transcultural counselling and psychotherapy* (pp. 220–230). Open University Press.

Hardin, G. (1968). The tragedy of the commons. *Science*, 162, 1243–1248.

Hart, S. (2010). *The impact of attachment*. W.W. Norton.

Hart, T. (2000). Deep empathy. In T. Hart & P. Nelson (Eds.), *Transpersonal knowing: Exploring the horizon of consciousness* (pp. 253–270). State University of New York Press.

Hauer, M. E., Fussell, E., Mueller, V., Burkett, M., Call, M., Abel, K., McLeman, R., & Wrathall, D. (2020). Sea-level rise and human migration. *Nature Reviews Earth & Environment*, 1, 28–39. https://doi.org/10.1038/s43017-019-0002-9.

Haule, J. (2011). *Jung in the 21st century* (2 vols.). Routledge.

Heidegger, M. (1978). *Being and time*. Blackwell. (Original work published 1927)

Hepburn, A., & Jackson, C. (2009). Rethinking subjectivity: A discursive psychological approach to cognition and emotion. In D. Fox, I. Prilleltensky, & S. Austin (Eds.), *Critical psychology: An introduction* (pp. 176–194). Sage.

Hillman, J. (1982). Anima mundi: The return of soul to the world. *Spring*, 71–83.

Hillman, J. (1995). A psyche the size of the Earth: A psychological foreword. In T. Roszak, M. E. Gomes, & A. D. Kanner (Eds.), *Ecopsychology: Restoring the Earth, healing the mind* (pp. xvii–xxiii). Sierra Club Books.

Hoffman, I. (1992). Some practical implications of a social constructivist view of the psychoanalytic situation. *Psychoanalytic Dialogues*, 2(3), 287–304. https://doi.org/10.1080/10481889209538934.

Holdgate, M. (2022). What does climate change really mean for Cumbria? Friends of the Lake District [website]. https://www.friendsofthelakedistrict.org.uk/news/what-does-climate-change-really-mean-for-cumbria.

House, R. (2003). *Therapy beyond modernity: Deconstructing and transcending profession-centred therapy*. Karnac.

House, R. (2010). *In, against and beyond therapy: Critical essays towards a 'post-professional' era*. PCCS Books.

House, R., & Totton, N. (Eds.). (1997). *Implausible professions: Arguments for pluralism and autonomy in psychotherapy and counselling*. PCCS Books.

Hull, C. (1943). *Principles of behaviour*. Appleton-Century.

Inguilli, K., & Lindbloom, G. (2013). Connection to nature and psychological resilience. *Ecopsychology*, 5(1), 52–55. https://doi.org/10.1089/eco.2012.0042.

Ioane, J., & Tudor, K. (2017). The fa'ásamoa, person-centred theory, and cross-cultural practice. *Person-Centered and Experiential Psychotherapies*, 16(4), 287–302. https://doi.org/10.1080/14779757.2017.1361467.

Ioane, J., & Tudor, K. (2022). Family-centred therapy: Implications of Pacific spirituality for person-centred theory and practice. *Person-Centered and Experiential Psychotherapies*. https://doi.org/10.1080/14779757.2022.2100812.

Israel, J. (2002). *The radical Enlightenment: Philosophy and the making of modernity 1650–1750*. Oxford University Press.

Israel, J. (2009). *A revolution of the mind: Radical enlightenment and the intellectual origins of modern democracy*. Princeton University Press.

Jacob, M. (2006). *The radical enlightenment: Pantheists, freemasons and republicans*. Cornerstone Book Publishers. (Original work published 1981)

Jaynes, J. (1976). *The origin of consciousness in the breakdown of the bicameral mind*. Houghton Mifflin.

Johnson, C. N., Balmford, A., Brook, B. W., Buettel, J. C., Galetti, M., Guangchun, L., & Wilmshurst, J. M. (2017). Biodiversity losses and conservation responses in the Anthropocene. *Science*, 356(6335), 270–275. https://doi.org/10.1126/science.aam9317.

Jung, C. G. (1964). *Man and his symbols*. Aldus Books.

Jung, C. G. (1971). Psychological types. In *The collected works of C.G. Jung, Vol. 6: Psychological types* (H. Read, M. Fordham, & G. Adler, Eds.; H. G. Baynes, Trans.). Princeton University Press. (Original work published 1921)

Jung, C. G. (1977). *Jung speaking: Interviews and encounters* (W. McGuire & R. F. C. Hull, Eds.; H. G. Baynes, Trans.). Princeton University Press.

Jung, C. G. (1979). The stages of life. In *The collected works of Carl Gustav Jung. Vol 8: The structure and dynamics of the psyche* (H. Read, M. Fordham, & G. Adler Eds.; R. F. C. Hull, Trans.; pp. 387–403). Routledge and Kegan Paul. (Original work published 1931)

Kahn, E. (1985). Heinz Kohut and Carl Rogers: A timely comparison. *American Psychologist*, 40, 893–904. https://doi.org/10.1037/0003-066X.40.8.893.

Kantor, J. R. (1924a). *Principles of psychology* (Vol.1). Knopf.

Kantor, J. R. (1924b). *Principles of psychology* (Vol.2). Knopf.

Kaplan, R., & Kaplan, S. (1989). *The experience of nature: A psychological perspective*. Ulrich's Bookstore.

Karter, J. M., & Kamens, S. R. (2019). Toward conceptual competence in psychiatric diagnosis: An ecological model for critiques of the DSM. In S. Steingard (Ed.), *Critical psychiatry* (pp. 17–69). Springer.

Kauffman, S. (2000). *Investigations*. Oxford University Press.

Kauffman, S. (2008). *Reinventing the sacred: A new view of science, reason, and religion*. Basic Books.

Kearney, R. (Ed.). (1984). Emmanuel Lévinas. In *Dialogues with contemporary continental thinkers: The phenomenological heritage* (pp. 47–70). Manchester University Press.

Kegan, R. (1983). *The evolving self: Problem and process in human development*. Harvard University Press.

Kegan, R. (1998). *In over our heads: The mental demands of modern life*. Harvard University Press.

Keil, W. W. (1996). Hermeneutic empathy in client-centered therapy. In U. Esser, H. Pabst, & G-W. Speierer (Eds.), *The power of the person-centered approach. New challenges—perspectives—answers* (pp. 65–80). GwG.
Keller, C. (1986). *From a broken web: Separation, sexism and self*. Beacon Press.
Keller, C. (2008). *On the mystery*. Fortress Press.
Key, D., & Tudor, K. (2023). *Ecotherapy: A field guide*. CONFER.
Keyes, C. L. M. (1998). Social well-being. *Social Psychology Quarterly*, 61(2), 121–140. https://doi.org/10.2307/2787065.
Keys, S. (2018). *Hope in despair: The shadows stand as a proof of the light*. Keynote speech delivered to the 13th World Conference for Person-Centered & Experiential Psychotherapy & Counseling, 6th–12th July 2018, Vienna, Austria.
Kidner, D. (2001). *Nature and psyche*. State University of New York Press.
Kierkegaard, S. (1941). *The sickness unto death*. Princeton University Press.
Kierkegaard, S. (1985). *Fear and trembling*. Penguin.
King, L., & Moutsou, C. (Eds.). (2010) *Rethinking audit cultures: A critical look at evidence-based practice in psychotherapy and beyond*. PCCS Books
King, M. (2003). *The Penguin history of New Zealand*. Penguin.
Kinsella, J. (2020). *Displaced: A rural life*. Transit Lounge Publishing.
Kirschenbaum, H. (2007). *The life and work of Carl Rogers*. PCCS Books.
Kirschenbaum, H., & Henderson, V. (1989). *The Carl Rogers reader*. Constable.
Klein, G. S. (1976). *Psychoanalytic theory: An exploration of essentials*. International Universities Press.
Klein, M. (1952). Notes on some schizoid mechanisms. In M. Klein, P. Heimann, S. Isaacs, & J. Riviere (Eds.), *Developments in psycho-analysis* (pp. 292–320). Hogarth Press.
Klein, M. (1975). Envy and gratitude. In *Envy and gratitude and other works (1946–1963)* (pp. 176–235). Free Press. (Original work published 1957)
Kohut, H. (1978). *The restoration of the self*. International Universities Press.
Komiya, N., & Tudor, K. (2016). "Reading the air", finding common ground: Reconsidering Rogers' therapeutic conditions as a framework for understanding therapy in Japan. *Asia Pacific Journal of Counselling & Psychotherapy*, 17(1&2), 26–38. https://doi.org/10.1080/21507686.2016.1157088.
Kot, G. (1999). Reapers and weepers: Interview with Tom Waits. *Chicago Tribune*.
Kramer, R. (1995). The birth of client-centered therapy: Carl Rogers, Otto Rank, and 'the beyond'. *Journal of Humanistic Psychology*, 35(4), 54–110. https://doi.org/10.1177/00221678950354005.
Kriz, J. (2008). *Self-actualization: Person-centred approach and systems theory*. PCCS Books.
Künkel, F. (1984). *Fritz Kunkel: Selected writings* (J. A. Sanford, Ed.). Paulist Press.
Laing, R. D. (1967). *Politics of experience and the bird of paradise*. Pantheon.
Lambert, M. (1992). Psychotherapy outcome research: Implications for integrative and eclectic therapists. In J. C. Norcross & M. R. Goldfried (Eds.), *Handbook of psychotherapy integration* (pp. 94–129). Basic Books.
Lambert, M. J., & Bergin, A. E. (1994). The effectiveness of psychotherapy. In A. E. Bergin & S. L. Garfield (Eds.), *Handbook of psychotherapy and behavior change* (4th ed.; pp. 143–189). Wiley.
Lao Tse. (1973). *Te tao ching* (G-F. Feng, & J. English, Trans.) Wildwood House. (Original work written 600 BCE)
Larsen, D., Edey, W., & LeMay, L. (2007). Understanding the role of hope in counselling: Exploring the intentional uses of hope. *Counselling Psychology Quarterly*, 20(4), 401–416. https://doi.org/10.1080/09515070701690036.

Lasch, C. (1979). *The culture of narcissism*. Warner Books.
Laszlo, E. (2003). *The connectivity hypothesis: Foundations of an integral science of quantum, cosmos, life, and consciousness*. State University of New York Press.
Laszlo, E. (2004). *Science and Akashic field: An integral theory of everything*. Inner Traditions.
Layard, R. (2005). *Happiness: Lessons from a new science*. Penguin.
Leberger, R., Rosa, I. M. D., Guerra, C. A., Wolf, F., & Pereira, H. M. (2020). Global patterns of forest loss across IUCN categories of protected areas. *Biological Conservation*, 241, 108299. https://doi.org/10.1016/j.biocon.2019.108299.
Lenton, T. M., Rockström, J., Gaffney, O., Rahmstorf, S., Richardson, K., Steffen, W., & Schellnhuber, H. J. (2019). *Climate tipping points—Too risky to bet against*. Nature Publishing Group.
Lévinas, E. (1983). *Die spur des anderen* [The trace of the other]. Albers.
Levins, R., & Lewontin, R. C. (1985). *The dialectical biologist*. Harvard University Press.
Lévy-Bruhl, L. (1985). *How natives think* (L. Clare, Trans.). Princeton University Press. (Original work published 1910)
Loewald, H. (1960). On the therapeutic action of psychoanalysis. *Journal of the American Psychoanalytic Association*, 41, 16–33.
Loewenthal, D., & Proctor, G. (Eds.) (2018). *Why not CBT? Against and for CBT revisited*. PCCS Books.
Louv, R. (2005). *Last child in the woods: Saving our children from nature-deficit disorder*. Algonquin Books.
Lovelock, J. (1987). *Gaia: A new look at life on Earth* (rev. ed.). Oxford University Press. (Original work published 1979)
Lovelock, J. (1991a). *Gaia: The practical science of planetary medicine*. Gaia Books.
Lovelock, J. (1991b). The Earth as living organism. In B. Willers (Ed.), *Learning to listen to the land* (pp. 11–16). Island Press.
Lovelock, J. (1996). *The ages of Gaia: A biography of our living Earth*. Oxford University Press. (Original work published 1988)
Lovelock, J. (2009). *The vanishing face of Gaia*. Penguin.
Lucas, G. (Director). (1977). *Star Wars: Episode IV—A new hope* [Film]. Lucasfilm.
Luquet, P. (1981). Le changement dans la mentalisation [The change in mentalisation]. *Revue Francais Psychoanalyique*, 45, 1023–1028.
Machado Assumpção, L., & Wood, J. K. (2001). Project estância Jatobá [The Jatobá home project]. *The Person-Centred Journal*, 8(1–2), 26–42.
Maclean, P. (1990). *The triune brain in evolution*. Springer.
Maclean, P., Campbell, D., & Boag, T. (1973). *A triune concept of the brain and behaviour*. University of Toronto Press.
Macleod, A., & McSherry, B. (2007). Regulating mental healthcare practitioners: Towards a standardized and workable framework. *Psychiatry, Psychology and Law*, 14(1), 45–55. https://doi.org/10.1375/pplt.14.1.45.
Macmurray, J. (1991a). *The self as agent. Vol. I. The form of the personal*. Faber & Faber. (Original work published 1957)
Macmurray, J. (1991b). *Persons in relation. Vol. II. The form of the personal*. Faber & Faber. (Original work published 1961)
Mahrer, A. (1983). *Experiential psychotherapy*. Brunner/Mazel.
Maller, C., Townsend, M., Prior, A., Brown, P., & St Leger, L. (2005). Healthy nature healthy people: 'Contact with nature' as an upstream health promotion intervention for populations. *Health Promotion International*, 21(1), 45–54. https://doi.org/10.1093/heapro/dai032.

Manchester, R. & Manchester, B. (1996). *The New Zealand Association of Psychotherapists/ Te Roopuu Whakaora Hinengaro: Notes towards a history.* NZAP.

Marx, K. (1973). *Grundrisse: Outlines of a critique of political economy.* Penguin. (Original work published 1839)

Marx, K. (1975). Economic and philosophical manuscripts. In *Karl Marx: Early writings* (R. Livingston & G. Benton, Eds.; pp. 279–400). Penguin. (Original work published 1844)

Marx, K., & Engels, F. (1971) *Manifesto of the Communist Party.* Progress. (Original work published 1848)

Masson, J. (1989). *Against therapy.* Fontana.

Mathews, F. (1991). *The ecological self.* Rowman & Littlefield.

May, R. (1977). *The meaning of anxiety.* The Ronald Press Company.

McCleary, R. A., & Lazarus, R. S. (1949). Autonomic discrimination without awareness. *Journal of Personality*, 18, 171–179.

McIlduff, E., & Coghlan, D. (1991). Dublin, 1985: Perceptions of a cross-cultural communications workshop. In E. McIlduff & D. Coghlan (Eds.), *The person-centered approach and cross-cultural communication: An international review* (Vol. I, pp. 43–59). Center for Cross-Cultural Communication.

McIlduff, E., & Coghlan, D. (1993). The cross-cultural communication workshops in Europe—Reflections and review. In E. McIlduff & D. Coghlan (Eds.), *The person-centered approach and crosscultural communication: An international review* (Vol. II, pp. 21–34). Center for Cross-Cultural Communication.

McIntyre, D. B. (1963). James Hutton and the philosophy of geology. In C. C. Albritton (Ed.), *The fabric of geology* (pp. 1–11). Addison-Wesley.

Mead, G. H. (1934). *Mind, self and society* (C. W. Morris, Ed.). University of Chicago Press.

Mearns, D. (1996). Working at relational depth with clients in person-centred therapy. *Counselling*, 7(4), 306–311.

Mearns, D., & Cooper, M. (2005). *Working at relational depth in counselling and psychotherapy.* Sage.

Merleau-Ponty, M. (1968). *Phenomenology of perception* (C. Smith, Trans.). Routledge and Kegan Paul.

Merry, T. (2002). *Learning and being in person-centred counselling* (2nd ed.). PCCS Books.

Mihaka, H. (2018). PCE2021—Promotional video. https://youtu.be/aZnBot5GrKU.

Miller, S., Hubble, M., & Duncan, B. (1995, March/April). No more bells and whistles. *The Family Therapy Networker*, 53–63.

Mills, I. (2019). *Climate of the heart: Only relatedness can save us.* Jubilation Books.

Mollot, G., Pantel, J. H., & Romanuk, T. N. (2017). The effects of invasive species on the decline in species richness: A global meta-analysis. In D. A. Bohan, A. J. Dumbrell, & F. Massol (Eds.), *Advances in ecological research* (pp. 61–83). Academic Press.

Moodley, R., Lago, C., & Talahite, A. (Eds.). (2004). *Carl Rogers counsels a black client: Race and culture in person-centred counselling.* PCCS Books.

Moreton-Robinson, A. (2019). Engaging the white possessive. *Kalfou*, 6(1), 68–72. https://doi.org/10.15367/kf.v6i1.231.

Morgan, S., & Juriansz, D. (2002). Practice-based evidence. *OpenMind*, 114, 12–13.

Morton, I. (Ed.) (1999). *Person-centred approaches to dementia care.* Winslow Press.

Mountford, C. P. (2006). Open-centred ecosophy or how to do environmentally interesting things with Dr Rogers' therapeutic conditions. In J. Moore & C. Purton (Eds.), *Spirituality and counselling: Experiential and theoretical perspectives* (pp. 99–115). PCCS Books.

Moustakas, C. (1990). *Heuristic research: Design, methodology and applications*. Sage.
Murphy, D., Cornelius-White, J., & Stephen, S. (Eds.). (2019). *Person-centered & Experiential Psychotherapies*, 18(2).
Murphy, G. (1947). *Personality: A biosocial approach to origins and structure*. Harper.
Murray, H. A. (1938). *Explorations in personality*. Oxford University Press.
Muthukrishna, M., & Henrich, J. (2016). Innovation in the collective brain. *Philosophical Transactions of the Royal Society*, B 371, 20150192. http://dx.doi.org/10.1098/rstb.2015.0192.
Myers, S. (1999). Empathy: Is that what I hear you saying? *Person-Centered Journal*, 6(2), 11–152.
Naess, A. (1973). The shallow and the deep, long-range ecology movement: A summary. *Inquiry*, 16, 95–100. https://doi.org/10.1080/00201747308601682.
Naess, A. (1989). *Environment, community and lifestyle: Outline of an ecosophy* (D. Rothenberg, Trans). Cambridge University Press.
Naess, A. (1995). Self-realization: An ecological approach to being in the world. In A. Drengson & Y. Inoue (Eds.), *The deep ecology movement: An introductory anthology* (pp. 13–30). North Atlantic Books.
Naydler, J. (1996). *Goethe on science: An anthology of Goethe's scientific writings*. Floris Books.
Neville, B. (1976). *Group climate, interpersonal functioning and learning* [Unpublished doctoral thesis]. La Trobe University.
Neville, B. (1996). Five kinds of empathy. In R. Hutterer, G. Pawlowsky, P. F. Schmid, & R. Stipsits (Eds.), *Client-centered and experiential psychotherapy: A paradigm in motion* (pp. 439–453). Peter Lang.
Neville, B. (1997). The person-centred ecopsychologist. *Person: Internationale Zeitschrift für Personzentrierte und Expereinzielle Psychotherapie und Beratung* [The International Journal for Person-Centered and Experiential Psychotherapy and Counselling], 1, 72–81.
Neville, B. (1999). The client-centered ecopsychologist. *The Person-Centered Journal*, 6(1), 59–74.
Neville, B. (2000). Addressing planetary pathology. *Psychotherapy in Australia*, 6(2), 10–21.
Neville, B. (2005). Reconnecting with Gaia. In P. Heywood, T. McCann, B. Neville, & P. Wills (Eds.), *Towards re-enchantment education: Education, imagination and the getting of wisdom*. Post Pressed Publishers.
Neville, B. (2007). What kind of universe? Rogers, Whitehead and transformative process. *Person-Centered & Experiential Psychotherapies*, 6(4), 271–285. https://doi.org/10.1080/14779757.2007.9688447.
Neville, B. (2012). *The life of things: Therapy and the soul of the world*. PCCS Books.
Neville, B. (2013a). Anxiously congruent: Congruently anxious. *Person-Centered & Experiential Psychotherapies*, 12(3), 223–236. https://doi.org/10.1080/14779757.2013.840671.
Neville, B. (2013b). Setting therapy free. *Person-Centered & Experiential Psychotherapies*, 12(4), 382–395. https://doi.org/10.1080/14779757.2013.855138.
Neville, B. (2014). Arts and health as an ecopsychological practice: Developing a conversation. *Journal of Applied Arts & Health*, 5(2), 273–280. https://doi.org/10.1386/jaah.5.2.273_1.
Neville, B., & McCann, P. (2013). Person-centered teacher advocates as culture brokers. *The Person-Centered Journal*, 20(1–2),19–39.
Neville, B., & Varney, H. (2014). Arts and health as an ecopsychological practice: Developing a conversation. *Journal of Applied Arts and Health*, 5 (2), 273–280. https://doi.org/10.1386/jaah.5.2.273_1.

New Zealand Association for Psychotherapists/Te Roopuu Whakaora Hinengaro. (2008). NZAP Conference 2008. www.nzap.org.nz/Pages/Conference/pages/intro-page.htm.

New Zealand Association for Psychotherapists/Te Rōpū Whakaora Hinengaro. (2018). Code of ethics. NZAP. https://nzap.org.nz/wp-content/uploads/2019/01/NZAP-Code-of-Ethics-2018.pdf.

Nietzsche, F. (1974). *The gay science* (W. Kaufmann, Trans.). Random House. (Original work published 1882)

Noel, J. R., & DeChenne, T. K. (1974). Three dimensions of psychotherapy: I-we-thou. In D. A. Wexler & L. N. Rice (Eds.), *Innovations in client-centered therapy* (pp. 247–257). Wiley.

Nordgren, P. H. (2001). Symphony No. 6 Interdependence. Op.107.

Nwoye, A. (2002). Hope-healing communities in contemporary Africa. *Journal of Humanistic Psychology*, 42(4), 58–81. https://doi.org/10.1177/002216702237124.

O'Leary, E. (1993). Empathy in the person-centred and gestalt approaches. *British Gestalt Journal*, 2, 111–114.

Online Etymology Dictionary. (2021). *Hope*. https://www.etymonline.com/.

Ornstein, R. (1997). *The right mind: Making sense of the hemispheres*. Harcourt.

Orr, D. W. (1992). *Ecological literacy: Education and the transition to a postmodern world*. State University of New York Press.

Owen, W. J. B., & Smyser, J. W. (2013). *The prose works of William Wordsworth* (Vol. 1). Lulu.

Paine, R. T. (1969). A note on trophic complexity and community stability. *The American Naturalist*, 103, 91–93.

Panksepp, J. (1998). *Affective neuroscience: The foundations of human and animal emotions*. Oxford University Press.

Parker, I. (1997). Discursive psychology. In D. Fox, I. Prilleltensky, & S. Austin (Eds.), *Critical psychology: An introduction* (pp. 284–298). Sage.

Parlett, M. (1991). Reflections on field theory. *The British Gestalt Journal*, 1, 69–81.

Perlesz, A. (1999). Complex responses to trauma: Challenges in bearing witness. *Australian and New Zealand Journal of Family Therapy*, 20(1), 11–19.

Perls, F. (1969). *Ego, hunger and aggression*. Vintage. (Original work published 1947)

Piaget, J. (1952). *The origins of intelligence in children*. International University Press. (Original work published 1936)

Pine, F. (1990). *Drive, ego, object and self: A synthesis for clinical work*. Basic Books.

Plotkin, B. (2008). *Nature and the human soul: Cultivating wholeness and community in a fragmented world*. New World Library.

Plumptre, A. J., Baisero, D., Belote, R. T., Vázquez-Domínguez, E., Faurby, S., Jędrzejewski, W., Kiara, H., Kühl, H., Benítez-López, A., Luna-Aranguré, C., Voigt, M., Wich, S., Wint, W., Gallego-Zamorano, J., & Boyd, C. (2021). Where might we find ecologically intact communities? *Frontiers in Forests and Global Change*, 4, 626635. https://doi.org/10.3389/ffgc.2021.626635.

Pointing, S., Buedel, B., Convey, P., Gillman, L., Koerner, C., Leuzinger, S., & Vincent, W. (2015). Biogeography of photoautotrophs in the high polar biome. *Frontiers in Plant Science*, 6, 692. https://doi.org/10.3389/fpls.2015.00692.

Poland, T. M., Patel-Weynand, T., Finch, D. M., Miniat, C. F., Hayes, D. C., & Lopez, V. M. (2021). *Invasive species in forests and rangelands of the United States: A comprehensive science synthesis for the United States forest sector*. Springer International Publishing. https://doi.org/10.1007/978-3-030-45367-1.

Pope, A. (2007). *Essay on man* (H. Morley, Ed.). Gutenberg. (Original work published 1732) https://www.gutenberg.org/files/2428/2428-h/2428-h.htm.

Porges, S. W. (2009). The polyvagal theory: New insights into adaptive reactions of the autonomic nervous system. *Cleveland Clinic Journal of Medicine*, 76(Supplement 2), S86–S90. https://doi.org/10.3949/ccjm.76.s2.17.

Porges, S. W. (2011). *The polyvagal theory: Neurophysiological foundations of emotions, attachment, communication, and self-regulation*. W. W. Norton & Company.

Pörtner, M. (2000). *Trust and understanding: The person-centred approach to everyday care for people with special needs*. PCCS Books.

Prigogine, I. (1980). *From being to becoming*. W.H. Freeman.

Proctor, B. W. (1877). Helvellyn. In H.W. Longfellow (Ed.), *Poems of place* (Vol. I; pp. 307–309). Macmillan & Co.

Proctor, G., Cooper, M., Sanders, P., & Malcolm, B. (Eds.). (2006). *Politicizing the person-centred approach: An agenda for change*. PCCS Books.

Prouty, G. F. (1976). Pre-therapy, a method of treating pre-expressive, psychotic and retarded patients. *Psychotherapy: Theory, Research and Practice*, 13(3), 290–295. https://doi.org/10.1037/h0088359.

Prouty, G. F. (1994). *Theoretical evolutions in person-centered/experiential therapy: Applications to schizophrenic and retarded psychoses*. Praeger.

Prouty, G. F., Van Werde, D., & Pörtner, M. (2002). *Pre-therapy*. PCCS Books.

Pyšek, P., & Richardson, D. M. (2010). Invasive species, environmental change and management, and health. *Annual Review of Environment and Resources*, 35, 25–55. https://doi.org/10.1146/annurev-environ-033009-095548.

Quinn, R. (1993). Confronting Carl Rogers: A developmental-interactional approach to person-centered therapy. *Journal of Humanistic Psychology*, 33(1), 6–23. https://doi.org/10.1177/0022167893331002.

Radin, D. (1997). *The conscious universe: The scientific truth of psychic phenomena*. HarperOne.

Radin, D. (2006). *Entangled minds: Extrasensory experiences in quantum reality*. Pocket Books.

Radin, D. (2009). *The conscious universe: The scientific truth of psychic phenomena*. HarperOne.

Rand, J. (2010). *Risk(s)* [Poem]. https://smartenglishnotes.com/2022/02/25/risks-poem-by-janet-rand-summary-analysis-questions-and-answers/.

Raskin, N. J., & Rogers, C. R. (1989). Person-centered therapy. In R. J. Corsini & D. Wedding (Eds.), *Current psychotherapies* (pp. 155–194). Peacock.

Rawlins, M. D. (2008). *De testimonio: On the evidence for decisions about the use of therapeutic interventions*. Royal College of Physicians.

Reason, P., & Rowan, J. (Eds.) (1981). *Human enquiry: A sourcebook of new paradigm research*. John Wiley.

Reed, C. (Director) (1949). The *third man* [Film]. London Films.

Rehfeld, K., Münch, T., Ho, S. L., & Laepple, T. (2018). Global patterns of declining temperature variability from the Last Glacial Maximum to the Holocene. *Nature*, 554, 356–359. https://doi.org/10.1038/nature25454.

Richards, K., & Jagger, M. (1969). You can't always get what you want [Song]. On *Let it bleed*. Decca.

Ripple, W. J., Wolf, C., Newsome, T. M., Galetti, M., Alamgir, M., Crist, E., Mahmoud, M. I., & Laurance, W. F. (2017). World scientists' warning to humanity: A second notice. *BioScience*, 67(12), 1026–1028. https://doi.org/10.1093/biosci/bix125.

Ritchie, J. (2008, April 17). *Recognising difference*. Panel presentation. NZAP Conference, Waitangi, New Zealand.

Rivers, S., Rodgers, B., May, J., & Tudor, K. (2022). On–and in–bicultural encounter. *Person-Centred & Experiential Psychotherapy*, 21(2). https://doi.org/10.1080/14779757.2022.2067782.
Roach, A. (1990a). I've lied [Song]. On *Charcoal Lane*. Aurura.
Roach, A. (1990b). Native born [Song]. On *Charcoal Lane*. Aurura.
Roach, A. (1997). Mother's heartbeat [Song]. On *Looking for butter boy*. Aurura.
Roach, A. (2002). All men choose the path they walk [Song]. On *The Tracker*. Mushroom.
Roach, A. (2007). Too many bridges [Song]. On *Journey*. Liberation.
Roach, A. (2012a). Into the bloodstream [Song]. On *Into the bloodstream*. Liberation.
Roach, A. (2012b). Wash my soul [Song]. On *Into the bloodstream*. Liberation.
Roach, A. (2012c). We won't cry [Song]. On *Into the bloodstream*. Liberation.
Roach, A. (2016a). Get back to the land [Song]. On *Let love rule*. Liberation.
Roach, A. (2016b). Let love rule [Song]. On *Let love rule*. Liberation.
Roach, A. (2018a). Dancing [Song]. On *Dancing with my spirit*. Mushroom Music Publishing.
Roach, A. (2018b). Heal the people, heal the land [Song]. On *Dancing with my spirit*. Mushroom Music Publishing.
Roach, A. (2019). Place of fire [Song]. On *Tell me why*. Bloodlines.
Rodgers, B., & Tudor, K. (2020). Person-centred therapy: A radical paradigm in a new world. *New Zealand Journal of Counselling*, 40(2), 21–35. https://www.nzac.org.nz/assets/Journals/Vol-40-No-2/Chapter_2_Person-centred_therapy.pdf.
Rodgers, B., Tudor, K., & Ashcroft, A. (2021). Online video-conferencing therapy and person-centred approach in the context of a global pandemic. *Person-Centered & Experiential Psychotherapies*, 20(4), 286–302. https://doi.org/10.1080/14779757.2021.1898455.
Rogers, C. R. (1942). *Counseling and psychotherapy: Newer concepts in practice*. Houghton Mifflin.
Rogers, C. R. (1946). Significant aspects of client-centred therapy. *American Psychologist*, 1, 415–422. https://doi.org/10.1037/h0060866.
Rogers C. R. (1947). Some observations on the organisation of personality. *American Psychologist*, 2(9), 358–368. https://doi.org/10.1037/h0060883.
Rogers, C. R. (1951). *Client-centered therapy*. Houghton Mifflin.
Rogers, C. R. (1957). The necessary and sufficient conditions of therapeutic personality change. *Journal of Consulting Psychology*, 21(2), 95–103. https://doi.org/10.1037/h0045357.
Rogers, C. R. (1958). The characteristics of a helping relationship. *Personnel and Guidance Journal*, 37, 6–16. https://doi.org/10.1002/j.2164-4918.1958.tb01147.x.
Rogers, C. R. (1959). A theory of therapy, personality and interpersonal relationships, as developed in the client-centred framework. In S. Koch (Ed.), *Psychology: A study of a science. Vol. 3: Formulation of the person and the social context* (pp. 184–256). McGraw-Hill.
Rogers, C. R. (1962). Some learnings from a study of psychotherapy with schizophrenics. *Pennsylvania Psychiatric Quarterly*, 2, 3–15.
Rogers, C. R. (1963). The actualizing tendency in relation to "motive" and to consciousness. In M. Jones (Ed.), *Nebraska symposium on motivation 1963* (pp. 1–24). University of Nebraska Press.
Rogers, C. R. (1967a). The characteristics of a helping relationship. In *On becoming a person* (pp. 39–57). Constable. (Original work published in 1958)
Rogers, C. R. (1967b). Dealing with breakdowns in communication—Interpersonal and intergroup. In *On becoming a person* (pp. 329–337). Constable. (Original work published in 1952)

Rogers, C. R. (1967c). *On becoming a person: A therapist's view of psychotherapy.* Constable. (Original work published 1961)

Rogers, C. R. (1967d). Persons or science? A philosophical question. In *On becoming a person* (pp. 199–224) Constable. (Original work published in 1955)

Rogers, C. R. (1967e). A process conception of psychotherapy. In *On becoming a person* (pp. 125–159). Constable. (Original work published in 1958)

Rogers, C. R. (1967f). Significant learning: In therapy and education. In *On becoming a person* (pp. 279–296). Constable. (Original work published 1959)

Rogers, C. R. (1967g). Some of the directions evident in therapy. In *On becoming a person* (pp. 73–106). Constable. (Original work published 1953)

Rogers, C. R. (1967h). A therapist's view of the good life: The fully functioning person. In *On becoming a person* (pp. 183–196). Constable. (Original work published in 1957)

Rogers, C. R. (1967i). 'This is me': The development of my professional thinking and personal philosophy. In *On becoming a person* (pp. 3–27). Constable. (Original work published in 1961)

Rogers, C. R. (1967j). 'To be that self which one truly is': A therapist's view of personal goals. In *On becoming a person* (pp. 163–182). Constable. (Original work published 1960)

Rogers, C. R. (1967k). Toward a theory of creativity. In *On becoming a person* (pp. 347–359). Constable. (Original work published 1954)

Rogers, C. R., (1968). Some thoughts regarding the current presuppositions of the behavioral sciences. In C.R. Rogers & W.R. Coulson (Eds.), *Man and the science of man* (pp. 55–72). Charles E. Merrill.

Rogers, C. R. (1969). *Freedom to learn.* Charles E. Merrill.

Rogers, C. R. (1973). *Carl Rogers on encounter groups.* Harper and Row. (Original work published 1970)

Rogers, C. R. (1982). A psychologist looks at nuclear war: Its threat, its possible prevention. *Journal of Humanistic Psychology*, 22(4), 9–20. https://doi.org/10.1177/002216788202200402.

Rogers, C. R. (1983). *Freedom to learn for the 80s.* Charles E. Merrill.

Rogers, C. R. (1986a). A client-centered/person-centered approach to therapy. In I. Kutash & A. Wolf (Eds.), *Psychotherapist's casebook* (pp. 197–208). Jossey-Bass.

Rogers, C. R. (1986b). Rogers, Kohut, and Erickson: A personal perspective on some similarities and differences. *Person-Centered Review*, 1(2), 125–140.

Rogers, C. R. (1990). What I learned from two research studies. In H. Kirschenbaum & V. L. Henderson (Eds.), *The Carl Rogers reader* (pp. 203–211). Constable.

Rogers, C. R. (1991). An open letter to participants of European workshops. In E. McIlduff & D. Coghlan (Eds.), *The person-centered approach and cross-cultural communication: An international review* (Vol. 1; pp. 11–13). Center for Cross-Cultural Communication.

Rogers, C. R. (1995a). Beyond the watershed: And where now? In *A way of being* (pp. 292–315). Houghton Mifflin. (Original work published 1977)

Rogers, C. R. (1995b). Do we need 'a' reality? In *A way of being* (pp. 96–108). Houghton Mifflin. (Original work published 1978)

Rogers, C. R. (1995c). Ellen West—and loneliness. In *A way of being* (pp. 164–180). Houghton Mifflin. (Original work published 1977)

Rogers, C. R. (1995d). Empathic: An unappreciated way of being. In *A way of being* (pp. 137–163). Houghton Mifflin. (Original work published 1975)

Rogers, C. R. (1995e). The foundations of a person-centred approach. In *A way of being* (pp. 113–136). Houghton Mifflin. (Original work published 1963 and 1978)

Rogers, C. R. (1995f). In retrospect—Forty-six years. In *A way of being* (pp. 46–69). Houghton Mifflin. (Original work published 1974)

Rogers, C. R. (1995g). My philosophy of interpersonal relationships and how it grew. In *A way of being* (pp. 27–45). Houghton Mifflin. (Original work published 1973)

Rogers, C. R. (1995h). Some new challenges to the helping professions. In *A way of being* (pp. 235–259). Houghton Mifflin. (Original work published 1973)

Rogers, C. R. (1995i). *A way of being*. Houghton Mifflin. (Original work published 1980)

Rogers, C. R. (1995j). The world of tomorrow, and the person of tomorrow. In *A way of being* (pp. 339–356). Houghton Mifflin. (Original work published 1980)

Rogers, C. R., & Freiberg, H. J. (1994). *Freedom to learn* (3rd ed.). Charles E. Merrill.

Rogers, C. R., & Russell, D. E. (2002). *Carl Rogers: The quiet revolutionary: An oral history*. Penmarin Books.

Rogers, N., Tudor, K., Embleton Tudor, L., & Keemar, K. (2012). Person-centred expressive arts therapy: A theoretical encounter. *Person-Centered & Experiential Psychotherapies*, 11(1), 31–47. https://doi.org/10.1080/14779757.2012.656407.

Roszak, T. (1992). *The voice of the earth: An exploration of ecopsychology*. Phanes Press.

Roszak, T., Gomes, M. E., & Kanner, A. D. (Eds.). (1995). *Ecopsychology: Restoring the Earth, healing the mind*. Random House.

Rowland, B. (2002). Depressed process: A person-centred view of depression. *Person-Centred Practice*, 10, 27–34.

Roy, B. (1988). Loss of power—Alienation. In B. Roy & C. Steiner (Eds.), *Radical psychiatry: The second decade* (pp. 3–13). http://www.emotional-literacy.com/rp0.htm.

Sabini, M. (2002). *The Earth has a soul*. North Atlantic Books.

Sacks, O. (1995). Foreword. In K. Goldstein (Ed.), *The organism* (pp. 7–14). Zone Books.

Samuels, A. (1989). *The plural psyche: Personality, morality, and the father*. Tavistock/Routledge.

Samuels, A. (1993). *The political psyche*. Routledge.

Samuels, A., & Williams, R. (2001). Andrew Samuels in conversation with Ruth Williams. *Transformations*, 13(Suppl.), 1–3.

Sanders, P., & Tudor, K. (2001). This is therapy: A person-centred critique of the contemporary psychiatric system. In C. Newnes, G. Holmes, & C. Dunn (Eds.), *This is madness too: Critical perspectives on mental health Services* (pp. 147–160). PCCS Books.

Saner, R. (1989). Culture bias of gestalt therapy: Made-in-USA. *The Gestalt Journal*, 12(2), 57–73.

Sapriel, L. (1998). Can gestalt therapy, self-psychology and intersubjectivity theory be integrated? *The British Gestalt Journal*, 7(1), 33–44.

Schmale, A. H. Jr. (1964). A genetic view of affects with special reference to the genesis of helplessness and hopelessness. *Psychoanalytic Study of the Child*, 19, 287–310. https://doi.org/10.1080/00797308.1964.11822870.

Schmid, P. F. (1998). Face to face: The art of encounter. In B. Thorne & E. Lambers (Eds.), *Person-centred therapy: A European perspective* (pp. 74–90). Sage.

Schmid, P. F. (2005). Authenticity and alienation: Towards an understanding of the person beyond the categories of order and disorder. In S. Joseph & R. Worsley (Eds.), *Person-centred psychopathology: A positive psychology of mental health* (pp. 75–90). PCCS Books.

Schmid, P. F. (2006). The challenge of the other: Towards dialogical person-centered psychotherapy. *Person-Centered & Experiential Psychotherapies*, 5(4), 240–254. https://doi.org/10.1080/14779757.2006.9688416.

Schmid, P. F. (2019). The power of hope: Person-centered perspectives on contemporary personal and societal challenges, *Person-Centered & Experiential Psychotherapies*, 18(2), 121–138. https://doi.org/10.1080/14779757.2019.1618371.

Schmid, P. F., & Mearns, D. (2006). Being-with and being-counter: Person-centered psychotherapy as an in-depth co-creative process of personalization. *Person-Centered & Experiential Psychotherapies*, 5(3), 174–190. https://doi.org/10.1080/14779757.2006.9688408.

Schneider, K. (2004). *Rediscovery of awe*. Paragon House.

Schopenhauer, A. (1958). *The world as will and representation* (E. F. J. Payne, Trans). Falcon Wings Press. (Original work published 1844)

Schopenhauer, A. (1994). On death and its relationship to the indestructibility of our inner nature. In W. Schirmacher (Ed.), *Philosophical writings* (pp. 278–294). Continuum.

Schore, A. N. (1994). *Affect regulation and the origin of the self: The neurobiology of emotional development*. Lawrence Erlbaum Associates.

Schwartz, J. (1999). *Cassandra's daughter: A history of psychoanalysis*. Penguin.

Scott-Holland, H. (1910). *Death: The king of terrors* [Sermon]. Delivered 15th May 1910, at St. Paul's Cathedral, London, UK.

Sela-Smith, S. (2002). Heuristic research: A review and critique of Moustakas's method. *Journal of Humanistic Psychology*, 42(3), 53–88. https://doi.org/10.1177/0022167802423004.

Semel, V. (1990). Confrontations with hopelessness: Psychoanalytic treatment of the older woman. *Modern Psychoanalysis*, 12, 215–224.

Shakespeare, W. (1998). *Pericles, prince of Tyre* (D. DelVecchio & A. Hammond, Eds.; rev. ed.). Cambridge University Press. (Original work published 1608)

Shakespeare, W. (2004). *All's well that ends well* (R. Fraser, Ed.; updated ed.). Cambridge University Press. (Original work published 1605)

Shaw, S., & Tudor, K. (2022). The Emperors' new clothes: The socialisation and regulation of health professions. *Journal of Interprofessional Education and Practice*, 28. https://doi.org/10.1016/j.xjep.2022.100519.

Sheldrake, R. (1981). *A new science of life*. Paladin.

Sheldrake, R. (1990). *The rebirth of nature: New science and the revival of animism*. Rider.

Sheldrake, R. (2012). *The science delusion: Freeing the spirit of enquiry*. Coronet.

Sherrard, E. M. (2020). *The book of Evan: The work and life of Evan McAra Sherrard* (E-book edition; K. Tudor, Ed.). Tuwhera Open Access Books. https://ojs.aut.ac.nz/tuwhera-open-monographs/catalog/book/2.

Shostrom, E. (Producer). (1965). *Three approaches to psychotherapy*. Psychological Films.

Siegel, D. J. (1999). *The developing mind: How relationships and the brain interact to shape who we are*. Guilford Press.

Singh, J., & Tudor, K. (1997). Cultural conditions of therapy. *The Person-Centered Journal*, 4(2), 32–46.

Skinner, B. F. (1948). *Walden two*. Hackett Publishing Company.

Slochower, H. (1984). Hope—Beyond hopelessness. *American Imago*, 41(3), 237–243.

Smart, S. M., Thompson, K., Marrs, R. H., Le Duc, M. G., Maskell, L. C., & Firbank, L. G. (2006). Biotic homogenization and changes in species diversity across human-modified ecosystems. *Biological Sciences*, 273(1601), 2659–2665. https://doi.org/10.1098/rspb.2006.3630.

Smith, G. H. (1997). *The development of kaupapa Māori: Theory and praxis* [Doctoral dissertation, University of Auckland]. ResearchSpace. https://researchspace.auckland.ac.nz/handle/2292/623.

Smith, L. T. (1999). *Decolonizing methodology*. Zed Books.

Smuts, J. (1987). *Holism and evolution*. Macmillan. (Original work published 1926)

Snell, T. (2012). Peak experiences in nature: Implications for psychological well-being and environmental behaviour [Unpublished doctoral thesis]. Monash University.
Snygg, D., & Combs, A. (1949). *Individual behaviour: A new frame of reference for psychology*. Harper and Brothers.
Stark, M. (1999). *Modes of therapeutic action: Enhancement of knowledge, provision of experience, engagement in relationship*. Jason Aronson.
Stark, M. (2017). *Relentless hope: The refusal to grieve*. International Psychotherapy Institute.
Statistics New Zealand. (2012). Te ao mārama 2012: A snapshot of Māori well-being and development. http://www.stats.govt.nz/browse_for_stats/people_and_communities/maori/te-ao-marama-2012/environment.aspx.
Steffen, W., Rockström, J., Richardson, K., Lenton, T. M., Folke, C., Liverman, D., Summerhayes, C. P., Barnosky, A. D., Cornell, S. E., Crucifix, M., Donges, J. F., Fetzer, I., Lade, S. J., Scheffer, M., Winkelmann, R., & Schellnhuber, H. J. (2018). Trajectories of the earth system in the Anthropocene. *Proceedings of the National Academy of Sciences* 115(33), 8252–8259. https://doi.org/10.1073/pnas.1810141115.
Steiner, C. (1981). *The other side of power*. Grove Press.
Steiner, L. R. (1974). Response to Rogers 'Challenges' [Letter]. *American Psychologist*, 29(5), 148.
Stern, D. N. (1985). *The interpersonal world of the infant: A view from psychoanalysis and developmental psychology*. Basic Books.
Stern, D. N. (1998). *The interpersonal world of the infant: A view from psychoanalysis and developmental psychology* (rev. ed.). Karnac Books.
Stern, D. N. (2004). *The present moment in psychotherapy and everyday life*. W.W. Norton & Co.
Stinckens, N., Lietaer, G., & Leijssen, M. (2002). The valuing process and the inner critic in the classical and current client-centered/experiential literature. *Person-Centered and Experiential Psychotherapies*, 1(1&2), 41–55. https://doi.org/10.1080/14779757.2002.9688277.
Stringer, C. (2016). The origin and evolution of Homo sapiens. *Philosophical Transactions of the Royal Society B: Biological Sciences*, 371, 20150237. https://doi.org/10.1098/rstb.2015.0237.
Sullivan, H. S. (1997). *The interpersonal theory of psychiatry*. Norton. (Original work published 1953)
Summers, G., & Tudor, K. (2000). Cocreative transactional analysis. *Transactional Analysis Journal*, 30(1), 23–40. https://doi.org/10.1177/036215370003000104.
Summers, G., & Tudor, K. (2021). Reflections on cocreative transactional analysis: Acceptance speech for the Eric Berne Memorial Award 2020. *Transactional Analysis Journal*, 51(1), 1–12. https://doi.org/10.1080/03621537.2020.1853345.
Swimme, B. (1996). *The hidden heart of the cosmos*. Orbis Books.
Szent-Gyoergyi, A. (1966). The drive in living matter to perfect itself. *Journal of Individual Psychology*, 22(2), 153–162.
Taft, J. (1973). *The dynamics of therapy in a controlled relationship*. Macmillan. (Original work published 1933)
Tallbear, K. (2019). Caretaking relations, not American dreaming. *Kalfou*, 6(1), 24–41. https://doi.org/10.15367/kf.v6i1.228
Taper, M. L., Böhning-Gaese, K., & Brown, J. H. (1995). Individualistic responses of bird species to environmental change. *Oecologia*, 101, 478–486. https://doi.org/10.1007/BF00329427.
Targ, R. (2004). *Limitless mind*. New World Library.

Teilhard de Chardin, P. (1959). *The phenomenon of man*. Harper & Brothers.
Teo, T. (2009). Philosophical concerns in critical psychology. In D. Fox, I. Prilleltensky, & S. Austin (Eds.), *Critical psychology: An introduction* (pp. 36–54). Sage.
Thorne, B., & Mearns, D. (2000). *Person-centred therapy today: New frontiers in theory and practice*. Google e-Book.
Thornton, A. (1998). Do a and o categories of 'possession' in Maori express degrees of tapu? *The Journal of the Polynesian Society*, 107(4), 381–393. https://www.jstor.org/stable/20706829.
Tillich, P. (1956). *Systematic theology* (Vol. 1). University of Chicago Press.
Timulak, L. (2007). Identifying core categories of client-identified impact of helpful events in psychotherapy: A qualitative meta-analysis. *Psychotherapy Research*, 17(3), 310–320. http://dx.doi.org/10.1080/10503300600608116.
Tolman, E. C. & Brunswik, E. (1935). The organism and the causal texture of the environment. *Psychological Review*, 42, 43–77. https://doi.org/10.1037/h0062156.
Totton, N. (2011). *Wild therapy: Undomesticating inner and outer worlds*. PCCS Books.
Totton, N. (2012). Wild therapy. In *Not a tame lion: Writings on therapy in its social and political context* (pp. 152–156). PCCS Books. (Original work published 2011)
Toukmanian, S. (2002). Perception: The core element in person-centered and experiential psychotherapies. In G. Wyatt & P. Sanders (Eds.), *Contact and perception* (pp. 115–132). PCCS Books.
Trisos, C. H., Merow, C., & Pigot, A. L. (2020). The projected timing of abrupt ecological disruption from climate change. *Nature*, 580, 496–501. https://doi.org/10.1038/s41586-020-2189-9.
Truax, C. B., & Carkhuff, R. R. (1967). *Toward effective counseling and psychotherapy: Training and practice*. Aldine.
Tuck, E., & Yang, K. W. (2012). Decolonization is not a metaphor. *Decolonization: Indigeneity, Education & Society*, 1(1), 1–40.
Tudor, K. (1996). *Mental health promotion: Paradigms and practice*. Routledge
Tudor, K. (1997a). Being at dis-ease with ourselves: Alienation and psychotherapy. *Changes*, 22(2), 143–150.
Tudor, K. (1997b). The personal is political—and political is personal: A person-centred approach to the political sphere. *Person Centred Practice*, 5(2), 4–10.
Tudor, K. (2000). The case of the lost conditions. *Counselling*, 11(1), 33–37.
Tudor, K. (2002, Summer). From the person of Carl Rogers to the person-centred approach. *ipnosis*, 6, 8–19.
Tudor, K. (2003). The neopsyche: The integrating Adult ego state. In C. Sills & H. Hargaden (Eds.), *Ego states* (pp. 201–231). Worth Reading.
Tudor, K. (2007). Training in the person-centred approach. In M. Cooper, M. O'Hara, P. Schmid, & G. Wyatt (Eds.), *The handbook of person-centred psychotherapy and counselling* (pp. 379–389). Palgrave.
Tudor, K. (2008a). Persoonsgerichte therapie: grondslagen en fundamentele inzichten [Person-centred therapy: Foundations and fundamentals]. *Tijdshrift Cliëntgerichte Psychotherapie*, 46(2), 122–134.
Tudor, K. (2008b). Psychological health: Autonomy and homonomy. In B. Levitt (Ed.), *Reflections on human potential: Bridging the person-centered approach and positive psychology* (pp. 161–174). PCCS Books.
Tudor, K. (2008c). Therapy is a verb. *Therapy Today*, 19(1), 35–37.
Tudor, K. (2008d). We cannot imagine without the other: Contact and difference in psychotherapeutic relating. *Forum* [The Journal of the New Zealand Association of Psychotherapists], *14*, 46–61.

Tudor, K. (2010). Person-centred relational therapy: An organismic prospective. *Person-Centred and Experiential Psychotherapies*, 9(1), 52–68. https://doi.org/10.1080/14779757.2010.9688504.

Tudor, K. (2011a). Rogers' therapeutic conditions: A relational conceptualization. *Person-Centered & Experiential Psychotherapies*, 10(3), 165–180. https://doi.org/10.1080/14779757.2011.599513.

Tudor, K. (Ed.). (2011b). *The turning tide: Pluralism and partnership in psychotherapy in Aotearoa New Zealand*. LC Publications

Tudor, K. (2011c). Understanding empathy. *Transactional Analysis Journal*, 41(1), 39–57. https://doi.org/10.1177/036215371104100107.

Tudor, K. (2012). Ebb and flow: One year on from '*The Turning Tide: Pluralism and Partnership in Psychotherapy in Aotearoa New Zealand*'. *Psychotherapy and Politics International*, 10(2), 170–177. https://doi.org/10.1002/ppi.1271.

Tudor, K. (2013a). "Be careful what you wish for": Professional recognition, the statutory regulation of counselling, and the state registration of counsellors. *New Zealand Journal of Counselling*, 33(2), 46–69.

Tudor, K. (2013b). From humanism to humanistic psychology and back again. *Self & Society*, 41(1), 35–42. https://doi.org/10.1080/03060497.2013.11084321.

Tudor, K. (2013c). Person-centered psychology and therapy, ecopsychology and ecotherapy. *Person-Centered & Experiential Psychotherapies*, 12(4), 315–329. https://doi.org/10.1080/14779757.2013.855137.

Tudor, K. (2014). Back to the future: Carl Rogers' 'new challenges' reviewed and renewed. *Self & Society*, 41(2), 17–24. https://doi.org/10.1080/03060497.2014.11084339.

Tudor, K. (2016). 'We are': The fundamental life position. *Transactional Analysis Journal*, 46(2), 164–176. https://doi.org/10.1177/0362153716637064.

Tudor, K. (2017a). Alienation and psychotherapy. In *Conscience and critic: The selected works of Keith Tudor* (pp. 58–70). Routledge. (Expanded version of original work published 1997)

Tudor, K. (2017b). The relational, the vertical, and the horizontal: A critique of "relational depth". In *Conscience and critic: The selected works of Keith Tudor* (pp. 191–201). Routledge. (Original work published 2014)

Tudor, K. (2018a). In(ter)dependence day: Lives mattering, freedom with responsibility, and social well-being. *Psychotherapy and Politics International*, 16(2), e1447. https://doi.org/10.1002/ppi.1447.

Tudor, K. (2018b). Person-centred therapy, a cognitive behavioural therapy. In D. Loewenthal & G. Proctor (Eds.), *Why not CBT? Against and for CBT revisited* (pp. 201–218). PCCS Books. (Original work published 2008)

Tudor, K. (2018c). *Psychotherapy: A critical examination*. PCCS Books.

Tudor, K. (2019). Cocreative counseling. *The Journal of Humanistic Counselling*, 58(2), 135–149. https://doi.org/10.1002/johc.12102.

Tudor, K. (Ed.). (2020a). *Claude Steiner, emotional activist: The life and work of Claude Michel Steiner*. Routledge.

Tudor, K. (Ed.). (2020-b). *Pluralism in psychotherapy: Critical reflections from a post-regulation landscape* [E-book]. Tuwhera Open Access Books. https://ojs.aut.ac.nz/tuwhera-open-monographs/catalog/book/1 (Original work published 2017)

Tudor, K. (2021). He tangata, he tangata, he tangata: A humanistic relational approach to a people-centred and experiential therapy in and of Aotearoa New Zealand. In *20/20 vision, 2020* [E-book]. Tuwhera Open Access Books. https://ojs.aut.ac.nz/tuwhera-open-monographs/catalog/book/6.

Tudor, K. (2022a). *Helvellyn* [Poem]. Unpublished manuscript.
Tudor, K. (2022b). There and back again: Re-envisioning "relationship therapy" as the centre of a contemporary, cultural, and contextual person-centred therapy. *Person-Centered and Experiential Psychotherapies*, 21(2), 188–206. https://doi.org/10.1080/14779757.2022.2066562.
Tudor, K. (2022c). 絆 *Kizuna: Bonds(絆) and binds(結び付き), connection(繋がり), competition(競争) and co-operation(協力)*. https://taaj.or.jp/program/conference-34/keinote-speech/.
Tudor, K., & Embleton Tudor, L. (1999). The philosophy of Temenos. *Self & Society*, 27(2), 32–37.
Tudor, K., & Hargaden, H. (2002). The couch and the ballot box: The contribution and potential of psychotherapy in enhancing citizenship. In C. Feltham (Ed.), *What's the good of counselling and psychotherapy? The benefits explained* (pp. 156–178). Sage.
Tudor, K., & Lewin, P. (2006). Fit for purpose: The organisation of psychotherapy training. *Self & Society*, 34(1), 33–40. https://doi.org/10.1080/03060497.2006.11083897.
Tudor, K., & Merry, T. (2002). *Dictionary of person-centred psychology*. Whurr.
Tudor, K., & Rodgers, B. (2020). The person-centred approach in Aotearoa New Zealand: A critical examination of a settler psychology. *Person-Centered & Experiential Psychotherapies*, 20(1), 84–101. https://doi.org/10.1080/14779757.2020.1846602.
Tudor. K., Rodgers, B., Smith, V. (2022). Tihei mauri ora—Contact, culture, and context. *Person-Centred & Experiential Psychotherapy*, 21(2). https://doi.org/10.1080/14779757.2022.2066563.
Tudor, K., & Summers, G. (2014). *Co-creative transactional analysis: Papers, responses and developments*. Karnac Books.
Tudor, K., & Worrall, M. (Eds.). (2004a). *Freedom to practise: Person-centred approaches to supervision*. PCCS Books.
Tudor, K., & Worrall, M. (2004b). Person-centred philosophy and theory in the practice of supervision. In K. Tudor & M. Worrall (Eds.), *Freedom to practise* (pp. 11–30). PCCS Books.
Tudor, K., & Worrall, M. (2006). *Person-centred therapy: A clinical philosophy*. Routledge.
Tudor, K., & Worrall, M. (Eds.). (2007). *Freedom to practise II: Developing person-centred approaches to supervision*. PCCS Books.
Ulloa, A. (2003). *The ecological native: Indigenous peoples' movements and Eco-governmentality in Colombia* [Unpublished dissertation]. University of California.
Van Belle, H. A. (1990). Rogers' later move towards mysticism: Implications for client-centered therapy. In G. Lietaer, J. Rombauts, & R. Van Balen (Eds.), *Client-centered and experiential psychotherapy in the nineties* (pp. 47–57). Leuven University Press.
Van Belle, H. A. (2005). Philosophical roots of person-centered therapy in the history of Western thought. *The Person-Centered Journal*, 12(1–2).
Van der Veen, F. (1970). Client perception of therapist conditions as a factor in psychotherapy. In J. T. Hart & T. M. Tomlinson (Eds.), *New directions in client-centered therapy* (pp. 214–222). Houghton-Mifflin.
Van Kalmthout, M. (1998). Person-centred theory as a system of meaning. In B. Thorne & E. Lambers (Eds.), *Person-centred therapy: A European perspective* (pp. 11–22). Sage.
van Kessel, W., & van der Linden, P. (1993). Die aktuelle Beziehung in der Klientenzentrierten Psychotherapie; der interaktionelle Aspekt. [The here-and-now relationship in client-centered psychotherapy.] *GwG-Zeitschrift* 90, 19–32.

Van Werde, D. (2002). The falling man: Pre-therapy applied to somatic hallucinating. *Person-Centred Practice*, 10(2), 101–107.
Vaughan, F. E. (1979). *Awakening intuition*. Anchor.
Vygotsky, L. (1962). *Thought and language*. MIT Press.
Waddington, C. (1962). *New patterns in genetics and development*. Columbia University Press.
Wainwright, A. (1955). Helvellyn. In *A pictorial guide to the Lakeland fells: Book one, the Eastern fells* (pp. 1–26). Westmoreland Gazette.
Warner, M. S. (1991). Fragile process. In L. Fusek (Ed.), *New directions in client-centered therapy: Practice with difficult client populations (Monograph Series 1)* (pp. 41–58). Chicago Counseling and Psychotherapy Center.
Warner, M. S. (1998). A client-centered approach to therapeutic work with disssociated and fragile process. In L. Greenberg, J. Watson, & G. Lietaer (Eds.), *Handbook of experiential psychotherapy* (pp. 368–387). The Guilford Press.
Warner, M. S. (2000). Person-centered psychotherapy: One nation, many tribes. *The Person-Centered Journal*, 7(1), 28–39.
Watson, J. B. (1913). Psychology is the behaviorist views it. *Psychological Review*, 20, 158–177. https://doi.org/10.1037/h0074428.
Watson, J. B. & MacDougall, W. (1929). The battle of behaviourism: An exposition and exposure. http://psychclassics.yorku.ca/Watson/Battle/.
Watson, N. (1984). The empirical status of Rogers's hypotheses of the necessary and sufficient conditions for effective psychotherapy. In R. F. Levant & J. M. Shlien (Eds.), *Client-centered therapy and the person-centered approach: New directions in theory, research and practice* (pp. 17–40). Praeger.
Weingarten, K. (2010). Hope in a time of global despair. *New Zealand Journal of Counselling*, 30(1). https://www.nzac.org.nz/assets/Uploads/Journals/Vol-30-No-1-Weingarten.pdf.
Wells, J., O'Donnell, L., Noah, P., Attie, E., Cahn, D., Singer, J., & Schmidt, L. (2005). *The West Wing*. Season 7. NBC.
Werner, H. (1948). *Comparative psychology of mental development* (rev. ed.). Follett.
Weyler, R. (undated). *Declaration of Interdependence: A brief chronology*. www.rexweyler.com/resources/green_declaration.html.
Wheeler, R. H. (1940). *The science of psychology* (2nd ed.). Crowell.
Whitehead, A. N. (1920). *The concept of nature*. Cambridge University Press.
Whitehead, A. N. (1948). *Essays in science and philosophy*. Rider and Co.
Whitehead, A. N. (1978). *Process and reality* (D. R. Griffin & D. W. Sherburne, Eds.; Corrected ed.). The Free Press. (Original work published 1929)
Whitehead, A. N. (1997). *Science and the modern world*. Free Press. (Original work published 1925)
Wikipedia. (2021). *Forestry in the United Kingdom*. https://en.wikipedia.org/wiki/Forestry_in_the_United_Kingdom.
Wikipedia. (2022). *Helvellyn*. https://en.wikipedia.org/wiki/Helvellyn.
Wilber, K. (1983). *Eye to eye*. Anchor.
Wilcox, C., Van Sebille, E., & Hardesty, B. D. (2015). Threat of plastic pollution to seabirds is global, pervasive, and increasing. *Proceedings of the National Academy of Sciences*, 112(38), 11899–11904. https://doi.org/10.1073/pnas.150210811.
Wilson, E. O. (1984). *Biophilia: The human bond with other species*. Harvard University Press.
Wilson, P. (2003). Landslides in Lakeland. *Conserving Lakeland*, 24–25.
Winnicott, D. W. (1957). Further thoughts on babies as persons. In *The child and the outside world: Studies in developing relationships* (pp. 134–140; Hardenberg, Ed.). Tavistock. (Original work published 1947)

Wohlleben, P. (2016). *The hidden life of trees: What they feel and how they communicate* (J. Billinghurst, Trans.). Black. (Original work published 2015)

Wood, J. K. (2006). What does it have to do with client-centred therapy? In G. Proctor, M. Cooper, P. Sanders, & B. Malcolm (Eds.), *Politicizing the person-centred approach: An agenda for change* (pp. 277–283). PCCS Books.

Woodard, W. (2014). Politics, psychotherapy, and the 1907 Tohunga Suppression Act. *Psychotherapy and Politics International*, 12(1), 39–48. https://doi.org/10.1002/ppi.1321.

Woof, P. (2015). Wordsworth learns to write elegy. *The Wordsworth Circle*, 46(2), 70–79.

World Resources Institute. (2005). Millennium ecosystem assessment, 2005: Ecosystems and human well-being: Wetlands and water synthesis. https://www.millenniumassessment.org/documents/document.358.aspx.pdf

Wyckoff, H., & Steiner, C. (Eds.) (1971). Alienation. Berkeley [Special issue]. *The Radical Therapist*, 2(3), 4.

Xu, C., Kohler, T. A., Lenton, T. M., Svenning, J-C., & Scheffer, M. (2020). Future of the human climate niche. *Proceedings of the National Academy of Sciences*, 117, 11350.

Yalom, I. (1980). *Existential psychotherapy*. Basic Books.

Yalom, I. D. (1995). *The theory and practice of group psychotherapy* (4th ed.). Basic Books.

Yunkaporta, T. (2019). *Sand talk: How Indigenous thinking can save the world*. Text Publishing.

Žižek, S. (2017). *The courage of hopelessness*. Akken Lane.

Index

Abram, D. 73, 77, 112, 158
acceptance 35, 75, 76, 82, 117; of anxiety 123; of hopelessness 117–129
Aczel, A. 25
adjustment, psychological: 21, 74
Adler, Alfred 17
Akhtar, S. 118, 129
Alexander, F. 123, 144
Alford, C. F. 10
alienation 2, 67, 70–71, 77, 79, 81, 109, 110, 127, 129, 145, 185; incongruence and 96–104
Alighieri, Dante 62, 64
Allport, Gordon 168
Amatuzzi, M. M. 66, 78
American Psychological Association 189
Angyal, A. 10, 68, 88, 89, 90,
Angyal, Andreas 17, 168
anxiety 2, 34, 73, 105–116, 122–123, 125 128; congruent 75, 116, 122; ecological 117, 128; species 77
Asay, T. P. 18
Assagioli, Roberto 39, 133, 168
Atwood, G. 86

Baldwin, L. V. 84
Barr, J. 144
Barrett-Lennard, G. T. 21, 64, 66, 68, 75, 78, 124, 147, 178
Bazzano, M. 20
becoming 5, 22, 58, 59, 61, 147, 169, 172, 173; and congruence 113–114; God as 59; nature as 23, 171; the process of 27, 173, 196; self 105, 113; of the universe 16, 18–20, 61, 111, 172, 173; of the whole system 58; of the world 56
being 5, 22–23, 91; anxiously congruent 105–116; in the between 25, 35; counter 91; embodied 36; with/in the environment 69; the ground of 48–64; the process of 91; of the universe 18–20; ways of 128; whole 180, 181
belonging 5, 22, 56, 71, 104, 113, 162, 187; and connection 22; to the land 96, 103; and mountains 147; with the planet 130; and unbelonging 152
Bergin, A. E. 82
Bergson, Henri 166, 172
Berne, E. 50, 93, 184
Berne, Eric 184
biodiversity; 65, 100, 102, 104, 109; threats to 99
Bion, W. R. 119
Birch, C. 25, 111, 166, 174
Blair, L. 65, 66, 68, 72
Bohart, A. C. 126
Bohm, D. 59, 61
Bohn, David 165, 166
Born, M. 175
Bowen, M. V.-B. 68
Bowen, Maria 198
Bozarth, J. D. 71, 126
brain 45–46, 52; bicameral 46; collective 145; development 89; left- 39, 40; right- 39, 40; social 145; three- 46; triune 45
Bregman, R. 90. 96
Breit, S. 55
Brown, M. 88
Brunswik, E. 88
Buber, M. 91, 124, 174, 175
Buber, Martin 17
Buechler, S. 128
Bühler, C. 17
Bühler, Charlotte 17
built environments 102
Byrne, N. 126

Cameron, R. 36
Caplow, T. 182
Capra, F. 111
Capra Fritjof 17, 165
Carkhuff, R. R. 15, 35,
Carper, B. 183
Castaneda, C. 183
catastrophe 18, 62, 63, 64; coping with 109–111
Ceballos, G. 99
challenges to science, old and new 180–191
Chalquist, C. 115
Charles, R. 26
Clark, P. U. 98
Clarkson, P. 61, 144, 189
climate change: 65, 98 – 99, 100, 102, 103, 161
Coats, L. L. 97
Cobb, J. 111
Cobb, John 58
Coghlan, D. 77
the Cold War 63
Combs, A. 54
condition(s), therapeutic 11, 35, 71–77; necessary and sufficient, 23, 67, 72, 81, 124, 146; the sixth 146–162
congruence 24, 35, 74–75, 76, 82, 105, 111, 113–114, 116, 117, 125, 147; ecocentric 114–115; philosophical 66
congruent, anxiously 105–116
connectedness 85, 92, 107, 153, 177; inter- 68; to nature 72
connection 56, 59–62, 78, 81; and belonging 22; to the land 194; loss of 115; with the natural world 115; non-sensory 112; and unbelonging 152; with the universe 34
Connell, R. 50
consciousness: earth-oriented 48; evolution of 20; human, stages of 130–143 *see also* mind; New Age 140; structure of 32–44, 133–135, 138–139; layered 45; order of 43; we-oriented 48
contact 24, 35, 72–73, 74, 81, 83–94, 185; ecological 75; in encounter 91–92
Cook, F. H. 59
Cooper, M. 46, 53, 67, 183
Cornelius-White, J. H. D. 20
Cornelius-White, Jeff 6, 193–194, 194–195
COVID-19 xi, 198
creative advance 20, 59, 112; co- 11, 87, 93, 124, 126, 188; 124; Eros 58; tendency 169, 177–179

Crisp, Ross 6, 194, 195, 196, 197
Crucifix, M. 98
Csikszentmihalyi, M. 27

Dalal, F. 16, 53, 185, 191
Damasio, L. 88, 89–90, 182
daring, a manifesto for 191
Darwin, C. 171
David Suzuki Foundation 85
de Bono, E. 188
DeChenne, T. K. 11
Dekar, P. R. 84
Dell, W. 46
de Quincey, C. 22, 61, 112, 174, 177
Descartes, René 16, 55, 63, 166, 171, 178
development, cognitive 32
Dewey, John 17
dialogue 11, 61, 91, 92, 126
differentiation 61, 74, 90; non- 33; of self 133
Dillon, G. 189
diversity 30, 90, 100; ecosystem 101; species 101
Donald, M. 33
Duncan, B. I. 126–127

ecology 1, 77; anxiety about 128; deep 68, 178
ecopsychology 69, 79, 145, 169, 178; and alienation 71; and person-centred psychology 65, 67–71, 197; tasks of 5
ecosystems 63, 97, 99–102; collapse of 102
ecotherapy 11, 49, 145; person-centred therapy as 65, 71–79
Education Amendment Act 1990 191
education 23, 163, 176, 181, 185, 190, 191, 196; soul in 30–31
Egan, G. 15
Egan, K. 32, 46
ego/Ego 53, 57, 63, 65, 87, 88, 140, 169; -boundaries 132; centred 135; -centric 10, 36, 48, 63, 132, 145; and consciousness 43–44, 48–49, 64, 138; -free(dom) 18, 43, 44, 48, 62, 64, 138; group- 132; as illusion 34; independent 59, 63; individual 34, 63, 131, 174; -less 48, 64, 131, 132, 138; and self-actualisation 178; state(s) 93, 94, 188; strength 121, 143; strong 22, 48; 'we'- 10
Eliot, T. S. 138, 191
Ellingham, I. 11, 14, 169, 177
Ellingham, Ivan 11

Embleton Tudor, L. 3, 4, 23, 66, 67, 72, 73, 147, 163, 181, 187,
Embleton Tudor, Louise 6, 194
empathy 23, 24, 25, 34, 35, 42, 75–76, 77, 82, 94, 110, 114, 121–122, 123, 124, 125, 127, 130, 176, 184; archaic 131; for the Earth 75–76; embodied 36; integral 137–143; magical 132; mental-rational 40; modes of 82, 143–145; mythical 38, 133–134; process of 94; visceral 36
encounter 11, 77–79, 86; contact in 91–92; group(s), 79, 196; interpersonal 124; therapeutic 20, 84; Thou-I 94
Engels, F. 84
Enlightenment: the 32, 169, 171; the other (radical) 16–18, 166
Einstein, Albert **112**
epistemology 5, 29, 30, 151, 180, 183, 184, 185
Estância Jatobá 78
evolution 19, 20, 57, 104, 165, 166, 167, 171–172, 181; biological 46; creative 114; cognitive 33; of culture 33; *homo* 102; of human consciousness 130–143; the nature of 96–97; of the universe 114
existence 10, 18, 49, 51, 53, 61, 68, 107, 114, 115, 117, 127; coping with 107–109; human 18, 61, 64, 108, 131; independent 49, 68; personal 10, 51, 53
existential 86, 108, 127, 128, 147, 168, 175, 178; anxiety 109, 113; fear 115; moment 23, 55; (psycho)therapy 107, 108, 139, 169
experience: moments of 23, 35, 56, 58; openness to 74
extensionality 74

Fairbairn, W. R. D. 144
fallacy: of dogmatic finality 14, 15, 29; of misplaced concreteness 14, 24; pre/trans 140, 143; of simple location 14, 60, 175
Feldenkrais, M. 88
Fernald, P. S. 88
Finke, J. 122
Fisher, A. 5, 66, 112, 173
fixity 27, 117
flow 20, 27, 28, 58, 78, 114, 168; evolutionary 28, 58, 72, 112, 114, 172–173
fluidity 27, 55, 117, 118
Fonagy, P. 87, 131
Fordham, M. 36
forest loss 100–101, 102, 162
Fossey, Dian 9

Fox, W. 64
Frankl, V. 108
Freiberg, H. J. 163
Freud, S. 49, 131, 182
Freud, Sigmund 10, 37, 42, 48, 130, 183
Fromm, E. 128

Gare, A. 16, 166
Gatto, J. T. 181
Gebser, J. 17, 32, 33, 35, 36, 43, 46, 63, 64, 130, 132, 134, 135, 138, 140
Gebser, Jean 3, 30, 34, 42, 44–45, 48, 62, 82, 136–137, 141, 145, 195, 196
Gendlin, E. 25, 39
Gendlin, Eugene 60, 196
Gentry, A. H. 100
Gibson, D. 147
Gillman, L. N. 100
Global Forest Watch 101, 161
Gloria 41–42, 122
Goldberg, A. 136
Goldstein, K. 10, 67, 88, 89, 181
Goldstein, Kurt 17, 168
Gomez, L. 182
Greenberg, J. R. 144
Greene, G. 126
Greening, T. 118
Greenway, R. 112
Grof, Christina 17
Grof, Stanislav 17
growth 19, 21, 27, 42, 58, 66, 128, 167, 168, 169, 173; and change 67, 70, 72; model 185; personal 58, 111; in plants 146; psychic 118; therapeutic 42, 105; trap 110
Guardini, R. 91
Guattari, Félix, 17

Haenga-Collins, M. 8, 77
Haggbloom, S. J. 190
Hakl, H. T. 17
Hall, C. 22, 88, 111
Hall, F. 7
Hardin, G. 103, 104
Hargaden, H. 87
Hart, S. 131
Hart, T. 26
Hartshorne, Charles 17
Hauer, M. E. 99
Haule, J. 99
Health Practitioners Competence Assurance Act 2003 187
Heidegger, M. 108, 112
Helvellyn 155–161

Henderson, V. 180
Henrich, J. 145
Hepburn, A. 111
Heraclitus 74
heteronomy 90
Hillman, J. 47, 69, 110, 133
Hoffman, I. 119, 128
Holdgate, M. 160, 162
hologram **59**
homonomy 89, 92, 162, 187,
hope: the challenges of **121**; charity and faith *119*; false 120; the hence of **121**; and hopelessness 117–118; idealised 118; relentless 118, 121, 122, 123, 128; springs eternal 118–120; springs external 127, 129; the thence of **121**; the whence of **121**
hopelessness 103; acceptance of 129; hope and 117–118; the necessity of 129; the privilege of 129
Horney, Karen 168
House, R. 37
Hull, C. 170

Ibn El Arabi, 'Abū 'Abdillāh Muḥammad 64
identity, mutual 60
imagining 14, 31, 39, 84–88, 93–95, 154, 155
incongruence 70–71, 73–74, 82, 105 114–115, 117, 122–123; and alienation 96–104; client 34, 77, 81, 82
indeterminacy 57
Inguilli, K. 72
intercausality 60
interdependence 84–88, 89; of organism and environment 22
interdisciplinarity 68, 69
intersubjectivity 61, 84–88, 94, 125, 177
intuition, 18, 26–27, 53, 94, 175, 176
Ioane, J. 8, 147
Israel, J. 16, 166

Jackson, C. 111
Jacob, M. 16, 166
Jagger, M. 118
James, William 17
Jaynes, J. 40, 46
Johnson, C. N. 99, 100
Jung, C. G. 32, 36, 40, 42, 44
Jung Carl Gustav, 130, 166, 195
Juriansz, D. 185, 189

Kahn, E. 136
Kamens, S. R. 185

Kantor, J. R. 67, 88
Kaplan, R. 115
Kaplan, S. 115
Karter, J. M. 185
Kauffman, S. 108–109, 112, 114, 172, 173
Kearney, R. 85
Kegan, R. 32, 38, 41, 43
Kegan, Robert 196
Keil, W. W. 121
Keller, C. 51, 49
Keller, Catherine 17, 58
Key, D. 65, 129
Keyes, C. L. M. 187
Keys, S. 124, 128
Keys, Suzanne 7
Kidner, D. 112, 115
Kierkegaard, S. 107
Kierkegaard, Søren 13, 108, 113
King, L. 189
King, M. 93
Kinsella, J. 151–152, 153, 154
Kirschenbaum, H. 13, 15, 180
Klein, G. S. 10
Klein, M. 36, 118
Kohut, H. 136
Kohut, Heinz 137
Komiya, N. 8, 147
Kot, G. 89
Kramer, R. 14
Kriz, J. 66, 68
Künkel, F. 10

Laing, R. D. 110
Lambert, M. J. 18, 82, 119
language 20–23, 55, 64, 86, 92, 94, 107, 151–153, 162, 168, 177; body 33; consciousness and 133, 139; and development 85; dominant 181, 184; Māori 76, 157, 159; and metaphor 39; perception and 73; process 92; psychological 49; of wholes (and holism) 69, 162, 181, 182, 191
Laozi 75, 174, 175
Larsen, D. 82
Lasch, C. 86
Laszlo, E. 112, 174
Laszlo, Ervin 179
Layard, R. 185
Lazarus, R. S. 83
Leberger, R. 100
Lemke, J. 25
Lenton, T. M. 98
Lévinas, E. 92, 184
Lévinas, Emanuel 85, 86

Levins, R. 68
Lévy-Bruhl, L. 36
Lewin, Kurt 77
Lewin, P. 4
Lewontin, R. C. 68
life: the good 13, 18, 27–28, 153, 173; positions 50–51, 85
Lilly, John 17
Lindbloom, G.
Lindzey, G. 22, 88, 111
Locke, John 16
Loewald, H. 72
Loewenthal, D. 185
Louv, R. 72
Lovelock, J. 68, 69, 110, 111
Lucas, G. 75
Luquet, P. 131

MacDougall, W. 52
Machado Assumpção, L. 78
Maclean, P. 45
Maclean, Paul 46
Macleod, A. 186
Macmurray, J. 10
Mahrer, A. 139, 141–142
Mahrer, Alvin 143
Maller, C. 115
Manchester, B. 182
Manchester, R. 182
Māori 76; culture 190; research methodology 185; whakataukī (saying) 104, 160; world (view) 96
Marx, K. 71, 84
Marx, Karl 185
Maslow, Abraham 17, 168 xx
Masson, J. 15
Mathews, F. 112
May, R. 113,
McCann, P. 7
McCann, Patricia 6, 196, 196
McCarthy, I. 126
McCleary, R. A. 83
McFague, Sally 17
McIlduff, E. 77
McIntyre, D. B. 68
McSherry, B. 186
Mead, G. H. 10
Mead, George Herbert 17
meaning 40, 45, 94, 108–109, 114, 126, 194; new 171; types of 61
Mearns, D. 53, 67, 175, 183
Medical Practitioners Act 1995 187
Merleau-Ponty, M. 60, 61, 177
Merleau-Ponty, Maurice 73, 77, 112

Merry, T. 3, 74
methodology 10, 11, 118, 124, 180; Māori research 185
Mihaka, H. 85
Miller, S. 127
Mills, I. 62, 64
mind: archaic 31, 33–35, 44; embodied 55; integral 31, 42–44; magical 31, 32, 35–38, 39; mental-rational 31, 40–42; mythical 31, 38–40, 42; rational 23, 44,
Mitchell, S. 144
Mollot, G. 101
Moodley, R. 77
Moreton-Robinson, A. 151
Morgan, S. 185, 189
Morton, I. 91
Mountford, C. P. 66, 68
Moustakas, C. 148
Moutsou, C. 189
Murayama, Magoha 17
Murphy, D. 120
Murphy, G. 88
Murray, H. A. 71
Muthukrishna, M. 145
Myers, S. 124

Naess, A. 57–58, 62, 68, 111, 112, 169, 178
Naess, Arne 3, 17, 64, 166, 178, 195
nature: of evolution 96–97; loss of 96–104; of nature 97–98
Naydler, J. 74
Neville, Alisoun 6, 82, 155–156
Neville, B. 3, 4, 19, 20, 65, 66, 68, 70, 72, 75, 77, 129, 176
Neville, Bernie 47; breadth and depth 197–198; the common man and 'Aussie bloke'; the educator 196; the in-between 196; one man, many tribes 197; the person; setting free 193–200; Trickster and brother 198
New Age 31, 132
new science 26, 185
Newton, Isaac 16, 63, 166, 168, 171, 178
New Zealand Association for Psychotherapists/Te Roopuu Whakaora Hinengaro 83, 182, 186
Nietzsche, F. 129
Noel, J. R. 11
Nordgren, P. H. 85
Nwoye, A. 120

O'Hara, Maureen 1, 6, 196, 198
O'Leary, E. 125

Online Etymology Dictionary 118
ontology 151, 180
organic: experience 21, 56; paradigm 19, 28, 113–114, 169; philosophy 14, 17, 20, 21–23; process 11, 21, 55–57
organism(s): experiencing 21, 70, 73, 74, 89, 113, 147, 162, 167
organismic: psychology 88–91; theory 22, 88
Ornstein, R. 46
Orr, D. W. 69, 74
(the) other/Other 10, 25, 44, 61, 62, 65, 69, 78, 83–95, 118, 124, 139, 141, 144; -than-human 150, 151; no 34; the personhood of 25; self and 34, 39, 60, 133, 134, 140, 142, 177; subjects 22, 56, 61, 177
Owen, W. J. B. 157

Paine, R. T. 97
Panksepp, J. 89
Parker, I. 111
Parlett, M. 86
perceiving: experiencing and 146–162; internal frame of reference 25
perception 14, 54–55, 56, 60, 88, 147; the client's 14, 41, 77, 146, 147; experience/ 93; extrasensory 175, 182; and language 73; of the self 53
people, whole 181–182
Perlesz, A. 126
Perls, F. 89
Perls, Fritz 168
person-centred: cosmology 24, 28, 168, 177; ecotherapy 65, 71–79
philosophy, process 23, 55, 166, 168, 175, 176
Piaget, J. 32
Pierce, Charles 17
Pine, F. 88
Plotkin, B. 2
Plumptre, A. J. 100
Pointing, S. 98
Poland, T. M. 101
pollution, plastic 101
Pope, A. 119, 120
Porges, S. W. 55
Pörtner, M. 81, 91
Prigogine, I.
Prigogine, Ilya 17, 165, 166
Proctor, B. W. 158–159
Proctor, G. 66, 185
professionalism 186–187, 191
Prouty, G. F. 81, 91

psychology: eco 5, 11, 65–79, 145, 169, 178; one-person 81, 120, **121**, 121–123, 125, 143; one-and-a-half-person 120, **121**, 123–124, 125, 143–144; organismic 88–91; person-centred; two-person **121**, 124–126, 144–145; two-person-plus 82, 90, **121**, 126–129, 145; we 10–11, 145
Pyšek, P. 101

Quinn, R. 15

Radin, D. 26, 176
Rand, J. 85
Rank, Otto 19, 168, 177
Raskin, N. J. 144
Rawlins, M. D. 189
reality 57, 59, 64, 78, 83, 84, 90, 108, 112, 132, 139, 166, 169, 174, 175, 176, 180, 183, 191, 196; explicate order of 59; new 64, 179; objective 54, 58, 141; and perception/perceptual field 54, 88, 137; process conception of 55, 56; single/unitary 64, 68, 90, 112, 134, 182–183; separate 183; social 91; transpersonal 143
Reason, P. 18
Reed, C. 126, 127
regard, unconditional positive 24, 35, 75, 76, 77, 124, 125, 129, 146, 147, 178
Rehfeld, K. 98
relation, in good 153–155
relationship: immediacy of 22, 44; therapeutic 11, 23–26, 28, 44, 61, 83, 84, 86, 123, 124, 126, 127, 130, 136, 139, 144–145, 147, 183, 188, 190
relating: therapeutic 23–26, 83–95, 126, 188
Richards, K. 118
Richardson, D. M. 101
Ripple, W. J. 97
Ritchie, J. 93
Rivers, S. 8
Rivers, Shirley 7
Roach, A. 8, 92
Roach, Archie 6
Rodgers, B. 8, 23, 84, 147, 183
Rodgers, Brian 6, 198
Rogers, C. R. 3, 5, 6, 10, 13, 14, 15, 17, 18, 19, 20, 21, 22, 23, 24, 25, 26, 27, 28, 35, 38, 40, 41, 42, 44, 51, 52, 53, 54, 55, 56, 58, 59, 62, 66, 67, 68, 70, 71, 72, 73, 74, 77, 78, 79, 81, 82, 83, 84, 87, 89, 90, 91, 92, 94, 105, 110,

111, 112, 113, 114, 117, 118, 122, 123, 124, 127, 135, 136, 137, 139, 141, 143, 144, 145, 146, 147, 163, 165, 168, 169, 170, 171, 172, 173, 174, 175, 176, 178, 179, 180, 181, 183, 184, 185, 186, 187, 188, 190
Rogers, N. 4
Rogers, Natalie 198
Romantic/ism 16, 19
Roszak, T. 69, 112, 115
Rowan, J. 18
Rowland, B. 129
Roy, B. 71
Rumi, Jalāl al-Dīn Muḥammad 64
Russell, D. E. 66, 185

Sabini, M. 42
Sacks, O. 88
Samuels, A. 36, 74, 189
Sanders, P. 3
Saner, R. 11
Sapriel, L. 92
Schmale, A. H. Jr. 117
Schmid, P. F. 11, 25, 61, 67, 94, 119, 124, 178
Schmid, Peter 82
Schneider, K. 107
Schopenhauer, A. 107, 114
Schopenhauer, Arthur 54, 107, 112
Schore, A. N. 84
Schwartz, J. 92
science: challenges to 180–191; a human 180, 183–185, 191; modern, dogmas of 63, 165–166, 180; new 26, 165 Newtonian 169, 183
Scott-Holland, H. 199–200
Segrera, Alberto 6, 194, 197
Sela-Smith, S. 148
self/Self: -actualisation 42, 65, 89, 105, 113, 187; concept 56, 81; (that) one truly is 105, 107, 111, 113–114; real 24, 112; as subject 11, 52–55
Semel, V. 120
sense, felt 39, 113
Shakespeare, W. 125, 128
Shaw, S. 182
Sheldrake, R. 57, 111, 165, 167, 172
Sheldrake, Rupert 166, 169, 176, 179
Sherrard, E. M. 2
Shostrom, E. 41
Siegel, D. J. 141
Singh, J. 23, 147
Skinner, B. F. 170
Slochower, H. 125

Smith, G. H. 185
Smith, L. T. 185
Smuts, J. 181
Smuts, Jan 17, 165
Smyser, J. W. 157
Snell, T. 115
Snygg, D. 54
space and time 25, 140,
species: declines and extinctions 99–100; invasive pest 101–102
Spinoza, Baruch 18, 20 64, 112, 166, 169, 178
Stark, M. 81, 87, 118, 120, 121. 122, 123, 124, 125, 143, 144
Statistics New Zealand 76
Steffen, W. 97, 98
Steiner, C. 127, 185, 191
Steiner, Claude 2
Steiner, L. R. 190
Stengers, Isabelle 17
Stern, D. N. 10, 24, 87, 92, 93, 188
Stern, Daniel 84
Stinckens, N. 91
Stolorow, R. 86
Stringer, C. 98
subception 56, 83
subject/object 39, 61, 134; dichotomy 22; differentiation 61; distinction 22, 61; duality 187
subjectivity 10, 18, 25, 26, 44, 45, 52, 53, 57, 60, 62, 63, 85, 86, 87, 113, 170; almost mystical 173–175; deconstruction of 69; independent 61; personal 25, 52, 58, 60; shared 61; *see also* intersubjectivity
suffering 113, 129; planet 105
Sullivan, H. S. 87
Summers, G. 11, 92, 126, 188
Swimme, B. 106
Szent-Gyoergyi, A. 171
Szent-Gyoergyi, Albert 17

Taft, J. 10, 14, 144
Taft, Jessie 17
Tallbear, K. 150, 151, 153, 154
Tallman, K. 126
Taper, M. L. 97
Targ, R. 176
Teilhard de Chardin, P. 174
Teilhard de Chardin, Pierre, 17
tendency: actualising; creative; formative 20, 28, 42, 58, 70, 75, 111, 113, 114, 167, 169, 170, 171, 173
Teo, T. 111
therapists: as designers 187–188

therapeutic action 87, 120–129; as modes of empathy 143–145
therapy(ies): eco 65, 71–79; non-Western 167; right-brain 39; setting free 165–179
things 23, 54, 56, 60, 63, 69, 73, 77, 94, 107, 114, 175, 177, 178, 183, 188; the life of 175; living 57, 89; the mind of 30–47; the relatedness of 59
Thorne, B. 175
Thornton, A. 159
Tillich, P. 91
time-freedom 43
Timulak, L. 119, 128
Titirangi 5, 7. 96
Tohunga Suppression Act 1907 187
Tolman, E. C. 88
Toolebewong, Mt xi, 7, 147, 148–155
Totton, N. 37, 69, 78, 189
Toukmanian, S. 147
transactional analysis (TA) 11, 184–185, 188
Trisos, C. H. 99
Truax, C. B. 15
Tuck, E. 150, 151
Tudor, K. 1, 2, 3, 4, 7, 8, 11, 14, 15, 20, 22, 23, 36, 37, 50, 51, 53, 61, 65, 66, 67, 68, 70, 72, 73, 81, 82, 85, 87, 88, 89, 90, 92, 93, 94, 121, 126, 127, 129, 130, 136, 144, 145, 147, 160, 168, 178, 181, 182, 183, 184, 185, 186, 187, 188
Tudor, Keith, 195, 198

Ulloa, A. 70
universe: as alive 18–20; being in the living 57–59

Van Belle, H. A. 14, 118
van der Linden, P. 124
Van der Veen, F. 147
Van Kalmthout, M. 70
van Kessel, W. 124
Van Werde, D. 81
Varney, H. 17
Vaughan, F. E. 26
vitalism 76, 166
Vygotsky, L. 10

Waddington, C. 174
Waddington, Conrad 166

Wainwright, A. 157
Warner, M. S. 124, 129, 197
Watson, J. B. 52, 170
Watson, John 53
Watson, N. 147
Weingarten, K. 125, 126
Wells, J. 1
'we': -go 10; ness 9, 11, 50; psychology 10–11, 145
Werner, H. 66, 88
West, Ellen 113
Weyler, R. 85
Wheeler, R. H. 67, 88
Whitehead, A. N. 14, 24, 35, 49, 56, 67, 174, 175
Whitehead, Alfred North 3, 13, 17, 19, 20, 55, 57, 58, 59, 60, 61, 64, 112, 166, 167, 172, 177, 179, 195, 196
Whyte, Lancelot 17
Wikipedia 100, 157
Wilber, K. 140, 143
Wilcox, C. 101
Williams, R. 189
Wilson, E. O. 114
Wilson, Edward 115
Wilson, P. 160
Winnicott, D. W. 10, 84
Wohlleben, P. 62, 73, 75
Wolini 10
Wood, J. K. 66, 78
Wood, John 198
Woodard, W. 187
Woof, P. 159
World Resources Institute 100
Worrall, M. 2, 4, 14, 20, 22, 23, 61, 66, 67, 68, 70, 72, 81, 88, 89, 90, 127, 136, 147, 168, 178, 181, 183, 185
Worrall, Mike 1, 3
Wurundjeri 148, 152, 154
Wyckoff, H. 127, 185

Xu, C. 99

Yalom, I. D. 108, 124
Yang, K. W. 150, 151
Yunkaporta, T. 151, 152

Zenji, Do-gen 64
Žižek, S. 128
Zohar, Danah 17
Zuangzi 64

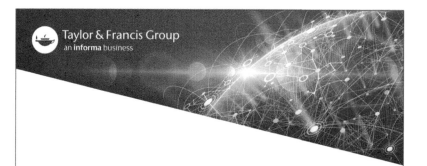